HOW TO IDENTIFY FLOWERING PLANT FAMILIES

*A Practical Guide
for Horticulturists and Plant Lovers*

JOHN PHILIP BAUMGARDT

TIMBER PRESS *Portland, Oregon*
in cooperation with
THE AMERICAN HORTICULTURAL SOCIETY
and THE RARE PLANT GROUP
of THE GARDEN CLUB OF AMERICA

© 1982 by Timber Press, Inc.
Fourth printing 1994
All rights reserved

Printed in Singapore

TIMBER PRESS, INC.
The Haseltine Building
133 S.W. Second Ave., Suite 450
Portland, Oregon 97204-3527, U.S.A.
phone 1-800-327-5680 (U.S.A. and Canada only)

Library of Congress Cataloging in Publication Data

Baumgardt, John Philip.
    How to identify flowering plant families.

    1. Angiosperms—Identification. 2. Plants—
Identification. I. Title.
QK495.A1B38   1982   582.13   82-10592
ISBN 0-917304-21-7

Contents

Dedicated with affection by
The Rare Plant Group to

Marion Rombauer Becker

for her unfailing enthusiasm and encouragement, and for her experience and support which made possible the undertaking of this publication.

Preface

Plant relationships, valuable information for the plantsman *per se*, also often yield clues to cultural requirements. These factors, plant identification and cultural success, supply the *raison d'etre* for this book. It is intended for home and professional gardeners and other non-botanically trained plantsmen, horticulturists, and plant lovers.

Horticulture (with no apology) makes little attempt to keep abreast of the constantly shifting plant classifications of taxonomic botanists. Plantsmen *use* classification systems as tools to pigeonhole their plants conveniently while taxonomists concern themselves with reconstructing the pigeonholes. Accordingly, the plant groups (families) described in this book largely are those found in current horticultural literature. Updated classifications are introduced in *Hortus III* and elsewhere. For the latest versions of classification it is necessary to go to the various botanical journals.

The basic techniques of flower analysis, flower diagrams, and flower formulas, as presented here apply to flowering plants right round the globe. The families included as examples occur natively or as introduced ornamentals in North America; because of my regional experience, many of them are found east of the Rocky Mountains to the exclusion of a few Western and Tropical North American families. As the emphasis is *technique*, any family serves to exemplify methods of study.

In preparing this manuscript I have dipped into old and new text books on plant identification and classification, into *Floras* of various parts of the United States, and into various other reference material. If you are interested in plant classification and identification you should do the same; any good library ought to have a Flora or Manual of local plants as well as that fine old classic, L.H. Bailey's *Standard Cyclopedia of Horticulture*, with its somewhat dated but superb synopsis of plant families at the beginning of Volume I. I also am indebted to Mrs. Katie Bourke for her many flower sketches. These are not botanically definitive drawings; the literature is full of that sort of thing for your rainy day reference work. These are the sort of sketches anyone can make in his field notebook, and I hope yours will be similar. Finally, I am indebted to the members of the Garden Club of America Rare Plant Group who encouraged me to prepare this manuscript; I hope they find it useful as they pursue their world wide plant studies.

J. P. B.

Barry County, Mo.
October, 1982

Introduction

Plant study holds its own as one of the oldest scientific disciplines. Those early botanical roots were grounded in practical applications: when men learned to plant, tend, and harvest a crop they could forego the nomadic necessity of following the natural movements of game for food; when they learned which plants were poisonous and which were curative, they could prevent or tend at least some of their ailments. Thus, agronomy and medicine were born. Agronomy stabilized at an early date, and each civilization knew and grew a few vegetables, some grain, some fiber plants. Each civilization also had its own medicinal plants. In some societies ethics grew apace and these plants were available for public use, but in some groups poisonous and drug plants were the closely guarded secret of an inner circle and so grew the witch doctor cults. In the western world agronomy and medicine (by and large, medical men were the botanists of the day) remained uncommonly stable from Greek and Roman days right into the Renaissance — excepting exotic probes into the Orient for spices. Then Columbus made his round trip and everything changed.

The European scientific community was intrigued by things from the New World; minerals, birds, animals, and especially, plants. Plants, because Europe was becoming over-crowded and promising food crops, fibers, and medicines were more than welcome. It helped that during the Renaissance the Church lost its iron grip on scientific thought, so men no longer felt themselves bound by the strictures of Aristotle, Pliny, and the Church fathers. Needless to say, this flood of new material to study posed logistical problems. How to classify it, how to store it, how to inter-relate it? It was just a matter of time until Linnaeus and his students made some degree of order out of the vast confusion. And with the order came a glimmering of natural relationships which would lead to Darwin. So we come to modern Botany.

We think of the great days of plant exploration as over because man has planted his foot or flag on almost every inch of terrestrial surface. As a matter of fact, the number of species yet to be identified, described, and classified, probably outnumbers those properly known. Not so much in the plant world as, say, the insect group, but still, there is a lot of plant study to be done. It is hard to believe that plants still grow which we do not know — and not necessarily in foreign lands, but in highly specialized habitats or overlooked corners close to home. It also is interesting to know that from the great age of exploration on, much of the best study was done by talented amateurs. It was so then, it was so in our Grandparents' day, and probably it is so today. Think of the poet Goethe — he did not spend all his time writing about the sorrows of young Werther or the odd behavior of Faust, or, wearing another hat, involving himself in municipal and state governments; he was a sound field botanist, collecting and classifying on his walks round the German countryside. Probably Conan Doyle enjoyed his field days because he armed Sherlock Holmes with a tin box (vasculum) and spud (digging tool) with which to improve his country holidays. In her younger days, my grandmother bicycled with friends — that must have been a sight, in those voluminous clothes — and the girls cycled to various bosky dells to collect ferns which they identified and pressed. It was the thing to do.

And so it goes today: capable amateurs poke off into the Turkish hinterland and bring prize collections to the Royal Horticulture Society; meanwhile botany is enriched. Talented amateurs ransack ground well trodden by earlier botanists in this country and discover or rediscover exciting plants. Possibly, it is only a matter of time before somebody wanders in with a branch of a shrub which will turn out to be the elusive *Franklinia alatamaha*, discovered once and never located again.

Modern botanical science is largely a laboratory and herbarium (collection of pressed plant specimens) discipline. Indeed, one sometimes wonders if many of the younger botanists have ever *seen* a living, growing plant. No doubt it is important to continue and to further scientific research, but when a botanist spends his entire career probing the insides of a single cell, or fails to recognize a plant unless it is properly pressed and dried (that sounds ridiculous but it is not all that far-fetched), something needs to be done to re-establish botanical contact with the great out of doors; with plants growing in their habitats or in a garden. This is an area which professional science seems willing to abandon to the amateur.

Plant societies, and horticulture and garden clubs, not infrequently become involved in hassles about plant identification, plant classification, and plant relationships. These arguments are usually readily resolved when somebody has the expertise to use classification techniques. For this, we can look to identification and classification methods of an earlier day. It is true that modern studies dealing with cytoplasmic and other internal relationships have to have the last word. But it is equally true that a person armed with the know-how to dissect a flower and define its structure (this is where flower formulas and diagrams come in), and to chase these characteristics through some sort of key to come to a proper binomial, can solve the problem. I grew up with flower diagrams and flower formulas, the handiest shorthand ways to jot down the characteristics of a plant or plant group. Before long, these symbols grouped themselves in my subconscience so that when I encountered an unknown species I somehow knew which family it was a part of. There are not so very many families, at least when dealing with familiar species, that the rankest amateur plantsman cannot learn their characteristics. And once you get to family, your identification problem is pretty well solved, for it is no great task to proceed to genus and species. Of course, you also will want to go the other way: to learn how and why families are grouped into orders, and to learn the relationship of these greater categories. But in my mind, it all starts with families. The late Dr. Edgar Anderson, creator of the theory of introgressive hybridization as a mechanism for the natural development of new species, once told me that, after all, a species is only a frame of mind. A botanist sits and thinks about which individual plants are in a given species and which

8

are not, and pretty soon he defines that species to his liking; before the ink is dry on his monograph another botanist has revised the entire group. Too many botanists today, apparently incapable of stepping outdoors to do a bit of original work with original material, spend their time reshuffling herbarium specimens so that no classification group is safe. A genus which has stood for a century is deleted; a family which is recognized right round the world is fragmented into a hundred families. We need not concern ourselves with this sort of pastime; at worst, it is merely an excuse to spend research money, and at best, some titillating bits of information are apt to fall out during the shuffle. Meanwhile, I hope that every gardener, every naturalist, everybody who loves plants, will join Aristotle, Pliny, Linnaeus, Goethe, Sherlock Holmes, and the rest of us in making an intellectual game out of sorting out plants. I hope this book about flower diagrams, flower formulas, and a few plant families will be of help.

THE PLANT KINGDOM

Microscopic germs and giant redwood trees are part of the plant kingdom. Scientists group the various members of the kingdom in several ways; a traditional system of classification, handy for beginning study, is presented here.

The Thallophytes. These are the "simplest" plant forms: the fungi (plants without chlorophyll, including bacteria, molds, mushrooms, bracket fungi, and so on) and algae (plants with chlorophyll, mostly aquatic, including seaweeds, pond-scums, some riverweeds, and more.) The thallophytes vary from unicellular to multiple-celled organisms with simple reproductive systems and little or no tissue differentiation so they have no veins, leaves, stems, roots, or flowers.

The Bryophytes. These are the mosses and liverworts; they contain chlorophyll and so are green. They show rudiments of tissue development but the reproductive systems are still primitive. The study of bryophytes is specialized but gratifying once you have learned to find your way through the botany which pertains to them.

The Pteridophytes. These are the ferns and club-mosses. Still with no true leaves (ferns have fronds) but with stems of a sort with primitive veins, and with "roots", the pteridophytes exhibit a more advanced life cycle. Many amateur botanists and horticulturists have been attracted by the beauty of ferns and club-mosses, and have produced quite a lot of sound data.

The Spermatophytes. These are the seed-bearing plants with true stems, roots, and leaves; some of them, the Gymnosperms, bear ovules in an exposed manner (gymnos = naked) and seeds are not enclosed in a carpel. Others, the Angiosperms, are the flowering plants with seeds enclosed in

9

carpels. It is a segment of this group with which we are concerned in this book. A great many plant families are found in the two sub-groups of Angiosperms; the tropical families tend to occur right round the equator with some notable exceptions. On the other hand, there is not a lot in common between the floras of the North Temperate and South Temperate zones, while the two Boreal regions again show differences.

The techniques used to classify flowering plants remain the same anywhere on the globe. When you learn how to analyze the monocots and dicots in your home garden, you will be able to analyze plants in (or from) China or Africa or Australia.

Presented here is a dichotomous key, a classifying tool consisting of a series of paired (dikhotomos = cut in two) statements. With plant in hand, choose the first or the second statement of the first pair of statements (consider only a single pair at a time) as describing your plant; then proceed to the next pair of statements under the one you chose, and so proceed through the key. Sometimes the choice is simple, as "plants green" versus "plants not green" but sometimes several characteristics are given so you must choose which statement of that pair comes closest to your plant. Sooner or later you may make a wrong choice; you will realize it down the line when no choices fit your plant. Back up and start over. Sometimes you cannot decide which of a pair to follow; mark that point and try one. If keying proceeds to a logical conclusion, good enough. But if you find yourself in a morass of choices which fail to match your plant, back up and try the other. At first, keying plants is difficult; as you become familiar with the key and its terms keying becomes easy. Wade in and keep trying; it is the only way to become adept.

A KEY TO SOME FLOWERING PLANT FAMILIES

I. Monocotyledonous Plants: Stems herbaceous in the North Temperate zone (woody and flexible in *Smilax*) without central pith but with fibrous vascular strands scattered throughout (a stem cross-section shows these as scattered dots). Leaves chiefly parallel-veined, sometimes with the lower portion (sheath) enwrapping the stem. Flower parts in 3's, more rarely in 2's, 4's, or 6's, but not 5's. Seedlings with a single cotyledon, often difficult to identify.

    a. Pistil of a single carpel, or if more, each carpel becoming distinct as fruit matures, or developing into an indehiscent, inferior ovary. Flower parts often of unequal numbers . . . . **b.**

        b. Flowers not in axils of regularly overlapping (imbricated) scales as grasses or sedges, nor on a fleshy axis as *Arum*, nor a branching axis as grasses or sedges . . . . **c.**

            c. Perianth scarcely developed (rudimentary) or modified to more or less persistent bristles or dry scales; flowers of a single sex, in heads or crowded spikes . . . . **d.**

                d. Flowers densely crowded in a terminal spike; perianth usually of slender bristles . . . . **Typhaceae.**

                d. Flowers in heads, radiating outward; perianth of scattered scales . . . . **Sparganiaceae.**

            c. Perianth leaf-like or petal-like, or none; flowers pefect or of a single sex . . . . **e.**

                e. Carpels free or becoming free at maturity . . . . . . **f.**

                    f. Perianth leaf-like or lacking; carpels single or few . . . . **g.**

                        g. Carpel one, or if more, free; aquatic plants with flowers in spikes, or clustered, or solitary; leaves often with flat blades and sheathing bases . . . . **h.**

                        h. Flowers in spikes or clustered, perianth lacking; carpels 1−4, free . . . . . **Zosteraceae.**

                        h. Flowers single, in leaf axils; pistillate flowers with a single carpel . . . **Najadaceae.**

                      g. Flowers in spikes or racemes, mostly perfect; with 3 leaf-like sepals and 3 leaf-like petals; leaves without blades, round . . . **Juncaginaceae.**

                    f. Perianth of 3 leaf-like sepals and 3 white or pink petals; carpels many . . . . **i.**

                        i. Stamens 3 or more; carpels numerous, free; 1-celled and mostly with one ovule, maturing into a nutlet (achene) . . . . **Alismataceae.**

                        i. Stamens 9 or more; carpels 6 or more, with many ovules, maturing into follicles . . . . **Butomaceae.**

e. Carpels united into an inferior compound ovary, often with 3 cells .... **Hydrocharitaceae.**

b. Flowers subtended by regularly overlapping scales, or on a fleshy, or leaf-like, axis .... **j.**

j. Flowers in the axils of overlapping scales, greatly reduced (stamens and pistils subtended by one or more specialized bracts, or by bristles), in dry spikes or heads; fruit indehiscent .... **k.**

k. Scales mostly paired; perianth indiscernable or rudimentary; flowers mostly perfect; stems often hollow, nodes solid, hard; leaves more or less linear, 2-ranked, sheath usually open .... **Gramineae.**

k. Scales usually single, perianth lacking or represented by bristles or scale-like sepals; flowers perfect or of one sex; stems mostly solid, 3-angled, nodes soft; grass-like leaves, when present, in 3 ranks, sheaths closed .... **Cyperaceae.**

j. Flowers crowded on a club-like fleshy or spongy structure (spadix) which may be enveloped by a leaf-like or colorful spathe; or minute flowers borne on tiny, mostly floating, fronds .... **l.**

l. Flowers crowded on a spadix with or without a spathe; perianth lacking, or 4 or 6 sepals, of one sex, sex separated, or perfect; fruit a berry; these commonly are leafy terrestrial plants; the family is largely tropical .... **Araceae.**

l. Flowers very rarely seen, nearly indiscernable; these are tiny acquatic plants mostly of a few fleshy fronds, mostly surface-floating, multiplying by budding .... **Lemnaceae.**

a. Pistil compound, of 3 carpels; flower whorls each of the same number of parts or multiples of the same number (3's and 6's usually) .... **m.**

m. Ovary superior or inferior; flowers regular or nearly so (except corolla irregular in *Commelina* and *Pontederia*); seeds with endosperm (reserve nutrient = "albumen") stored around the embryo .... **n.**

Endosperm mealy .... **o.**

o. Ovary superior, with one cell .... **Xyridaceae.**

o. Ovary superior, mostly 2–3 cells .... **p.**

p. Flowers of a single sex, very small, in dense heads ... . **Eriocaulaceae.**

p. Flowers perfect .... **q.**

q. Epiphytic (non-terrestrial); plants with scurfy leaves .... **Bromeliaceae.**

q. Plants rooting in the soil or aquatic; leaves not scurfy .... **r.**

r. Flowers with green sepals and colored petals; plants terrestrial, brittle-fleshy, or soft .... **Commelinaceae.**

r. Flowers with uniformly colored perianth; plants terrestrial or aquatic, mostly tough-leathery when mature .... **Pontederiaceae.**

n. Endosperm fleshy or horny; ovary superior or inferior .... **s.**

    s. Ovary superior (except in *Aletris* and some species of *Zygdanus*) .... **t.**

        t. Flowers small; sepals and petals brown or green, scale-like; leaves grass-like .... **Juncaceae.**

        t. Flowers mostly showy; sepals resembling white or colored peals (leaf-like in *Trillium*); leaves various but rarely grass-like; mostly with bulbs or rhizomes .... **Liliaceae.**

    s. Ovary partly or wholly inferior .... **u.**

        u. Stamens 3, opposite the inner perianth segments .... **Haemodoraceae.**

        u. Stamens 6 (in American species) or 3 opposite the outer perianth segments .... **v.**

            v. Twining vines; flowers small, greenish, mostly of one sex; leaves broad, strongly veined; fruit a winged capsule . ... **Dioscoriaceae.**

            v. Erect perennial herbs; flowers often showy, perfect; leaves linear .... **w.**

                w. Stamens 6, facing outward (extrorse) .... **Amaryllidaceae.**

                w. Stamens 3, facing inward (introrse) .. **Iridaceae.**

m. Ovary inferior; flowers irregular (except in **Burmanniaceae**); seeds minute, with little or no endosperm (except **Marantaceae**) .... **x.**

    x. Leaves pinnately veined; perianth very irregular, petaloid; one fertile stamen with others as petaloid stamenodia; seeds with perisperm (nutrients stored outside the embryo sac **Marantaceae.**

    x. Leaves with parallel veins or stem leaves reduced to scales; fertile stamens 3, free, or 1 or 2 fused to the style .... **y.**

        y. Flowers regular; stem leaves reduced to scales; stamens 3, free .... **Burmanniaceae.**

        y. Flowers irregular; corolla with 1 petal (lip) unlike the other 2; stamens 1−2 fused to the style .... **Orchidaceae.**

II. Dicotyledonous Plants: Stems herbaceous or woody, with central pith; if woody, inner secondary tissue (wood) separated from outer secondary tissue (bark) by a cambium layer which produces a new layer of wood and of bark annually. In herbaceous and woody stems the vascular tissues are arranged cylindrically, not scattered. Leaves usually net-veined, sessile or with a petiole, not with a sheath. Flower parts in 2's, 3's, 4's, or 5's, or multiples. Embryos with 2 cotyledons ("seed-leaves", as the two halves of a peanut or bean, the "hinge" being the embryo axis).

II_1. Petals lacking or rudimentary, or, if present, free (a few species show some basal fusion of petals; in these, the anthers do not open by apical pores). See page 23 for II_2.

    a. Petals lacking or rudimentary .... **b.**

b. Flowers chiefly staminate or pistillate (rarely perfect), commonly in catkins (aments), and without a discernable perianth, or rarely with a bracteose perianth . . . . **c.**

    c. Plants mostly herbaceous; stems jointed; leaves alternate, heart-shaped; flowers perfect, crowded into a terminal spike, and appearing petal-like . . . . **Saururaceae.**

    c. Trees or shrubs; staminate and pistillate flowers in separate catkins, or mixed; perianth not petaloid . . . . **d.**

        d. Pistil of 2 united carpels which mature to a many-seeded capsule; seeds hair-tufted . . . . **Salicaceae.**

        d. Pistil of one carpel; few or one ovule; fruit a 1-seeded nut, samara, or drupe . . . . **e.**

            e. Ovary superior or naked; staminate flowers with no perianth; fruit a drupe or 1-seeded nut . . . . **f.**

                f. Wood dense and heavy; style formed or with 2 stigmas; fruit a waxy nut . . . . **Myricaceae.**

                f. Wood porous and light; style simple, fruit a drupe . . . . **Leitneriaceae.**

            e. Ovary more or less inferior, staminate flowers with or without a perianth . . . . **g.**

                g. Leaves odd-pinnate; ovary with one ovule . . . . . .
. . . . **Juglandaceae.**

                g. Leaves simple; ovary with several ovules; fruit a nut or samara . . . . **h.**

                    h. Pistillate flowers in short clusters or elongated catkins; pistil with 2 styles; ovary with 2 cells and 2−6 ovules . . . . **Corylaceae.**

                    h. Pistillate flowers solitary or clustered; pistils with 2 styles, ovary with 3−7 cells each with 1−2 ovules . . . . **Fagaceae.**

b. Flowers perfect or of a single sex, rarely in catkins, with or without a calyx . . . . **i.**

    i. Seeds with little or no nutrient reserves accompanying the embryo; ovary superior; fruit indehiscent; leaves with sepals . . . . **j.**

        j. Trees, shrubs, rarely herbs; leaves alternate; fruit a samara, or nutlet embraced by fleshy, juicy calyx tissue but not a dry nutlet . **k.**

            k. Trees with bland, watery sap . . . . **Ulmaceae.**

            k. Trees with milky sap . . . . **Moraceae.**

        j. Mostly herbs; leaves opposite or alternate; fruit a dry achene . . . . **l.**

            l. Leaves mostly opposite, rarely alternate, lobed or dissected; flowers of one sex, pistillate flowers with a single sepal embracing the ovary; style or stigma 2 . . . . **Cannabinaceae.**

            l. Leaves opposite or alternate but unlobed; calyx of pistillate flowers cup-shaped or tubular or with 2−5 lobes; one style and stigma . . . . **Urticaceae.**

14

i. Seed with ample nutrient reserve surrounding the embryo (except in certain seashore members of the **Chenopodiaceae**) .... **m.**

    m. Ovary more or less inferior .... **n.**

        n. Ovary with one cell; fruit indehiscent, a drupe, nut, or berry; plants parasitic .... **o.**

            o. Root parasite; leaves green, simple, mostly alternate, not leathery; fruit a drupe or nut .... **Santalaceae.**

            o. Branch parasite; leaves green or brown, leathery or reduced to scales; fruit a berry .... **Loranthaceae.**

        n. Ovary with several (mostly 6) cells; fruit a dehiscent capsule; calyx tubular or capanulate with 3 lobes; leaf blades entire, broad, often cordate .... **Aristolochiaceae.**

    m. Ovary superior .... **p.**

        p. Fruit a triangular or lens-shaped nutlet; stipules sheathing, at least in early stages .... **Polygonaceae.**

        p. Fruit a capsule, berry, or other, but not a nutlet ...... **q.**

            q. Ovary, or each carpel, with one ovule; fruit indehiscent or circumscissile .... **r.**

                r. Flower parts inserted spirally, not in whorls; perianth leaf-like or non-green, dry-membranous; leaves without stipules, mostly alternate .... **s.**

                    s. Flowers without subtending bracts; calyx green, leaf-like .... **Chenopodiaceae.**

                    s. Flowers with dry-membranous subtending bracts; calyx similar .... **Amaranthaceae.**

                r. Flower parts mostly in whorls; some part of perianth petal-like .... **t.**

                    t. Sepals petaloid; leaves without stipules ... **u.**

                        u. Calyx tubular or funnel-shaped, petaloid; fruit a nutlet, leaves opposite . **Nyctaginaceae.**

                        u. Calyx of free, petaloid sepals; fruit a many-seeded berry; leaves alternate .. **Phytolaccaceae.**

                    t. Sepals leaf-like or dry-membranous; leaves mostly opposite, with or without stipules .... **Caryophyllaceae.**

            q. Ovary with many ovules; fruit a capsule ... **Aizoaceae.**

a. Petals commonly present, lacking in a few genera*, or represented by showy, petal-like sepals; flowers mostly perfect .... **v.**

---

*petals lacking in **Ceratophyllaceae**, in many **Ranunculaceae**, in *Calycocarpum*, in **Lauraceae**, in **Podostemaceae**, in *Liquidambar*, in *Sanguisorba*, in *Xanthoxylum*, in **Euphorbiaceae**, in **Callitricaceae**, in **Empetraceae**, in **Buxaceae**, in some **Aceraceae**, in some **Rhamnaceae**, in **Thymeleaceae**, in **Elaeagnaceae**, in some species of *Ludwigia*, and in *Nyssa*.

v. Ovary mostly superior (rarely on an urn-shaped receptacle or surrounded by a fleshy disc) .... **w.**

w. Stamens inserted on the receptacle (hypogynous) or mostly so .... **x.**

x. Pistil compound, mostly with one (rarely 3–5) cell; ovules several to many, basal or attached to central column; flower parts in whorls; *or* several simple pistils (carpels) or if pistil compound, with more than one cell and at least some flower parts inserted spirally .... **y.**

y. Pistil compound, with numerous ovules; flower parts in whorls or cycles .... **z.**

z. Sepals or calyx lobes 2, stamens 5–many, inserted opposite the petals when of equal number; plants succulent or fleshy .... **Portulacaceae.**

z. Sepals or calyx lobes 4–5, stamens 4–10, inserted alternate to the petals when of equal number .... **Caryophyllaceae.**

y. Pistil simple (often numerous and spirally arranged) *or* compound with more than one cell; stamens numerous, inserted spirally or less commonly, in whorls .... **aa.**

aa. Flowers without a true perianth but with a green calyx-like involucre; fruit a nutlet; aquatic plants with dissected leaves in whorls .... **Ceratophyllaceae.**

aa. Flowers with calyx, with or without a corolla .... **bb.**

bb. Aquatic herbs growing from perennial rhizomes with peltate or cordate floating or immersed leaves; ovules on the sides of the ovary but not on the ventral seam (when solitary, pendant from the summit); *This traditional family commonly is divided into more logical families* .... **Nymphaeaceae.**

bb. Plants mostly terrestrial (but some aquatic in **Ranunculaceae**); leaves not as above; ovules on restricted placentae; carpels maturing the nutlets, follicles, berries, or drupes .... **cc.**

cc. Non-aromatic herbs or shrubs; sap mostly acrid, bitter, often poisonous; these without oil ducts in woody tissue .... **dd.**

dd. Plants with non-twining stems (but some with leaf tendrils, as *Clematis*); flowers mostly perfect (not so in some *Clematis* and *Thalictrum*) . ... **ee.**

ee. Anthers not opening by valves (lids); fruit a nutlet, capsule, or berry, with non-arillate seed .... **Ranunculaceae.**

ee. Anthers opening by apical valves (except **Podophyllaceae** which today often is in a separate family); fruit a capsule or a berry .... **Berberidaceae.**

dd. Plants with twining stems, dioecious, flowers small, greenish; simple leaves palmately lobed or marginally peltate; fruit a drupe with distinctive seeds .... **Menispermaceae.**

cc. Aromatic trees and shrubs with oil ducts in the wood .... **ff.**

ff. Stamens many, spirally inserted; anthers without lifted valves .... **gg.**

gg. Sepals 3−several, petals numerous (sepals and petals sometimes similar); pistils several to many; fruit not pulpy .... **hh.**

hh. Pistils on elongated axis; fruit aggregate, cone-like; leaves alternate .... **Magnoliaceae.**

hh. Pistils on a hollowed or concave receptacle; leaves opposite .... **Calycanthaceae.**

gg. Sepals 3; petals 3 or 6; pistils few to several, maturing into a pulpy fruit .... **Annonaceae.**

ff. Stamens 6−12 in whorls, opening by raised lids; fruit a drupe .... **Lauraceae.**

x. Pistil of 2 to many carpels united closely into a single ovary; placentation parietal (ovules inserted on walls of the ovary); all flower parts in whorls .... **ii.**

ii. Plants with ordinary leaves (not specialized as insect traps); flowers terminal or axillary but not scapose; sepals 2 or 4 (7 in **Resedaceae**) .... **jj.**

jj. Sepals 2, very rarely 3−4 (presently there is a question about these sepals, and a suggest that, in fact, they are bracts; also, as treated here, this family includes **Fumariaceae** which can be distinguished by irregular flowers with 6 stamens, **Papaveraceae** by regular flowers and 8 to any stamens) .... **Papaveraceae.**

jj. Sepals 4−7 .... **kk.**

kk Sepals and petals 4 each; flowers more or less regular. **ll.**

ll. Stamens 6 or more, equal or nearly so; capsule 1-celled with 2 valves but no partition; leaves with stipules; inflorescence with bracts .... **Capparidaceae.**

ll. Stamens 6, 2 short and inserted lower than the other 4 (tetradynamous); capsule 2-celled with transverse partition (sometimes indehiscent or articulated); stipules and bracts often lacking .... **Cruciferae.**

kk. Sepals and petals 4−7; irregularly compressed around the hypogynous disc; stamens numerous .... **Resedaceae.**

ii. Plants with insect-trapping leaves (bottle-shaped, spoon-shaped with sticky hairs, etc.); flowers on scapes rising from a basal rosette of leaves, sepals 5, rarely 4, persistent .... **mm.**

mm. Leaves tubular, hollow and hooded; ovary and capsule 5-celled, with a single umbrella-like style and stigma .... **Sarraceniaceae.**

mm. Leaves not tubular and hollow, but spoon-shaped with sticky glandular hairs on the blade; ovary and capsule mostly 1-celled; styles 3–5, each 2-parted .... **Droseraceae.**

w. Stamens not hypogynous but perigynous (inserted on the floral-cup), epigynous (inserted above the ovary), or inserted on or at the base of a hypogynous disc .... **nn.**

nn. Pistil simple (one carpel), solitary, or several (rarely more or less united); stamens mostly perigynous; sepals more or less basally connate or fused with a concave receptacle .... **oo.**

oo. Aquatic plants resembling liverworts; flowers with a spathe-like involucre .... **Podostemaceae.**

oo. Plants not thalloid, but with roots, stems and leaves, terrestrial .... **pp.**

pp. Seeds with endosperm, usually copious .... **qq.**

qq. Carpels of the same number as calyx segments, distinct or basally united; endosperm scanty; plants succulent .... **Crassulaceae.**

qq. Carpels mostly fewer than sepals, mostly 2; plants non-succulent herbs or trees .... **rr.**

rr. Fruit a dry capsule or berry, seeds few to many in each cell. In this treatment are included here: *Penthorum*, the saxifrages, *Parnassia*, *Philadelphus*, *Decumaria*, *Hydrangea*, *Itea*, and *Ribes*, now variously considered as separate families .... **Saxifragaceae.**

rr. Fruit a woody capsule adnate to the calyx, one seed in each of the 2 cells; shrubs or rarely trees .... **Hamamelidaceae.**

pp. Seeds with no endosperm (see **Crassulaceae**, above) or with very little, except for *Physocarpus* in **Rosaceae** .... **ss.**

ss. Trees with broad leaves, exfoliating bark; tiny monoecious flowers in spherical heads .... **Platanaceae.**

ss. Herbs or woody plants with perfect flowers (dioecious in *Aruncus*, some species of *Fragaria*, *Gleditsia*, *Gymnocladus*, et al.); corolla usually showy, rarely lacking .... **tt.**

tt. Pistils simple, one to several, distinct, or united in an enclosing floral tube, or single and maturing to a drupe; flowers regular .... **Rosaceae.**

tt. Pistil simple, maturing to a legume with one to several seeds, dehiscent along both sides or a loment with indehiscent segments; flowers regular, small, in dense heads, stamens often numerous (**Mimosaceae**); or flowers partially or nearly regular, stamens ten or fewer (**Cassiaceae**, etc.); or papilionaceous (butterfly-like, as sweet pea), stamens ten or five (**Fabaceae**, etc.) .... **Leguminosae.**

nn. Pistil compound, of several closely united carpels; calyx usually of free sepals .... **uu.**

uu. Stamens few, rarely more than twice as many as the sepals; hypogynous disc often well developed .... **vv.**

vv. Stamens as many as sepals (1–12), and opposite them **ww.**

ww. Stamens often monadelphous or glandular at the base, or borne on the base of the perianth; ovules pendulous, with the raphe toward the axis of the ovary .... **xx.**

xx. Land plants; stamens several .... **yy.**

yy. Flowers with calyx and corolla; perfect (rarely polygamous or dioecious) .... **zz.**

zz. Flowers regular (symmetrical) .... **aaa.**

aaa. Flowers perfect; American species herbacious .... **bbb.**

bbb. Leaves not pinnately compound ..
.... **ccc.**

ccc. Leaves simple, entire, narrow; capsule not splitting and coiling ......
Linaceae.

ccc. Leaves palmate or trifoliate, or palmately lobed or dissected .... **ddd.**

ddd. Leaves palmately compound; stamens twice or thrice the number of petals and of unequal lengths; capsule splitting at five sutures .... **Oxalidaceae**

ddd. Leaves not compound but lobed or variously dissected; stamens of equal length; capsule slender, splitting and coiling when ripe .... **Geraniaceae.**

bbb. Leaves pinnately compound ......
.... **Zygophyllaceae.**

aaa. Flowers perfect or polygamous or of one sex; American species woody .... **eee.**

eee. Leaves aromatic or pungent; punctate-dotted; flowers with prominent hypogynous disc ...... **Rutaceae.**

eee. Leaves not punctate; pinnate-compound .... **fff.**

fff. Leaves once pinnate; flowers in terminal panicles; filaments free, fruit a samara .... **Simaroubaceae.**

fff. Leaves twice pinnate; flowers in axillary panicles; monadelphous; fruit a drupe ... **Meliaceae.**

19

zz. Flowers very irregular with, usually, 3 herbaceous sepals and 2 lateral, petaloid, sepals which are winglike; petals mostly 3; stamens mostly 8 .... **Polygalaceae.**

yy. Flowers mostly apetalous, rarely polypetalous; of one sex; often with highly modified petal-like glands; ovary of 3 carpels; juice milky .... **Euphorbiaceae.**

xx. Mostly aquatic plants; stamens one; flower without perianth, naked or enclosed in membranous bracts in leaf axils . **Callitrichaceae.**

ww. Stamens mostly inserted on or at the base of a hypogynous disc; ovules pendulous with raphe away from the axis of the ovary or ascending with vertical raphe .... **ggg.**

ggg. Flowers regular or mostly so .... **hhh.**

hhh. Flowers apetalous; sepals sometimes petaloid; flowers unisexual or polygamous; leaves evergreen; woody shrubs or perennial herbs .... **iii.**

iii. Stamens 4−7; flowers often in spikes .... **Buxaceae.**

iii. Stamens mostly 3; low heath-like plants . **Empetraceae.**

hhh. Flowers usually with corolla, perfect, polygamous or of one sex .... **jjj.**

jjj. Delicate annuals; flower parts in 3's; fruit 3 achenes ....
.... **Limnanthaceae.**

jjj. Trees, shrubs, or woody vines .... **kkk.**

kkk. Pistil with one cell, 3 styles and stigmas ....
.... **Anacardiaceae.**

kkk. Pistil with 2 or more cells .... **lll.**

lll. Leaves simple and pinnately veined .... **mmm.**

mmm. Seeds without colorful arils .... **nnn.**

nnn. Flowers in racemes, perfect, fruit a capsule .... **Cyrillaceae.**

nnn. Flowers axillary; dioecious or polygamous; fruit a berry-like drupe ... **Aquifoliaceae.**

mmm. Seed with colorful aril; fruit a thickened capsule .... **Celastraceae.**

lll. Leaves simple and palmately veined, or compound .... **ooo.**

ooo. Leaves opposite .... **ppp.**

ppp. Flowers perfect, pistil 3-carpellate; capsule inflated, 3-lobed ...... **Staphylaceae.**

ppp. Flowers dioecious or polygamous; pistil 2-carpellate; fruit a pair of winged samaras ....
.... **Aceraceae.**

ooo. Leaves alternate .... **qqq.**

qqq. Leaves mostly palmately compound; flowers showy, irregular; in a thryse or panicle; fruit a leathery capsule ....
.... **Hippocastanaceae.**

20

qqq. Leaves pinnate or bipinnate; fruit a drupe or inflated capsule .... **Sapindaceae.**

ggg. Flowers very irregular; calyx with spurred or saccate sepal; succulent valves of dehisced capsule coiling; brittle herbs with enlarged nodes .... **Balsaminaceae.**

vv. Stamens as many as the sepals and alternate with them; flowers cyclic; carpels 2–5 .... **rrr.**

rrr. Shrubs, small trees, or vines with pinnately veined simple leaves; petals 4–5, or none; fruit a drupe or capsule .. **Rhamnaceae.**

rrr. Woody vines with tendrils, rarely shrubs; simple leaves palmately veined, usually lobed; petals falling early; fruit a berry .... **Vitaceae.**

uu. Stamens numerous to very numerous (except in some **Guttiferae**, in **Elatinaceae**, 5 in **Violaceae**, and 5 in **Passifloraceae** with many sterile filaments); hypogynous disc scarcely or not at all developed .... **sss.**

sss. Sepals or calyx lobes meeting but not overlapping in the bud (valvate); placentae united in the axis; pubescence mostly stellate . **ttt.**

ttt. Sepals deciduous; stamens in several clusters; anthers 2-celled .... **Tiliaceae.**

ttt. Sepals persistent; filaments of stamens united in a tube through which the style extrudes; anthers 1-celled ... **Malvaceae.**

sss. Sepals or calyx lobes imbricated or convolute; placentae usually parietal, sometimes basal or axile .... **uuu.**

uuu. Styles 3 or 5, distinct; placentae mostly basal or axile; seeds without endosperm .... **vvv.**

vvv. Trees or shrubs with pinnately veined, alternate (rarely opposite) exstipulate, simple leaves; showy flowers terminal or axillary; fruit a woody capsule, 5-celled .... **Theaceae.**

vvv. Shrubs or terrestrial, aquatic, or marsh herbs with opposite or whorled leaves, *or* shrubs with very small, heath-like alternate leaves; capsule 1–5-celled .... **www.**

www. Shrubs or herbs with opposite exstipulate leaves which are mostly pellucid-punctate; flowers showy mostly with 5 sepals and petals; very many stamens .. **Guttiferae.**

www. Opposite or whorled leaves with stipules, or very small exstipulate leaves .... **xxx.**

xxx. Small aquatic or marsh herbs with axillary flowers; capsule 2–5-celled .... **Elatinaceae.**

xxx. Shrubs with heath-like foliage; flowers tiny, in slender racemes; stamens 5; capsule 1-celled .... **Tamaricaceae.**

uuu. Styles united entirely or nearly to the summit or one; placentae parietal; seeds mostly with endosperm .... **yyy.**

yyy. Sepals distinct, mostly persistent .... **zzz.**

zzz. Flowers regular but 2 outer sepals much smaller than inner 3, stamens numerous .... **Cistaceae.**

zzz. Flowers very irregular, commonly spurred (sometimes cleistogamous); stamens 5 .... **Violaceae.**

yyy. Sepals more or less united into a floral cup .. **aaa.**

aaaa. Mostly vines; flowers with fringed crown in the calyx throat; ovary free from floral cup; stamens 5 filaments united to enwrap the very long ovary stalk .... **Passifloraceae.**

aaaa. Mostly herbs with harsh or adhesive pubescence; floral cup adherent to the ovary; stamens numerous; on floral cup .... **Loasaceae.**

v. Ovary inferior, adnate to the floral cup (sometimes only partially) *or* ovary quite enclosed in a tubular or campanulate floral cup .... **a.**

a. Plants fleshy, spiny with spines of 2 sorts in areoles or pulvinii, and with tiny or no leaves (except *Pereskia*); mostly with numerous sepals and petals inserted above a 1-celled ovary; stamens numerous on the floral cup .... **Cactaceae.**

a. Plants herbaceous, or trees, or shrubs, without spines in areoles or pulvinii; not cactus-like .... **b.**

b. Sepals and petals (when present) rarely more than 5; flowers not in umbels nor small and numerous in corymbs; stamens in 2 whorls, mostly inserted on the perianth; style one (except in **Haloragaceae** with 3−4 stigmas) .... **c.**

c. Ovary merely enclosed in, not adnate to, the tubular or campanulate floral cup .... **d.**

d. Petals usually lacking but calyx, petaloid; ovary 1-celled .... **e.**

e. Shrubs or trees with non-scurfy leaves .... **Thymelaeaceae.**

e. Shrubs or trees with scurfy leaves .... **Elaeagnaceae.**

d. Herbs or woody plants; corolla mostly present; ovary 2−6-celled .... **Lythraceae.**

c. Ovary inferior, with calyx and corolla epigynous, or at least the base of the ovary adnate to the floral cup .... **f.**

f. Herbs, shrubs, or trees; flowers with more than one stamen .... **g.**

g. Trees with simple, alternate, exstipulate leaves and small, greenish flowers in terminal or axillary heads .... **Nyssaceae.**

g. Trees, shrubs, or herbs with showy flowers, or aquatic plants with small, green or reduced flowers .... **h.**

h. Herbs or tropical woody plants with showy, perfect flowers; anthers with apical pores .... **Melastomataceae.**

h. Herbs (mostly) and some aquatic or marsh plants; anthers not dehiscing through apical pores .... **i.**

     i.   Plants aquatic, floating leaves with inflated petioles, submersed leaves pinnatifid; flowers among the floating leaves perfect; calyx 4-lobed; petals and stamens perigynous .... **Hydrocaryaceae.**

     i.   Plants not as above .... **j.**

        j.   Plants terrestrial or aquatic; flowers showy; with parts in 4's, less commonly in 2's, 3's, 5's, or 6's; ovary with 2−4 cells, many ovules .... **Onagraceae.**

        j.   Plants mostly aquatic; flowers greenish; indehiscent fruit with 3−4 cells each with one seed .... **Haloragaceae.**

   f.   Soft aquatic plants with small, apetalous flowers; style threadlike with stigma in a longitudinal groove; one large stamen .... **Hippuridaceae.**

b.   Sepals small or reduced; petals 5 or 4; stamens in a single whorl; flowers mostly in umbels or many-flowered corymbs .... **k.**

   k.   Stamens 5; mostly distinct styles 2−5; flowers in umbels or panicles or racemes of small umbels .... **l.**

     l.   Fruit a berry-like drupe .... **Araliaceae.**

     l.   Fruit dry when mature, splitting into 2 mericarps .... **Umbelliferae.**

   k.   Stamens 4; one style, one stigma; flowers not in umbels .... **Cornaceae.**

II$_2$Petals more or less united (distinct or barely coherent in early families, as all or some **Clethraceae, Pyrolaeae, Ericaceae, Primulaceae** (no corolla in *Glaux*), **Styracaceae, Asclepiadaceae, Oleaceae** (no corolla in *Fraxinus)*, **Cucurbitaceae**, and *Galax* in **Diapensiaceae** .... **a.**

   a.   Pistil with superior ovary, *or* if inferior, with anthers opening by apical pores or slits .... **b.**

     b.   Stamens mostly free from the corolla, or adnate only at its base (as in **Diapensiaceae**), as many as corolla lobes and alternate with them, or twice as many .... **c.**

        c.   Stamens free from corolla or merely adnate at its base, not monadelphous .... **d.**

          d.   Corolla with petals always free (polypetalous); ovary 3-celled; fruit a capsule; deciduous shrubs with stellate pubescence .... **Clethraceae.**

          d.   Corolla with petals united (sympetalous) or free; ovary mostly 2−5-celled; mostly evergreen perennials or low shrubs, or saprophytes with no green tissue .... **e.**

            e   Herbs or sub-shrubs, evergreen or saprophytic; here are included the saprophytes *Monotropa* and *Hypopitys* (corolla polypetalous) and *Pterospora* and *Monotropsis* (corolla gamopetalous) which sometimes form the family **Monotropaceae** .... **Pyrolaceae.**

e. Shrubs or trees, evergreen or rarely deciduous; calyx free from the ovary and fruit a capsule *or* ovary inferior and fruit a berry (the latter family **Vacciniaceae** of some authors), *or* drupaceous; corolla mostly sympetalous; well-developed hypogynous disc; ovary 2−10-celled .... **Ericaceae.**

c. Stamens inserted at corolla sinuses (between the lobes), or united in a 10-part tube (monadelphous); .... **Diapensiaceae.**

b. Stamens inserted directly onto the corolla epipetalous .... **f.**

f. Epipetalous stamens as many as corolla lobes and opposite them, *or* twice as many or more .... **g.**

g. Herbs with exstipulate simple leaves; flowers regular, perfect, mostly sympetalous .... **h.**

h. Style one; fruit a capsule .... **Primulaceae.**

h. Styles 5; fruit an achene or utricle ..... **Plumbaginaceae.**

g. Shrubs or trees with simple, alternate leaves; flowers regular; perfect, polygamous, or dioecious .... **i.**

i. Stamens as many as corolla lobes; ovary superior; style one; plants with milky juice (latex) .... **Sapotaceae.**

i. Stamens twice as many as corolla lobes, or more .... **j.**

j. Trees with no latex; flowers of 1 sex or polygamous; styles 2−8 .... **Ebenaceae.**

j. Flowers mostly perfect; style one, simple or lobed . **k.**

k. Stamens in clusters; pubescence simple .... **Symplocaceae.**

k. Stamens in a single series; pubescent stellate or scurfy .... **Styracaceae.**

f. Epipetalous stamens as many as corolla lobes or fewer, and alternate with them .... **l.**

l. Carpels two, united or distinct below the united styles; stamens 2 or 4−5; leaves mostly opposite .... **m.**

m. Flowers perfect or of one sex, regular; stamens (mostly 2) fewer than corolla lobes (or corolla lacking) and alternating with the carpels .... **Oleaceae.**

m. Flowers with 4−5 calyx lobes, corolla lobes, and stamens; epipetalous .... **n.**

n. Stigmas distinct; ovary one, compound; juice not milky .... **o.**

o. Ovary 2-celled; leaves stipulate or petiole bases joined by a stipular line .... **Loganiaceae.**

o. Ovary one-celled; leaves not stipulate (this includes some authors' **Menyanthaceae** which can be separated from **Gentianaceae** by leaves basal or alternate, aquatic or marsh plants) ...... **Gentianaceae.**

n. Stigmas united; ovaries mostly 2, or united with 2 placentae; juice milky .... **p.**

p.   Styles united; stamens with distinct filaments; pollen loose, of free grains .... **Apocynaceae.**

p.   Styles distinct but carpels united by stigmatic body; stamens monadelphous (filament tube forming the floral column); pollen in waxy pollinia or in granular masses   **Asclepiadaceae.**

l.   Compound pistil (except one carpel in **Phrymaceae**) with a single ovary and 2−5 cells or placentae (ovary divided in *Dichondra* and deeply 4-lobed in **Boraginaceae** and **Labiatae**); flowers regular or irregular; stamens distinct, mostly epipetalous .... **q.**

q.   Corolla regular (irregular in *Echium*); stamens as many as corolla lobes, 4−5 .... **r.**

r.   Ovary round, not 4-lobed; carpels not separating into nutlets on maturity .... **s.**

s.   Ovary 2-celled, rarely 3−4 celled; style one, entire, cleft, or 2-parted; mostly twining vines .... **Convolvulaceae**

(This treatment includes in **Convolvulaceae** the **Dichondraceae**, ovary completely divided into 2 carpels, and the **Cuscutaceae**, white or amber parasitic vines with leaves reduced to scales).

s.   Ovary not 2-celled (except *Hydrolea*); herbs, not twining vines .... **t.**

t.   Ovary 3-celled; stigmas 3, slender ... **Polemoniaceae.**

t.   Ovary one-celled (except *Hydrolea*); style one, lobed or divided .... **Hydrophyllaceae.**

r.   Ovary deeply 4-lobed around the style, but actually 2-celled, or not lobed in *Heliotropium*; nutlets separating on maturity .... **Boraginaceae.**

q.   Corolla mostly irregular, often more or less bilabiate, sometimes nearly regular, dry (regular and petaloid in **Solanaceae**); stamens mostly fewer than corolla lobes, 2 or 4, but 5 in **Solanaceae** .... **u.**

u.   Corolla petaloid, carpels 2 with one to many ovules ...... **v.**

v.   Carpels with 1−2 ovules .... **w.**

w.   Ovary not lobed, with 2 or 4 cells; style apical .... **Verbenaceae.**

w.   Ovary 4-lobed around the style, lobes maturing into nutlets .... **Labiatae.**

v.   Carpels with several to many ovules (some **Acanthaceae** with only 2) .... **x.**

x.   Flowers regular or nearly so; stamens same number as corolla lobes (4 plus 1 in Petunia); fruit a berry or capsule .. .. **Solanaceae.**

x.   Flowers markedly irregular .... **y.**

y.   Plants terrestrial with green stems and leaves; capsules not elastically dehiscent .... **z.**

> **z.** Placentae axile; ovary and capsule 2-celled ... . **Scrophulariaceae.**
>
> **z.** Placentae parietal; ovary with one cell or seemingly divided by intrusion of placentae or false septa .... **aa.**
>
>> **aa.** Trees, shrubs, or woody vines, seeds large, mostly winged .... **Bignoniaceae.**
>>
>> **aa.** Annual soft-leaved herbs, seeds never winged .... **Martyniaceae.**
>
> **y.** Plants non-green (root parasites) or aquatic or marsh-dwelling, or if green and terrestrial, with elastically dehiscent pods .... **bb.**
>
>> **bb.** Plants root parasites, non-green; leaves reduced to colored scales .... **Orobanchiaceae.**
>>
>> **bb.** Plants with chlorophyll .... **cc.**
>>
>>> **cc.** Aquatic or marsh plants with one-celled ovary; placenta free central . **Lentibulariaceae.**
>>>
>>> **cc.** Terrestrial plants with 2-celled ovary and capsule; elastically dehiscent; placentae axile .. .. **Acanthaceae.**

u. Corolla dry-scarious or membranous, or if petaloid, with one carpel, one ovule .... **dd.**

> **dd.** Corolla petaloid; carpel one with a single ovule .... **Phrymaceae.**
>
> **dd.** Corolla dry-scarious or membranous; ovary 2-celled or falsely 3—4-celled; ovules 1—several .... **Plantaginaeae.**

a. Pistil with inferior ovary, sometimes only partially so .... **ee.**

ee. Anthers free .... **ff.**

> **ff.** Stamens as many as corolla lobes and alternate with them (one fewer in *Linnaea*), *or* twice as many; ovary compound with ovules (one or many) in each cell .... **gg.**
>
> **gg.** Stamens as many as corolla lobes .... **hh.**
>
>> **hh.** Leaves stipulate, mostly simple, entire, usually blackening on drying; chiefly a tropical and warm climate family .... **Rubiaceae.**
>>
>> **hh.** Leaves mostly exstipulate, often serrate, not blackening when dry .... **Caprifoliaceae.**
>
> **gg.** Stamens twice as many as corolla lobes; rosetted leaves ternate-compound .... **Adoxaceae.**
>
> **ff.** Stamens usually fewer than corolla lobes; ovary a single cell and one ovule, or if 3-celled, 2 cells empty .... **ii.**
>
>> **ii.** Ovary 3-celled, 2 cells empty; calyx merely a ring, or developing into pappus-like plumes .... **Valerianaceae.**
>>
>> **ii.** Ovary one-celled; flowers densely capitate, involucrate, each embraced by a pair of bracteoles forming an epicalyx .... **Dipsacaceae.**

ee. Anthers mostly united (but no so in *Campanula* and *Specularia*) or in several genera of **Compositae** as here presented .... **jj.**

> **jj.** Flowers not in involucrate heads; juice mostly milky; flowers regular or irregular .... **Campanulaceae.**
>
> > (Some authors separate **Campanulaceae**, with flowers regular, and **Lobeliaceae**, flowers irregular.)
>
> **jj.** Flowers in involucrate heads .... **Compositae.**
>
> > This inclusive treatment of **Compositae** is altered sometimes to separate out, variously, **Chicoraceae** with flowers all ligulate and juice milky, **Ambrosiaceae** with flowers all tubular or only the outer ones ligulate, stamens distinct, and juice rarely milky, and **Compositae** with anthers united into a tube around the style.)

What Plant Is That?

Gardeners and natural history enthusiasts share a mutual problem. What tag goes on each plant — garden ornamental or wildflower? We need names for plants to be able to enjoy them fully. How can you look up library references dealing with a plant that strikes your fancy if you do not know its name? How can you intelligently discuss a plant without knowing its name? Names are essential. We have to learn all about them.

Taxonomy is the science of classification. Plant taxonomists classify plants according to their relationship to other plants. For example, if a non-woody (that is, herbaceous) perennial plant has flowers with five separate sepals, and five separate petals, and numerous stamens, and a central cluster of simple pistils, and all of these floral parts are inserted on the same plane — that is, none is above or below another so far as basal attachment is concerned — then there is just one thing that plant can be. It has to be a buttercup. Of course, there are many kinds of buttercups: tall ones and short ones, small-flowered and large-flowered ones, attractive ones and weedy ones. But all of them have the same basic flower structure.

Throughout the world more than 150,000 different species of plants have been identified. These group together into more than 37,000 genera. For example, the slippery elm, the American elm, the September elm, the winged elm, the Chinese elm, and the Siberian elm all are separate, recognizable *species*. But they have features in common that make all of them recognizable as elms. The various species group together in the elm *genus* (plural, *genera*). Several species of hackberries make up the hackberry genus. Elm, hackberry, planer-tree and several other genera group together to form the elm *family*. In this family we find some 140 species grouped together in twelve or thirteen genera, depending on which authority we consult.

It is handy to be able to look at a plant and say "That is in the elm family," or "That is in the buckwheat family." If you are able to learn plant family characteristics — say, key traits for 100 families or perhaps a few more you can pigeonhole most American flowering plants you meet into the correct family. Once you know the family, determining genus and species is no great problem.

When you walk into a room you are able to tell the piano from the television and these from the bookcase because of their characteristics. Without thinking, your mind runs through an analysis of characteristics. The thing with a row of black and white keys, a music rack, and a table-like or upright form has to be a piano. Why not an organ? No array of foot pedals, no rows of stops near the keyboard. You do not have to think all of this out. Your mind does it automatically.

Study the characteristics of plant families, and soon you will be automatically classifying at least some of the plants you encounter with similar automatic analyses. Is it an herbaceous or not too woody plant with simple leaves and with every stem joint (node) wrapped in a tissue-paper-like membrane? Surely it is in the buckwheat family, because no other plants have this peculiar structure. Are there four petals, separate, arranged cross-fashion, and two groups of stamens, four long ones and two short ones? Is the pistil composed of two carpels as indicated by the two stigmas at the top? Surely it is in the mustard family. Having decided that the plant is in the mustard family it takes no great search to determine if it is an *Arabis*, a bitter-cress, a stock, a wall-flower, or some other relative.

It is tempting to plunge right into these easy field characteristics. But that method leads to chaos. You have to learn a new vocabulary. You need to know how botanists group plants according to natural relationships. You need to learn all of the parts of a flower and all of the ways these parts can be put together. Armed with this tool kit of new words — facts concerning plant relationships and flower structure — you can tackle descriptions of a list of plant families with considerable understanding. Before long you will see features that group *Clematis,* columbine, aconite, *Delphinium, Anemone,* and marsh-marigold together in the buttercup family just as surely as you know that spinnets, virginals, harpsichords, and grand pianos all are related.

Variations in Flowers

COMPLETE AND PERFECT FLOWERS

A complete flower is one with calyx, corolla, stamens, and pistil — that is, all parts are present. A flower lacking either of the floral envelopes or the stamens or the pistil is said to be incomplete.

A perfect flower is one with both stamens and a pistil, that is, a flower capable of reproduction within itself. If either stamens or pistil are lacking, the flower is said to be imperfect. Flowers with only stamens and no pistil are called staminate flowers and flowers with only pistils but with no stamens are said to be pistilate flowers.

The following chart illustrates the relationship of flower parts and the terminology which describes their presence (or absence).

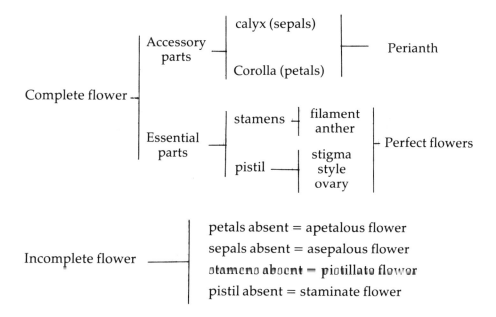

Complete flower
- Accessory parts
  - calyx (sepals)
  - Corolla (petals) — Perianth
- Essential parts
  - stamens — filament, anther
  - pistil — stigma, style, ovary — Perfect flowers

Incomplete flower
- petals absent = apetalous flower
- sepals absent = asepalous flower
- stamens absent = pistillate flower
- pistil absent = staminate flower

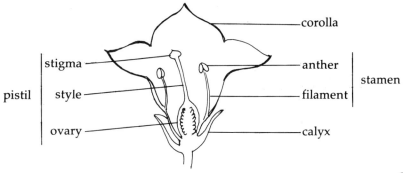

pistil — stigma, style, ovary

corolla, anther, filament, calyx — stamen

Two more terms very commonly used in describing the flowers of a plant have to do with staminate and pistillate flowers. A plant is said to be *monoecious* when the stamens and pistils are in separate flowers on the same individual plant. Corn is a good example of this sort of thing; the tassel is composed only of male (staminate) flowers, while the ears are composed of female (pistillate) flowers. Monoecious means literally one household, thus suggesting that single plant is capable of reproduction though a single flower on the plant is not. The other term is *dioecious*, used to describe a species with individual plants of one sex only. American holly is a good example of this; some plants produce only male (staminate) flowers while other plants produce only female (pistillate) flowers. Two plants are required for reproduction.

Acanthaceae Acanthus Family (p. 56)
Ruellia strepens Wild-petunia

Amaryllidaceae Amaryllis Family (p. 64)
Lycoris radiata Short-tube Lycoris

Galanthus nivalis Snowdrop

Araceae Arum Family (p. 72)
Arisaema atrorubens Jack-in-the-pulpit

Berberidaceae Barberry Family (p. 82)
Epimedium pinnatum Barrenwort

Asclepiadaceae Milkweed Family (p. 78)
Asclepias tuberosa Butterfly Weed

Boraginaceae Borage Family (p. 88)
Lithospermum canescens Puccoon

Calycanthaceae
Sweet-shrub Family (p. 93)
Calycanthus fertilis Pale Sweet-shrub

Campanulaceae Bellflower Family (p. 96)
Campanula garganica Serbian Bellflower

Campanula portenschlagiana
(= *C. muralis*) Dalmatian Bellflower

Caprifoliaceae
Honeysuckle Family (p. 102)
Lonicera flava Yellow Honeysuckle

Viburnum tomentosum
Doublefile Viburnum

Caryophyllaceae Pink Family (p. 104)
Silene regia Royal Catchfly

Cistaceae Rock-rose Family (p. 110)
Helianthemum nummularium cultivar
Sun-rose Cultivar

Compositae Composite Family (p. 114)
Centaurea montana Mountain Knapweed

Hymenopappus scabiosaeus
No common name; biennial; uncommon plant.

Cirsium undulatum album
White-flowered Wavy-leaf Thistle

Senecio plattensis Prairie Ragwort

Cornaceae Dogwood Family (p. 118)
Cornus florida Flowering Dogwood

Cucurbitaceae Gourd Family (p. 124)
Cucumis sativus cultivar
Garden Cucumber Cultivar
Female flower right; male flower left

Elaeagnaceae Oleaster Family (p. 136)
Elaeagnus umbellata Autumn-olive

Euphorbiaceae Spurge Family (p. 140)
Euphorbia corollata Flowering Spurge

Ericaceae Heath Family (p. 138)
Rhododendron cultivars
Exbury Azalea Cultivars

Geraniaceae Geranium Family (p. 146)
Erodium manescavii Pyrenees Heronbill

Iridaceae Iris Family (p. 158)
Crocus speciosus and *C. speciosus alba*
Autumn-flowering Crocuses

Crocus chrysanthus 'E. A. Bowles'
E. A. Bowles Crocus

Hippocastanaceae
Horse-chestnut Family (p. 154)
Aesculus pavia Red Buckeye

Leguminosae Pulse Family (p. 166)
Baptisia Hybrid *B. australis × leucantha*
Hybrid Wild-indigo

Schrankia uncinata Sensitive Brier

Lupinus polyphyllus, Russell Hyrid
Russell Lupin

Baptisia leucophaea
Buffalo Pea or Long-bracted Wild Indigo

Liliaceae Lily Family (p. 170)
Allium christophii (= *A. albopilosum*)
Star-of-Persia

Fritillaria meleagris Guinea Flower
Type species and var. *alba*

Camassia scilloides Wild-hyacinth

Chionodoxa luciliae Glory of the Snow

Labiatae Mint Family (p. 162)
Monarda russeliana Wild Bergamot

Linaceae Flax Family (p. 172)
Linum perenne Perennial Flax

Malvaceae Mallow Family (p. 178)
Hibiscus rosa-sinensis cultivar
Chinese Hibiscus cultivar

Nyctaginaceae
Four-o'clock Family (p. 188)
Mirabilis jalapa Four-o'clock

Nymphaeaceae Water-lily Family (p. 190)
Nelumbo nucifera cultivar
Sacred Lotus cultivar

Phytolaccaceae Pokeweed Family (p. 204)
Phytolacca americana Pokeweed

Onagraceae
Evening-primrose Family (p. 194)
Ludwigia alternifolia Seedbox

Oenothera speciosa
White Evening-primrose

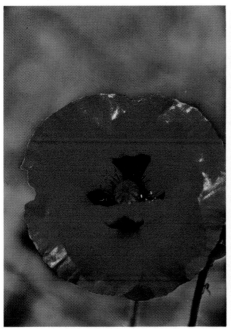 

Papaveraceae Poppy Family (p. 200) *Chelidonium majus* Greater Celandine
Papaver rhoeas Corn Poppy

Passifloraceae
Passion-flower Family (p. 202)
Passiflora incarnata   *Passiflora incarnata* var. *alba*
Passion-flower, Maypop   Passion-flower, Maypop

Plumbaginaceae
Plumbago Family (p. 210)
Plumbago capensis Cape Plumbago

Polygonaceae Buckwheat Family (p. 216)
Polygonum aubertii Silver Lace-vine,
Fleece vine

Polemoniaceae Phlox Family (p. 212)
Phlox divaricata var. *laphamii* forma *candida*
White Wild Sweet William

Rosaceae Rose Family (p. 230)
Rosa setigera Prairie Rose

Ranunculaceae Buttercup Family (p. 224)
Anemone blanda Grecian Windflower

Helleborus niger Christmas-rose
(opening white, aging to pink)

Clematis × *jackmanii* 'The President'
The President Hybrid Clematis

Scrophulariaceae Figwort Family (p. 242)
Veronica teucrium Germander Speedwell

Solanaceae Nightshade Family (p. 244)
Lycopersicon esculentum Tomato

Violaceae Violet Family (p. 266)
Viola pedata Bird's foot Violet

Flower Functions

THE FLOWER IN A PLANT'S LIFE-CYCLE

Nature designs each species to reproduce itself; higher plants accomplish this by seeds in most cases. Annual plants complete their life-cycle in one year. A seed germinates, makes a seedling which grows into a leafy plant which soon flowers and when the flower is pollinated, eventually seed is set and the plant dies. A biennial plant takes two years to accomplish the same thing. The first year's growth includes the seed to seedling to leafy plant stages, and early the following growing season the plant blooms and sets seed, then dies. Perennial plants go on year after year, blooming and setting seeds, but at least some part of the plant persists. Thus, we know herbaceous perennials which are the ones which die back to the ground so that only the root system persists to send up new leafy, flowering shoots year after year. The grasses and border perennials such as chrysanthemums, shasta daisies, bleeding-hearts, daylilies, irises, and the like are typical herbaceous perennials. Other perennial plants develop wood in the stems and branches and the above-ground portions live on year after year. Trees and shrubs are actually woody perennials, but usually we just refer to them as woody plants with the understanding that they are long-lived.

Strangely, living "stuff" persists in resisting ultimate destruction. If a plant is imperiled by some sort of catastrophe — say, a change in grade or severe storm damage — it may, quite out of season, attempt to flower and set at least a few viable seeds before it dies. A river bottom species such as the velvet plant, which is a weedy, invasive annual, grows into a sizeable plant, knee to waist-high, before flowering. By the time frost kills it, it may be head-high. But if flood waters destroy the early crop and keep the land inundated for a long time, in late summer or early fall exposed seeds will germinate, make only seed-leaves and a rather crippled flower with only a few ovules, completing the life-cycle in less than a month rather than the usual eighty or ninety days.

The flower, then, is the apex of the plant's life-cycle, or rather, the seed which develops from the flower and insures continuity of the species. Gardeners have long since learned that many blooming plants, especially annuals and biennials, can be kept in flower by the simple expedient of removing spent flowers as they wilt, and so preventing the development of seeds. Nature requires seeds, so the plants rebloom. Let's take a look at what goes on in a flower to make the seed crop develop.

A flower has sepals which collectively are referred to as the calyx; petals which collectively are referred to as the corolla; stamens which are the male organs of the flower, and carpels making up the pistil which is the female organ of the plant. Stamens and pistils are normally involved in reproducing the species.

Pollination refers to the transfer of pollen from the anther portion of the stamen to the stigma portion of the pistil. Some flowers produce quantities of light, airy pollen which become wind-borne and pollination is pure happenstance. Plants which depend on wind-borne pollen for pollination often have large anthers, feathery or well-developed and often extended stigmas, and not uncommonly the flowers of these are rather plain as compared to the larger, brightly colored and showy blossoms of insect pollinated plants. Plants which are not pollinated by wind-borne pollen usually depend on some sort of creature — usually an insect — to transfer pollen from the anthers to the stigmas. In many cases such pollen is heavy and may be waxy or sticky. Often stigmas are blunt and may be quite sticky. Flowers of these often are larger and showy or if small, are in clusters, so insect pollinators are attracted. Many intriguing unique arrangements exist where specialized flower structure guarantees pollination or where a specific insect and a specific plant are intimately involved with the perpetuation of both species. In the former cases think of some of the pea flowers where one of the ten stamens is cocked like the hammer of a pistol and when an invading insect intent on nectar deep in the blossom triggers the stamens, the insect is dusted with pollen which then is transferred to the stigma as he backs from the nectary to go to another flower — and some pollen will be carried along. A specific moth is required to successfully transfer pollen in yucca blossoms; the moth oviposits eggs in one carpel of the flower's compound pistil, so when we examine capsules of the yucca we usually find that one entire row of seeds has been devoured by the larvae of the moth, but the remaining seeds are fertile due to proper pollination. Milkweed flowers actually entangle insects which visit them, wrapping pollen clusters round their legs to be carried to neighboring blossoms.

Fertilization follows pollination. The stigmatic surface is moist, with a solution of various substances including sugars, proteins, and growth substances. When pollen grains of a compatible species land on the stigma, these substances in the solution stimulate the pollen grains to "germinate". A bulge develops in the outer wall of the pollen grain, this "bubble" elongates (it now is called a germ tube) and shoves its way downward through the cells of the stigma and style, penetrates through the cells of the carpel walls, protrudes through the cavity (locule) of the ovary to the exposed portion of an ovule (the micropile), and eventually reaches the egg cell within the ovule. While the germ tube has been developing and elongating two sperm cells have formed within it and these move toward the tip. When the tip end of the germ tube reaches the egg cell it opens and out come the sperm cells. One of the sperm cells fuses with the egg cell and this fusion is known as fertilization. The other sperm cell moves further into the embryo sac to fuse with two polar nuclei and the product of this triple fusion will be the endosperm tissue, rich in stored food materials, which will nurture the embryo either during development or later at germination.

The fertilized egg (product of egg cell and sperm cell fusion) is called a zygote. The zygote undergoes repeated cellular division, cellular specialization occurs, and an embryo develops. The embryo is a rudimentary plant; it lies enclosed in concentric layers of tissue — endosperm, nucellus, testas

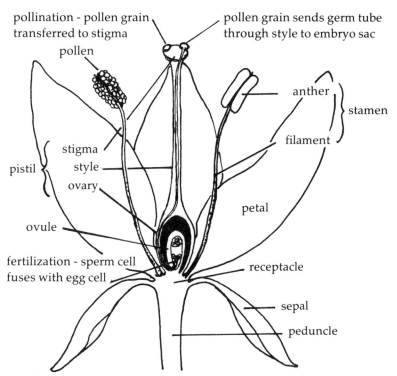

pollination - pollen grain transferred to stigma

pollen grain sends germ tube through style to embryo sac

pollen

anther

stamen

filament

stigma

pistil

style

ovary

ovule

petal

fertilization - sperm cell fuses with egg cell

receptacle

sepal

peduncle

(the inner and outer seed coats) — which make up the seed, and the seed is enclosed in some sort of fruit which protects it during development.

Seeds vary greatly in composition and structure. The embryo may be large — as in the case of legumes where the fleshy cotyledons, filled with stored food reserves are "hinged" by the axis of the rudimentary plant, *radicle* (root to be) pointing downward and *plumule* (leafy shoot to be) pointing upward — or very small as in orchid seeds which are only a few cells in a scant wrapping of a few more cells, the whole almost microscopic. The nutritive layers, endosperm (the product of triple fusion) and nucellus (maternal tissue surrounding the embryo sac) may be well developed (either or both) or virtually used up or undeveloped (either or both). The inner and outer seed coats usually are fused into a single often brittle or leathery protective layer. Where the stalk of the seed (the placental attachment) breaks away a scar persists called the *hilum*, there may be a ridge adjacent the hilum formed by the fusion of seed coats and placental attachment, the *raphe*, and at one end of the hilum may be a very tiny pore, the remnant of the micropile through which the germ tube entered prior to fertilization.

As a flower is pollinated and germ tubes develop usually the blossom begins to wilt; as egg cells are fertilized and the growth of embryos in ovules progresses, the ovary portion of the pistil enlarges to form some sort of fruit. It may be a berry, as a tomato or blueberry, it may be a drupe, as a cherry or plum, it may be a pepo as a melon or gourd, a samara as an elm fruit, a nut as an acorn, or any of many other fruit forms. Fruits are often handy key characters and it pays to know all about them.

The following list briefly describes commonly encountered fruits as well a structures called fruits. Fruit terms are based on the pericarp which is the thickened ovary wall. The pericarp may develop in three layers, each varying among plants. The outer layer, exocarp, consists usually of a single layer of cells but sometimes it is several layers thick; the "skin" of a tomato is a good example. The middle pericarp layer is called the mesocarp which may vary from a single layer of cells to a very thick and fleshy or fibrous mass of tissue; the "meat" of a peach is an example. The endocarp, the innermost pericarp layer, is the most variable of the three; it may be just one cell deep and almost jelly-like or skin-like, or it may be thicker and fleshy or hard and woody; the shell of a walnut is endocarp.

A. *Simple Fruits.* Consisting of a single matured ovary, plus in few species, adhering sepals, stamens, even petals, the simple fruit, in its several types, is the commonest fruit. Simple fruits are classified as follows:

1. Fleshy Fruits. All or most of the pericarp is more or less soft and fleshy at maturity.

a. Berry. The entire pericarp becomes fleshy though the exocarp may be a thin, often tough, skin. Examples: blueberry, banana, grape, tomato.

aa. Hesperidium. A berry with a distinct, leathery rind. Examples: grapefruit, lemon, orange.

bb. Pepo. A berry with a hard, not separating rind.

b. Drupe. The exocarp is thin, skin-like; the mesocarp is fleshy, meaty, or juicy; the endocarp is hard and stony, forming a "pit" or "stone" which contains one, or rarely two or three, seeds each with a thin, papery seed-coat. Examples: apricot, cherry, olive, peach, walnut.

2. Dry Fruits. The entire pericarp matures to become dry, usually hard or brittle. Note that the table vegetables among these are eaten in a tender, immature stage in most cases.

a. Dehiscent Fruits. These split open at definite seams or at definite points at maturity; they contain one to several seeds; commonly encountered dehiscent, dry fruits are further classified as:

aa. Follicle. Fruit consists of a single carpel (simple ovary) which, when dry, splits open along a single seam. Example: aconite, columbine, delphinium, peony, spirea.

bb. Legume. Fruit consists of a single carpel which, when dry, splits open along two longitudinal seams. Examples: Albizia, bean, locust, pea, soybean.

Loment. A legume which, upon maturity breaks into single seeded segments (articles), as Desmodium.

cc. Silique. Usually tube-like fruit consisting of two carpels which separate length-wise at maturity, to reveal the papery partition (replum) which separates the valves. Examples: Draba, money-plant, radish, shepherd's purse.

Silicle. A stubby silique, as Alyssum, woad.

dd. Capsule. Fruit consists of sometimes two

but usually three or more carpels. Capsules split any of several ways to free the several to many seeds; septicidal dehiscence, seams along the carpel margins; loculicidal dehiscence, seam dorsal to the locule and not where carpels unite; circumscissile dehiscence; seam opening around the capsule (as opposed to lengthwise seams), as exemplified by poppy. A special case is the Pyxis or Pyxidium, where circumscissile dehiscence occurs and a "lid", the upper portion of the capsule, falls away, as Anagallis, plantain, and Portulaca. In a few families capsules open by more or less terminal pores, a condition described as poricidal dehiscence, and exemplified by snapdragon. Typical capsules are evening-primrose, lily, tulip, violet, and Yucca.

   b.   Indehiscent Fruits. These do not split open along definite seams or at definite points at maturity, often they contain only one or two seeds, usually they are papery, horny, or woody.

      ee.   Achene (Nutlet). Fruit contains only one seed which is separated from the ovary wall except at a single, often minute point. Examples: buttercup, dandelion, strawberry, sunflower, silver-lace vine. Sedges and reeds produce achenes, a handy point of distinction from the grain-bearing grasses.

      ff.   Caryopsis (Grain). Fruit contains only one seed which is completely fused to the endocarp, making distinctions between seed-coat (testa) and ovary wall (pericarp) difficult. Examples: corn, grass "seeds" of all sorts, oats, rice, wheat. It is important to learn that a grain of corn, grass, rice, etc., is a complete *fruit*, not just a seed.

      gg.   Samara. Fruit with one or two seeds, pericarp with a lateral, flattened outgrowth which forms a wing-like structure. Example: single-seeded, circumferal wing, elm, wafer-ash; single or double-seeded, lateral-winged, ash, maple.

      hh.   Schizocarp. Fruit of two fused carpels, usually, which split apart at maturity, each portion containing a single seed which often is fused with the endocarp. Examples, carrot, dill, harbinger-of-spring, lovage, navelwort, water-hemlock.

      ii.   Nut. Fruit one-seeded, similar to an achene with a more-thickened, hard pericarp. Example: acorn, hazelnut.

B   *Aggregate Fruits.* An aggregate fruit is composed of several distinct ovaries from a single flower (borne on the same receptacle). The individual ovaries may develop into drupes, as the individual globules (druplets) of raspberries (the entire raspberry is an aggregate fruit), or into achenes (nutlets) as in the burr-like fruits of certain buttercups. The blackberry is a special case, depending on authority; the white core develops from the receptacle, so technically, there is reason to call a blackberry an accessory fruit (see below); modern authorities tend to include it with the aggregate fruits.

C.   *Multiple (Compound) Fruits.* A multiple fruit develops from a cluster of several, often many, matured ovaries from several separate flowers which are crowded closely into an inflorescence. The fruitlets of a multiple fruit may be berries, drupes, or nutlets, rarely another sort of simple fruit. Examples: mulberries, Osage-orange, pineapple.

D. *Accessory Fruits.* Fruits consist of matured ovary or ovaries plus other flower parts — usually the floral cup or receptacle or both — which adhere to or partially or entirely enclose the ovary or ovaries. The most typical accessory fruit probably is the Pome; the ovary walls develop into a pericarp which is partly horny, partly fleshy, and the entire ovary then is surrounded intimately by more fleshy tissue derived from the floral cup. Examples are apple, pear, and quince; the core and immediately surrounding edible tissue is pericarp while most of the fruit is from the floral cup. Some authorities place the fig in this category but others classify it as a multiple fruit. The edible portion of a fig is fleshy receptable tissue; tiny, crowded flowers inside the hollow, pear-shaped receptacle bear individual ovaries, one-seeded, each of which matures to a tiny achene (nutlet), the gritty structures in a fig. Similarly, a strawberry is receptacle material, this time cone-shaped, which becomes fleshy and juicy, bearing on its surface, partially embedded, tiny achenes, each of which is a true fruit having developed from the many separate pistils of the strawberry flower.

Certain plant families can be spotted by their fruits, or in some cases, the fruits are a strong pointer toward a certain family. The Cruciferae produce siliques and silicles; the Umbelliferae produce schizocarps; the primitive buttercups produce individual achenes or achenes clustered into aggregate fruits while more advanced members of the Ranunculaceae bear follicles. Legumes and loments are typical of the Leguminosae. Nutlet grouping and arrangement can help in separating borages, mints and a few other plants.

Floral Diagram Technique

The floral diagram presents an interpretation of a flower sliced flat across (cross or transverse section) as you look down on it. If an almost open bud is cut across the resulting cut face will provide a fairly good pattern for a floral diagram. The idea of the diagram, then, is to show the proper relationships of the component parts of a flower in a stylized sketch.

To make diagrams of flowers you need to become adept at cutting (actually or mentally) cross-sections of buds and flowers and in sketching the various parts as they relate one to another. If the flower is complete, there will be an outer whorl of sepals, an inner whorl of petals, one or more whorls of stamens, with the pistil or pistils in the center, also cut across to show internal details. Every taxonomist has his own method of stylizing the various parts. An easy way to begin is to show the sepals as elongated, solidly-shaded crescents, the petals as open (unshaded) crescents, the stamens as cross-sections of the anthers (here you can use considerable latitude because anthers are shaped differently in various flowers and a more or less accurate transverse section makes your sketch more valuable), and the pistil as an interpretation of the flower's ovary, as shown by exterior form (angle-sided or round), thick or thin-walled, and if at all possible, internal seed arrangement (placentation).

Radially symmetrical flowers such as the lily, iris, buttercup, primrose, or cactus are easily illustrated; the real trick is to become adept at sketching true circles very lightly, which will serve as guides for the concentric whorls of flower parts. Zygomorphic flowers such as grasses, orchids, peas, mints, and some of the composites require a bit more doing in order to keep proportions right. But when well done, the floral diagram of an irregular flower is exceptionally valuable in showing fusion of the various parts as well as relationships in position.

To begin, look at this diagram of an imaginary flower.

The outer whorl shows five sepals; the next inner whorl shows five petals which alternate with the sepals, next five stamens alternating with the petals, and finally, in the center, a simple pistil with a single ovule showing no attachment to the pistil wall, thus suggesting basal placentation. There is more to be read into this; as the sepals are shown with no lateral connections it is to be assumed that the flower is polysepalous, that is, each sepal is distinct; the corolla likewise is polypetalous. The stamens are inserted either on a floral cup or below the ovary as they show no attachment to the petals, and the pistil is composed of a single carpel.

The Sepals

The following diagrams show various arrangements of sepals:

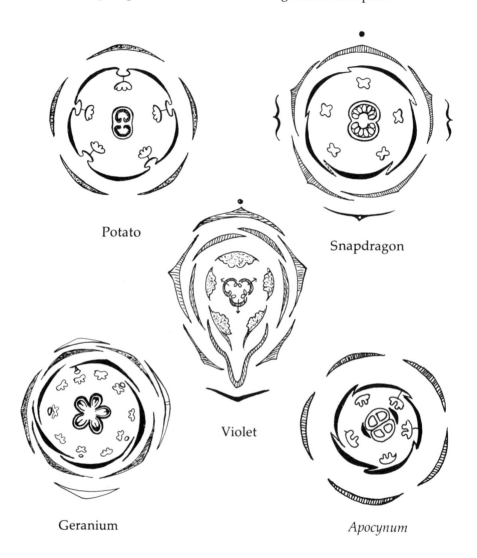

Potato

Snapdragon

Violet

Geranium

Apocynum

The flower of the potato is regular; the calyx is of five distinct sepals which neither overlap nor closely touch. The construction is simple, as shown. Snapdragon flowers are zygomorphic, but the calyx is considerably more regular than the corolla; while the pistil, corolla, and epipetalous stamens are bilaterally symmetrical, the sepals are not quite mirror images on the two halves of the flower. The five sepals of the geranium flower are imbricated, that is, some sepals completely overlap some others; even so, the flower is considered to be radially symmetrical. Flowers of the spurred violas and violets are constructed to accommodate the nectar-secreting sac (spur) which projects beyond the calyx even when the flower is in tight bud. The flowers of *Apocynum* are regular, and the calyx is synsepalous, with the joined sepals furled at least in the bud, as shown.

The Petals

Petals, in the floral diagram, are not as interesting as the sepals because their position and form are apt to be relatively symmetrical, either showing radial symmetry or bilateral symmetry. Still, it is important to get position correct, and if there is some special feature that can be suggested, include it, as for example, the papery, crinkled texture of poppy petals, or the thickened and ribbed petals of balsam, or the in-rolled though united petals of lilac.

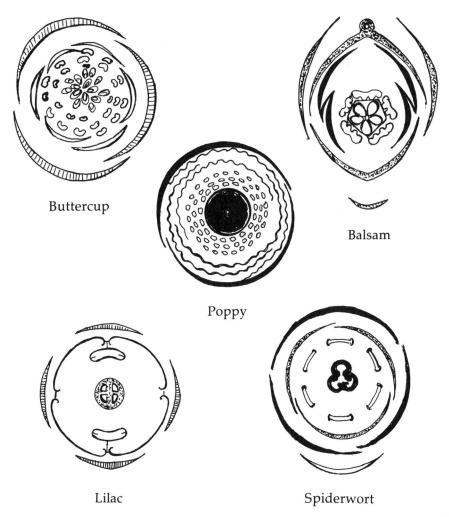

Buttercup

Poppy

Balsam

Lilac

Spiderwort

The Stamens

Even the most staid botanist seems to let himself go when drawing stamens in his floral diagrams. In the literature one sees them in all shapes and sizes, and in flowers such as buttercups, mallows, and poppies, where stamens are very numerous, in a diagram at least fifteen or so should be drawn in; often there are dozens. The form usually is taken from a cross-section of the anther; but in special cases such as the milkweeds and orchids, various schematic presentations are found in the literature. Two of each are shown below:

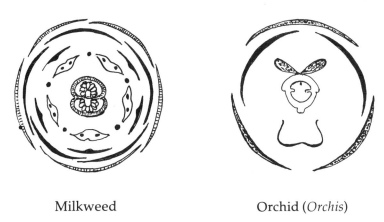

Milkweed   Orchid (*Orchis*)

The insertion of stamens, unless indicated by special notation remains unknown in a floral diagram unless the stamens are epipetalous. When stamens are inserted on the petals as shown for potato, snapdragon, and others, and below for trumpet-creeper and bluebell, a line connects the stamen symbol to the petal symbol:

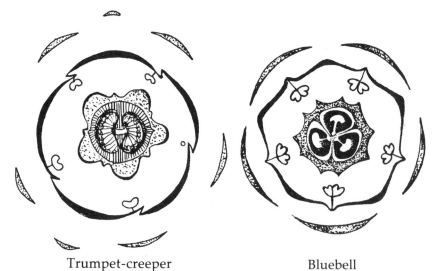

Trumpet-creeper   Bluebell

Not infrequently some stamens are non-functioning, represented by an aborted organ in its proper position; in such cases it is best to indicate the position of the sterile stamen using an × or else shade the fertile stamens and show the sterile ones in outline only. Sometimes sterile filaments are found more or less at random among the fertile stamens in which case the fertile stamens are shown in a normal way and the sterile filaments are ignored or, better, indicated by tiny circles.

Probably the three most important points to make when indicating stamens are (1) number, especially when only a few stamens are present, (2) position, whether opposite the inner whorl of petals or alternating with the petals, and also properly positioned in relation to the sides of the pistil if it is not round, and (3) whether epipetalous or not.

The Pistil

Pistils are shown dozens of ways; no author uses a single symbol for the ovary cross-section because there is so much variation among species and families. If the pistils are many and tightly clumped, as in buttercups, indicate simple units tightly aggregated as shown in the diagram above. Where only a few distinctly separate carpels (simple pistils) are found in a flower, they may be shown as in the diagram, below, for sedum:

Sedum

Where the pistil is compound, make every effort to get the ovary cross-section correct as to shape, ovary wall thickness, number of cells (locules), and placentation. Ovules in the ovary are illustrated in dozens of ways, but

43

the simple presentation, as shown below for evening-primrose and for lythrum usually is quite adequate. For many flowers it is necessary to resort to close-up work to get the ovary right; select a past-mature flower, use a sharp single-edged razor blade to make a cross-section cut, and study the resulting exposed ovary with a 10 × hand lens.

Evening-primrose   Lythrum

Auxiliary Structures

As you examine diagrams by various authors you will find structures outside the whorl of sepals. Most commonly these are either configurations much like the sepals, in which case they represent bracts which consistently subtend the flowers — sometimes there is only one as shown above in diagrams for snapdragon and spiderwort — or there may be more as shown in a highly detailed diagram (botanical) for the male flowers of alder, below:

When the auxiliary organ is shown as a simple circle to one side of the flower usually the indication means "stem" in one sense or another and suggests that the flowers are in a tight spike or spikelet. Commonly auxiliary structures are not diagramed save for some of the monocots with greatly modified flowers such as the grasses and the dicots with greatly reduced flowers such as those of the willow family, walnut family, birch family, beech family and so on.

Floral Formula Technique

The floral formula is a visual device to summarize the relationships of flower parts. It is based on symbols identifying the sepals collectively (calyx), the petals collectively (corolla), the stamens, and the pistil; which are, in the order given, Ca, Co, S, and P. As a matter of fact, in writing the symbols in this manner, Ca Co S P, we have written the beginnings of a floral formula because such a line of symbols indicates that the flower at hand is complete (all parts present) and inserted on the receptacle.

The use of small superscript numbers puts more information into the formula. As an example, assume the flower at hand is composed of five distinct sepals, five distinct petals, five stamens and a pistil composed of a simple carpel. We now can write:

$$Ca^5 \, Co^5 \, S^5 \, P^1$$

The indication is obvious as to number of flower parts and their insertions. When no indication of irregular form is shown we assume that the flower is regular (radially symmetrical = "wheel-like") as opposed to irregular (zygomorphic), as a pansy or sweet pea blossom.

Many flowers show fusion of some parts. Sepals may be partially or completely united laterally; petals may be joined into a floral tube (as snapdragon), into a funnel (as petunia), or into various other patterns; stamens may be united by the filaments (as mallows) or by the anthers (as tomato) or by both; pistils often consist of partially or completely united carpels. The fusion of various parts is indicated by a complete or interrupted ring round the superscript numbers. Thus:

$$Ca^{\underline{5}} \, Co^{\textcircled{5}} \, S^{10} \, P^{\textcircled{2}}$$

indicates a flower with all floral parts inserted on the receptacle, the calyx of 5 sepals partially united, a corolla of five completely united petals, ten separate stamens, and a compound pistil consisting of two fused carpels.

Various taxonomists have elaborated on these indications of fusion. As you delve into plant classification and look at the formulas of various specialists you soon find that each author uses some "shorthand" symbols peculiar to his own method. But a little study soon makes clear his meaning. Some symbols are relatively constant throughout the field of taxonomy. For example, consider a group of three rather uncomplicated plant families:

$$\overline{Ca^{3-\infty} \, Co^{0-\infty} \, S^{\infty} \, P^{\infty}}$$

Ach Fol Bac

Ranunculaceae

(1)

(2)

Magnoliaceae

$$\overline{Ca^{x} \, Co^{x} \, S^{\infty} \, P^{\infty}}$$

Sam Fol

$$\overline{Ca^5 \, Co^5 \, S^{\infty} \, P^{\underline{5-\infty}}}$$

Bac Cap

Malvaceae

(3)

45

First, we have to remember that we are dealing here with plant *families*, not with individual species; accordingly, each formula must account for the various possibilities of flower structure within its family. Second, we now have added more critical information dealing with fusion of parts and identifying the kinds of fruits typical of the three families.

The buttercup family, **Ranunculaceae**, exhibits features considered as primitive; all insertions are hypogynous as indicated by the straight line configuration of calyx, corolla, stamens and pistils, that is, sepals, petals, and stamens are inserted on the receptacle below (*hypo* = below) the ovary. The calyx of representatives of this family may consist of as few as three sepals (separate) or as many as, say, fifteen or more as indicated by the symbol∞, generally used to indicate infinity, or in taxonomy, some number over the usual multiples typical for the species or family at hand. In **Ranunculaceae**, flowers of the tassel-rue (or false bugbane) have three to five sepals, commonly four. Species of meadow-rue have four or five sepals. *Anemonella* flowers commonly have five to ten petal-like sepals, in *Isopyrum* the number sometimes goes as high as twenty. Petals often are lacking not only among the buttercups but also in species of *Clematis*, *Anemonella*, *Thalictrum*, *Hepatica*, and *Anemone*, but some buttercups and species of *Actaea* have ten or more petals. In primitive flowers the stamen number usually is large and often is indefinite; the numbers of stamens in different flowers from the same buttercup, *Isopyrum*, or *Trollius* plant may vary, though stamens are always numerous. Also, in primitive flowers usually the pistils are simple and there are several to many of them. Only a few of the more elaborate flowers in **Ranunculaceae** have a consistent number of pistils — genera such as **Aquilegia** (5) and **Actaea** (1). The abbreviations below the base line of the **Ranunculaceae** family formula are Ach = achene, Fol = follicle, and Bac = baccate (berry-like). These describe the various fruits found in the family.

The magnolia family, **Magnoliaceae**, also is considered primitive; it has many characteristics similar to those of the buttercup family; the affinities become apparent when we compare flower formulas (1) and (2). In the magnolia group, the number of sepals is small but indefinite, as indicated by the Ca^x. Similarly, petals are seldom numerous, and the number is not constant. Usually flowers of plants in this family have many stamens and many simple pistils. Floral parts like those in **Ranunculaceae** are hypogynous. Fruit may be a samara as indicated by Sam (the winged fruit of *Liriodendron* is an example), or a follicle (the individual leathery segments of a magnolia "cone", which open along a single seam to release a seed, are follicles). One short-coming of the floral formula becomes apparent at this point. While the buttercup family species mostly are herbaceous, species of **Magnoliaceae** mostly are woody. The formulas of the families do not account for the distinction between two rather closely related families.

The mallows, members of the **Malvaceae**, formula (3), are slightly more elaborated than the two previously discussed families. The numbers of sepals and petals are constant and the individual parts are separate, not fused. The stamens, however, do exhibit some fusion. Notice the half-circle enclosing the base of the superscript for indefinite large number. This indicates that the filaments of the many stamens are laterally joined while the anthers are free. Had the arc covered only the top of the superscript it would have indicated joined anthers with free filaments, while a complete circle would, of course, have indicated total lateral fusion. Anyone who has examined a flower of hollyhock or hibiscus can easily recall the tassel of stamens, filaments joined, anthers free, encircling the extruded style of the pistil, which is the outstanding field characteristic for the mallow family. In mallows, the pistils often are confusing; from a field standpoint it is relatively safe to say that lateral fusion is sufficiently complete to speak of carpels of a compound pistil, yet in many instances the stigmas (and often styles) are separate. We indicate this by a partial circle enclosing the base of the superscript for pistils; for some species (various tropical hibiscus species) we could justify complete encirclement of the superscript. In general, we have to remain vague when an arc below the superscript for pistils occurs, and conclude that carpels are more or less united.

Flower parts are not always inserted on the same plane. In simple flowers such as those of the buttercups, stamens, petals, and sepals are inserted below the ovary of the pistil (on the same plane) and so the pistil is described as superior and the condition is said to be hypogynous. When you dissect a hypogynous flower you will note that, indeed, the base of the stamens, petals, and sepals are more or less "tucked in" under the ovary. An epigynous flower has an inferior ovary; the lower part, at least, of the pistil is more or less submerged in a mass of tissue and the stamens, petals, and sepals seem to arise above it. Iris flowers, daffodils, and bellflowers, among others, are epigynous. Hypogyny and epigyny are shown clearly in a floral formula, thus:

$$\frac{Ca^{4-5} \, Co^{4-5} \, S^{4-10} \, P^{(2-5)}}{Cap \ Ber \ Dr} \qquad (1) \qquad \textbf{Ericaceae}$$

$$\frac{Ca^3 \, Co^3 \, S^3}{P^{③}} \bigg/ Cap \qquad (2) \qquad \textbf{Iridaceae}$$

Formula (1), **Ericaceae**, indicates typical hypogyny; the formula reads as follows: calyx of 4 or 5 sepals, joined basally, corolla of 4 or 5 petals at least basally but often completely joined, stamens separate, 4 to 10, pistil compound with 2 to 5 carpels, ovary superior, fruit a capsule, berry, or drupe. Formula (2) **Iridaceae**, indicates typical epigyny; the formula reads: calyx of 3 separate sepals, corolla of 3 separate petals, stamens separate, 3, pistil compound with 3 carpels and (note location in the diagram) inferior, fruit a capsule. In the case of **Ericaceae**, the current trend is to separate out a group as family **Vacciniaceae** and with pistil superior or inferior in remaining genera.

The position of stamens in a flower is a critical feature in taxonomic studies; in a floral formula the position can be illustrated graphically. Often stamens are hypogynous, that is, the filaments insert below the ovary. Such a condition is clearly shown in the formulas for **Ericaceae** and **Iridaceae**, above. Stamens are inserted on the corolla in many flowers, particularly those where petals are joined to form a tube as in snapdragon. This stamen position is described as *epipetalous* (epi = upon), and is illustrated in a diagram as follows:

Scrophulariaceae
$$\frac{S^{2-4\cdot5}\ \ Ca^{\circledS}Coz^{\circledS}p^{\circled{2}}}{Cap}$$

This formula indicates a more or less regular calyx of 5 united sepals, a zygomorphic (irregular) corolla or 5 united petals, a pistil with ovary superior of 2 carpels, and, for the snapdragon family, 2 to five stamens inserted on the corolla, that is, epipetalous. Furthermore, the simple bar below S indicates that the epipetalous stamens alternate with the lobes of the corolla. If the bar is blocked at one end (commonly the right end) as S, epipetalous stamens are inserted opposite the corolla lobes, as in primrose family members:

Primulaceae
$$\frac{S^5\ \ Ca^{\circledS}\ Co^{\circledS}\ p^{\circled{1:5}}}{Cap}$$

Another easily illustrated condition of stamens, using the floral formula, is grouping. Stamens sometimes are *diadelphous*, that is, two sets of two, shown as S^{2+2} or sometimes there is a possibility of variation, as stamens 2 and 2, or stamens 2 only, shown as $S^{2+2(2)}$. Fusions of stamens are indicated as $S^{\circled{10}}$, 10 stamens fused laterally by anthers and filaments; $S^{\widehat{10}}$, 10 stamens fused by anthers only; or $S^{\underset{10}{\smile}}$, 10 stamens fused by filaments only.

The pistil always is indicated by P, and in general, the actual significance of superscript numbers relates to the condition of the ovary. The floral diagram does not account for the presence or absence of a style or styles or the form of stigma or stigmas. While the form and organization of the pistil remain critical to plant classification, there is nothing beyond the ordinary in graphic presentations in floral formulas. Because fine points of classification often depend on variations in the pistil, careful attention to the various possibilities remains important. Thus, flowers of members of the night-shade family, **Solanaceae**, and the phlox (sweet william) family, **Polemoniaceae**, are remarkably similar *except for the pistil*:

Solanaceae
$$\frac{S^5\ \ Ca^{\circledS}\ Co^{\circledS}\ p^{\circled{2}}}{Ber\ Cap}$$

Polemoniaceae
$$\frac{S^5\ \ Ca^{\circledS}\ Co^{\circledS}\ p^{\circled{3}}}{Cap}$$

Ovary lobes, too, are important, as shown graphically in the plant formula:

(1) **Scrophulariaceae**
$$\frac{S^{2-4\cdot5}\ \ Ca^{\circledS}Coz^{\circledS}\ p^{\circled{2}}}{Cap}$$

(2) **Labiatae**
$$\frac{S^{2+2\ (2)}\ \ Ca^{\circledS}\ Coz^{\circledS}p^{\circled{2}}}{1-4\ Nutlets}$$

(3) **Boraginaceae**
$$\frac{S^5\ \ Ca^{\circled{4-5}}\ Co^{\circled{4-5}}p^{\circled{2}}}{1-4\ Nutlets}$$

Ovaries in members of the snapdragon family (1) are scarcely lobed — though in many garden snapdragons an indication of the two carpels is somewhat visible; the accepted way to show the pistil in a diagram is simply as 2 united carpels. Beginning taxonomists often have trouble distinguishing the mints (2) and the borages (3) because both have ovaries deeply 4-lobed, but two carpellate. The obvious distinction, here, lies in the remaining floral parts; note that while the corolla of the **Labiatae** is zygomorphic, and with diadelphous or only 2 stamens, the corolla of **Boraginaceae** is regular, with 5 epipetalous stamens. Members of **Boraginaceae** often are confused with the closely related **Hydrophyllaceae** and **Verbenaceae**. For practice, draw up floral diagrams for several species of each of these and compare them to get the distinguishing features clearly fixed. In the field students often encounter a problem because the corolla falls early from some members of **Boraginaceae** leaving only the deeply lobed pistil; in this case, leaf characteristics usually separate the specimen from the mints and pistil and style characters will separate out members of the water-leaf and verbena families.

Having seen formula examples from simple plant families such as those of the buttercups and magnolias, as well as formulas of some of the more evolved families such as the mints, borages, and snapdragons we can draw some general conclusions regarding the plant kingdom. Scientists tell us that families with flowers composed of all parts inserted in a hypogenous position, *and often in a spiral arrangement rather than concentric circles* exhibit a "primitive" condition. The needled, cone-bearing plants (conifers) far predate flowering plants; examine a pine cone to see the spiral arrangement of the segments of that fruiting structure. Then examine the fruiting structure of a member of the magnolia family and you will see a similar spiral arrangement. When you dissect the flower of a magnolia or liriodendron the spiral insertion of parts is fairly obvious. If the flower of a member of the rose family is stripped down it can be seen clearly that the various parts are in rings; an outer whorl or cycle of sepals, one (or more) of petals, next the stamens, often in several whorls, and finally, in the middle, the pistil. Such an arrangement is described as cyclic and is considered to be more evolved than the spiral arrangement.

Fusions and insertions of some floral parts above others also is considered to be more advanced. The madder family, **Rubiaceae**, is considered to be a late-comer (highly evolved); the formula is:

$$\frac{S^{4\text{-}5}}{\frac{Ca^{2\text{-}6}\,Co^{(4\text{-}5)}}{P^{(2)}\,^{(1\text{-}8)}}} \quad \text{Rubiaceae}$$

$$Cap\ Ber\ Dr$$

This three-tiered formula indicates that madders have epigynous flowers, that is, the ovary is inferior as indicated by the pistil location below the line of calyx and corolla. The calyx consists of 2 to 6 free sepals, the 4 or 5 petals are united into a tubular corolla, the 4 or 5 stamens are inserted in the throat of the corolla, alternating with the corolla lobes. The inferior ovary is composed of 1 to 8 carpels, usually 2. The fruit of the madders may be a capsule, a berry, or a drupe.

Very early in the course of drawing up floral formulas for individual species the beginning student of flower structure will find that his formulas do not exactly match those given in various texts for the family in which his species belongs. In fact, in studying floral formulas in various texts some differences will be distinguished. This is as it should be; the formula for a plant family has to be more or less generalized to encompass the several variations of flowers found in that family. The point is, it pays, when working with flower formulas, to be as exact as possible when composing a formula for a specific flower, but when fitting that formula into a family, remain open-minded, realizing that every plant family includes considerable variation of flower design.

There is nothing hard and fast about drawing up floral formulas so long as accuracy is there. A field notebook is just as valuable as the information it conveys to the person using it. One person may scribble a few words alongside his formulas to clarify a specific point — as, with the phloxes or morning-glories "corolla furled in the bud", or with the poppy family members "two sepals fall as flowers open". These personal notes make a formula more meaningful. The author, as a student, was disturbed by the apparent unaccountability in the floral formula for the perigynous condition, that is, where the ovary is superior but all the sepals, petals, and stamens insert on the floral cup rather than directly under the ovary on a flat receptacle. And so, for perigynous flowers, the author to this day tends to use a broken line rather than a solid one to underscore certain **Rosaceae** and other formulas, a technique certainly not included in any standard taxonomic texts.

This is a book about techniques for studying plant families. Most readers know, however, that families are assembled into Orders, and that it is at this level that relationships are most clearly defined. Every classifier, when adept at floral formulas at the specific and family levels, ought to become familiar with plant relationships at the Order level as presented in various plant taxonomy texts.

SYMBOLS AND ABBREVIATIONS USED IN FLOWER FORMULAS

Symbols and abbreviations are the botanist's shorthand; these are traditional, using abbreviations of familiar terms; some authors tend to be more technical, as K = calyx, C = corolla, A = stamens (androecium), and G = pistil (gynoecium).

Ca   calyx, sepals
Ca^0 sepals lacking
$Ca^{5-\infty}$ sepals 5 to many
Ca^{4-5} sepals 4 or 5
Ca^6 sepals 6
$Ca^\times$ sepals several but of indefinite number
$Ca^{\circledS}$ sepals somewhat united, 5
$Ca^{\circledS}$ sepals united, 5
Ca^P calyx a pappus
$Caz^{\circledS}$ 5-part, irregular (zygomorphic) calyx
Co   corolla, petals (corolla symbols similar to those for the calyx, above)
S   stamens
S^∞ stamens many
$S^{\circledS}$ stamens 5, united by the filaments
$S^{\circledS}$ stamens 5, united by the anthers

S^{2+2} stamens 4, in pairs
$S^{2+2(2)}$ stamens 4, in two pairs, or only 2
P   pistil, carpel
P^1 pistil 1 or carpel 1
$P^\times$ simple pistils (carpels) several
P^∞ simple pistils (carpels) many
$P^{\circledS}$ compound pistil of 5 carpels closely united
$P^{\circled{2}}$ compound pistil of 2 carpels, but ovary 4-lobed
$P^{\circled{1:5}}$ compound pistil of 5 carpels but ovary with one cell
$P^{\circled{1:4-5}}$ compound pistil of 4 or 5 carpels, ovary single-celled
$P^{\circled{5-\infty}}$ carpels 5 to many, only somewhat (usually basally) united

Ach	achene	Bac	baccate
Ber	berry	Cap	capsule
Br	bract	Dr	drupe
Di	dioecious	Fol	follicle
Evg	evergreen	Mult	multiple fruit
Mo	monoecious	Pf	flowers perfect
Pg	polygamous	Sam	samara
Sc	scale	Spat	spathaceous
Suc	succulent	Ut	utricle
U	flowers unisexual		

A Partial Plant Families List

BASED ON NORTH AMERICAN NATIVE SPECIES

* Families marked with an asterisk are included in the text of this book.

Monocotyledoneae
Typhaceae, Cat-tail
Sparganiaceae, Burr-reed
Zosteraceae, Pondweed
Najadaceae, Naiad
Juncaginaceae, Arrow-grass
Alismataceae, Water-plantain
Butomaceae, Flowering-rush
Hydrocharitaceae, Frog's-bit
*__Gramineae__, Grass
*__Cyperaceae__, Sedge
*__Araceae__, Arum
Lemnaceae, Duckweed
Xyridaceae, Yelloweyed-grass
Eriocaulaceae, Pipewort
*__Bromeliaceae__, Pineapple
*__Commelinaceae__, Spiderwort
Pontederiaceae, Pickerelweed
Juncaceae, Rush
*__Liliaceae__, Lily
Haemodoraceae, Bloodwort
*__Dioscoriaceae__, Yam
*__Amaryllidaceae__, Amaryllis
*__Iridaceae__, Iris
*__Marantaceae__, Arrowroot
Burmanniaceae, Burmannia
*__Orchidaceae__, Orchid

Dicotyledoneae
Saururaceae, Lizard's-tail
*__Salicaceae__, Willow
*__Myricaceae__, Wax-myrtle
*__Juglandaceae__, Walnut
*__Corylaceae__, Hazel
*__Fagaceae__, Beech
*__Ulmaceae__, Elm
*__Moraceae__, Mulberry
*__Cannabinaceae__, Hemp
*__Urticaceae__, Nettle

Santalaceae, Sandalwood
Loranthaceae, Mistletoe
*__Aristolochiaceae__, Birthwort
*__Polygonaceae__, Buckwheat
*__Chenopodiaceae__, Goosefoot
*__Amaranthaceae__, Amaranth
*__Nyctaginaceae__, Four-o'clock
*__Phytolaccaceae__, Pokeweed
*__Aizoaceae__, Carpetweed
*__Portulacaceae__, Purslane
*__Caryophyllaceae__, Pink
*__Ceratophyllaceae__, Hornwort
*__Nymphaceae__, Water-lily
*__Ranunculaceae__, Buttercup
*__Berberidaceae__, Barberry
Menispermaceae, Moonseed
*__Magnoliaceae__, Magnolia
*__Calycanthaceae__, Calycanthus
*__Annonaceae__, Custard-apple
*__Lauraceae__, Laurel
*__Papaveraceae__, Poppy
*__Capparidaceae__, Caper
*__Cruciferae__, Mustard
*__Resedaceae__, Mignonette
*__Sarraceniaceae__, Pitcher-plant
*__Droseraceae__, Sundew
Podostemaceae, Riverweed
*__Crassulaceae__, Orpine
*__Saxifragaceae__, Saxifrage
*__Hamamelidaceae__, Witch-hazel
*__Platanaceae__, Plane-tree
*__Rosaceae__, Rose
*__Leguminosae__, Pulse
*__Linaceae__, Flax
*__Oxalidaceae__, Wood-sorrel
*__Geraniaceae__, Geranium (Cranesbill)
Zygophyllaceae, Caltrop
*__Rutaceae__, Rue
Meliaceae, Mahogany

Simaroubaceae, Quassia
*Polygalaceae, Milkwort
*Euphorbiaceae, Spurge
Callitrichaceae, Water-starwort
*Buxaceae, Box
Limnanthaceae, False Mermaid
Anacardiaceae, Cashew
Cyrillaceae, Cyrilla
*Aquifoliaceae, Holly
*Celastraceae, Staff-tree
*Aceraceae, Maple
*Hippocastanaceae, Buckeye
Sapindaceae, Soapberry
*Balsaminaceae, Touch-me-not
*Rhamnaceae, Buckthorn
*Vitaceae, Vine (Grape)
*Tiliaceae, Linden
*Malvaceae, Mallow
*Theaceae, Tea (Camellia)
*Guttiferae, St. John'sworth
Elatinaceae, Waterwort
*Tamaricaceae, Tamarisk
*Cistaceae, Rock-rose
*Violaceae, Violet
*Passifloraceae, Passion-flower
Loasaceae, Loasa
*Cactaceae, Cactus
*Thymelaeaceae, Mezereum
*Elaeagnaceae, Oleaster
*Lythraceae, Loosestrife
*Nyssaceae, Sour Gum
Melastomataceae, Melastoma
IIydrocaryaceae, Water chestnut
*Onagraceae, Evening-primrose
Haloragidaceae, Water-milfoil
Hippuridaceae, Mare's-tail
*Araliaceae, Ginseng
*Umbelliferae, Parsley
*Cornaceae, Dogwood
*Clethraceae, White-alder
*Pyrolaceae, Wintergreen
*Ericaceae, Heath
Diapensiaceae, Diapensia
*Primulaceae, Primrose
*Plumbaginaceae, Leadwort
Sapotaceae, Sapodilla

*Ebenaceae, Ebony
Symplocaceae, Sweetleaf
*Styracaceae, Styrax
*Oleaceae, Olive
Loganaceae, Logania
*Gentianaceae, Gentian
*Apocynaceae, Dogbane
*Asclepiadaceae, Milkweed
*Convolvulaceae, Convolvulus
*Polemoniaceae, Polemonium
*Hydrophyllaceae, Waterleaf
*Boraginaceae, Borage
*Verbenaceae, Vervain
*Labiatae, Mint
*Solanaceae, Nightshade
*Scrophulariaceae, Figwort
*Bignoniaceae, Bignonia
Martyniaceae, Martynia
Orobanchaceae, Broom-rape
Lentibulariaceae, Bladderwort
*Acanthaceae, Acanthus
Phrymaceae, Lopseed
*Plantaginaceae, Plantain
*Rubiaceae, Madder
*Caprifoliaceae, Honeysuckle
Adoxaceae, Moschatel
*Valarianaceae, Valarian
*Dipsaceae, Teasel
*Cucurbitaceae, Gourd
*Campanulaceae, Bellflower
*Compositae, Composite (Aster)

Pronunciation Guide

achene	uh KEEN	petal	PEH tl
anther	AN th(u)r	pistil	PISS tl
apetalous	a PET uh lus	pistillate	PISS tuh late
asepalous	a SEE puh lus	plumule	PLUME yewl
asexual	a SEX yew(u)l	pollen	PAHL l(e)n
biennial	bye EN ee ul	pollination	pahl leh NAY shun
calyx		pome	pome
(pl. calyces)	KAY lix,	pyxidium	pick SID ee um
	KAY luh seez	pyxis	PICKS iss
carpel	KAR pul	radicle	RAD uh cull
caryopsis	CAR ry OP sis	raphe	RAY fee
corolla	kuh RAHL uh,	receptacle	ruh SEP tuh cull
	ko RAHL uh	replum	REP lum
dioecious	die EE shus	samara	sa MA ruh
drupe	droop	schizocarp	SKIT zo carp
embryo	EM bree oh	sepal	SEE pl
endocarp	ENN doh carp	silicle	SILL uh cl
endosperm	EN doh sperm	silique	sigh LEEK
epigynous	eh PIGE uhn us	species	SPEE seez
epipetalous	eh peh PET uh lus	stamen	STAY m(u)n
exocarp	EX oh carp	staminate	STAY muh nate
filament	FILL uh m(u)nt	stigma	STIG muh
follicle	FAHL ih cl	style	stile
genera	JEH nuh ruh	testa	TESS tuh
genus	GEE nus	zygomorphic	zy go MORE fick
herbaceous	her BAY shus	zygote	ZY goat
hesperidium	hess peh RID ee um		
hilum	HI lum		
hypogynous	high POGE uh nus		
legume	LEH gyum		
locule	LOW kyul		
loment	LO ment		
mesocarp	MEH zo carp		
micropyle	MY crow pile		
monoecious	Mo NEE shus		
nucellus	new SELL us		
ovary	OH vah ree, OH vuh ree		
pepo	PEE poh		
perennial	pu REN ee ul		
perianth	PEH ree anth		
pericarp	PEH reh carp		

Plant Families

Acanthaceae Acanthus Family

Mostly a tropical family with some species in the Mediterranean Basin, N. America, and Australia, the Acanthuses are mostly herbs and shrubs, rarely trees, and some climbers; in general, leaves are opposite or sometimes whorled, rarely alternate, usually simple, sometimes entire but sometimes large and quite lobed, even spine-tipped, *without* stipules. Often nodes (stem joints) are swollen. Flowers of most are not showy, but some are grown especially for their blooms or for their inflorescences with or without showy, colored bractioles; usually flowers are in a raceme or clustered in leaf axils or in tight, terminal spike-like inflorescences which may be quite showy; complete, hypogynous; calyx synsepalous, 5-cleft (rarely 4-part) or rarely reduced to a ring; corolla sympetalous, with a distinct tube and often 2-lipped (the upper lip may be obsolete, undeveloped, as in *Acanthus*) but sometimes nearly regular, with a flaring limb, 5, rarely 4-lobed, hypogynous; stamens commonly didynamous, rarely 2 with or without 1 or 2 stamenoids, epipetalous; compound pistil of 2 closely united carpels with a single, long style and mostly 2 stigmas or capitate, ovary superior on a hypogynous disc, 2-celled, with 1 to many ovules in each cell. Fruit a capsule, often much flattened contrary to the valves and partition. The juice of these is often mucilaginous and slightly bitter but not toxic.

This is a difficult family to characterize because plant habit varies greatly, some being climbers, some marsh plants, many of woodlands, or some of dry areas as steppes and desert borders. Start in the field with the basic flower analysis; typically, 5-part synsepalous calyx; 5-part, zygomorphic or nearly regular sympetalous corolla with didynamous or diandrous stamens, and a superior ovary with a long, slender style, simple stigma or 2-lobed; the 2-celled ovule with usually 2 to 4 seeds is distinctive; with your hand lens study the tiny stalk (funiculus) which attaches ovules to placentae as often the **Acanthaceae** species show strange outgrowths on this structure, and they are, indeed, characteristic, but scarcely easy field characters. To become more familiar with these in the garden examine inflorescences of the black-eyed-susan vine, *Thunbergia alata*, acanthus, *Acanthus molls* or other species as available, and any of the native species of genera such as *Ruellia*, *Justicia*, and *Dianthera* as even these few show an amazing range of general anatomy. In the conservatory or in your plant room examine the shrimp plant, *Beloperone guttata*, *Crossandra*, *Aphelandra*, *Jacobinia* and similiar sorts with showy or pronounced bracteoles at each flower in the inflorescence, and then look at some of the tender species with more nearly regular flowers such as *Eranthemum* which look very unlike their relatives. It takes a lot of study to understand the make-up of **Acanthaceae**. Features used to distinguish genera and species are exceptionally complicated and confusing!

Among the more common conservatory, plant room, garden, and native U.S. genera of **Acanthaceae** are:

Acanthus	*Beloperone*	*Dicliptera*
Anisotes	*Blepharis*	*Eranthemum*
Aphelandra	*Crossandra*	*Fittonia*
Barleria	*Dianthera*	*Graptophyllum*

Hemigraphis   *Jacobinia*   *Peristrophe*
Hygrophila   *Justicia*   *Ruellia*
Hypoestis   *Mackaya*   *Ruttya*
Isotheca   *Paulowilhelmia*   *Strobilanthes*

Acanthaceae

A.

B.

$$\frac{S^{2+2(2)}}{Ca^{(4-5)(0)} \, Coz^{(2+2 \, or \, 3)} \, P^{(2)}} {Cap}$$

Acanthus Family

A. Field sketch of Bear's-breech, *Acanthus mollis*. **B.** Floral formula for the **Acanthaceae**.

57

Aceraceae Maple Family

Two genera with about 200 species, mostly in the genus *Acer*, make up this small family of trees and shrubs with watery, rarely milky, saccharine sap. These are mostly mountain or upland species from the northern hemisphere; the greatest number of species occuring from the eastern Himalaya Moutains to central China. Leaves opposite, simple or palmately lobed or pinnately compound, exstipulate. Flowers in axillary or terminal cymes or racemes, actinomorphic (regular), mostly staminate or pistillate, or perfect (often bisexual flowers intermixed with monoecious ones); flowers greatly reduced; calyx colored, 5–(rarely 4 to 12) lobed or parted, imbricated; corolla of as many petals as sepals, or none, with short claws, and inserted on the margin of a perigynous or hypogynous disc; stamens 3 to 12, mostly 8, separate, inserted at the edge of the disc; compound pistil with a single style and 2 stigmas, laterally compressed, ovary superior, 2-celled, and 2-lobed, 1 or 2 ovules in each cell. Fruit a samara.

The opposite, often palmately lobed leaves with no stipules, the sweet bark, and the peculiar, flattened form of the 2-celled ovary usually suffice in the field to identify members of this family. The winter bud and leaf-scar characters also make good identification characteristics. Formerly, this family was included with the **Sapindaceae**, but separates out due to leaf and flower characteristics.

The two genera in **Aceraceae** are *Acer* (with samaras winged only on one side) and *Dipteronia* (winged all round).

Many species of *Acer* (maple) are of great ornamental value, including several of the rather small-structured species seldom seen in America.

E.

$$\frac{Ca^{4-5} Co^{4-5(0)} S^{4-10} P\textcircled{2}}{Samara}$$

Maple Family

A. Sketch of *Acer negundo*, box-elder, showing typical opposite leaf arrangement and a flower cluster. **B.** Staminate flower of maple. **C.** Pistillate flower of maple. **D.** Winged fruits, paired, of maple. **E. Aceraceae** family formula.

Aizoaceae Fig-marigold Family

Also known as the Carpet-weed or Ice-plant Family, most of the 2,500 species in 130 genera which make up this very diversified family are native to South Africa with a few generally African and others native to or introduced to North America and Europe. The plants mostly are succulent, many almost cactus-like, a few are erect or prostrate sub-shrubs, and a few are rather ordinary-looking herbaceous plants. Leaves usually are opposite or whorled, rarely alternate, usually with no stipules, never with spines, and mostly entire, or reduced to minute scales. Flowers showy but not so in American species, regular, perfect, but with only a single whorl of perianth segments (sepals) which are free or variously united, usually 4 or 5. The stamens alternate with the sepals and may equal them in number, or they may divide to give the appearance of several to many stamens, in which case the outer ones become sterile, staminoid or even petaloid, to produce quite a showy effect. The ovary is superior to inferior, with 2 to many cells (rarely 1-celled). The stigmas equal the number of cells in the ovary of the pistil.

From a field standpoint this is not an important family and it is a rather difficult one because of the diversity of characteristics. The greatest confusion comes in with the Purslane Family, but the Purslanes often have petals and have a 1-celled ovary. Look for the fleshy stems and leaves (not so in some of the American species), the apetalous flowers often with a showy perianth (not so in the American species) and sometimes with a fringe of stamens which includes staminoids and petaloids toward the outside.

Some of the horticulturally important members of the **Aizoaceae** are:

Aizoon	*Gibbaeum*	*Pleiospilos*
Argyroderma	*Glottiphyllum*	*Sesuvivum*
Cheiridopsis	*Lithops*	*Stomatium*
Conophytum	*Mesembryanthemum*	*Tetragonia*
Faucaria	*Mollugo*	*Titanopsis*
Geocarpon	*Pharnaceum*	*Trianthema*

* Sometimes in its own family.

Many of the above-listed genera include ornamental species grouped horticulturally under "cacti and succulents", a most unfair treatment as these Fig-marigolds are their own thing, and well worth knowing. Spend some time in the botanic garden studying them until you come to know them well. The American genera, *Sesuvium*, sea-purslane, and *Trianthema*, also sea-purslane, are coastal species, the latter growing in alkaline waste ground, the former on damp sands. *Mollugo*, carpetweed or Indian-chickweed, introduced from Europe and spreading rapidly westward, is a mean-to-control summer annual. Probably you never will see tiny *Geocarpon minimum*, a winter annual which occurs only very rarely in sandy barrens of southwestern Missouri. *Tetragona tetragonioides*, New Zealand-spinach, is a more or less edible species, the young shoots of the crisply succulent trailing stems being used, and the fruits of *Mesembryanthemum edule*, the hottentot-fig, are eaten in Africa. The relatively recent discovery and subsequent classification and reclassification of the "living stones" of Africa have added many new genera to the above list (these are marvelously interesting plants) and also, the genus *Mesembryanthemum* has been re-worked and somewhat fragmented in recent years. Refer to the latest edition of A.B. Graf's *Exotica* for an outstanding pictorial review of the ornamental members of **Aizoaceae**.

Aizoaceae

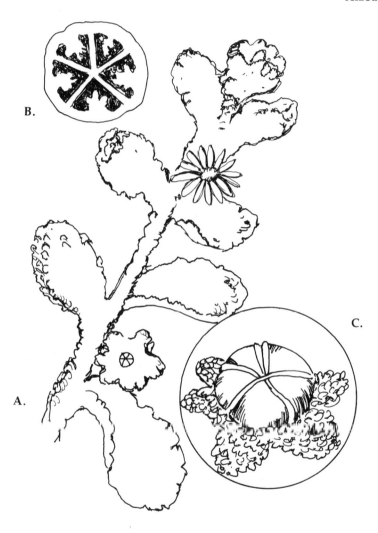

Ice Plant Family

A. Field sketch of *Mesembryanthemum*, indicating succulent character of stems and leaves. **B.** Cross-section of ovary, indicating five carpels each with peripheral placentation. **C.** Enlargement of a typical Ice Plant fruit.

Amaranthaceae Amaranth Family

Throughout the landmasses of the world, excepting arctic and antarctic regions, various members of the Amaranth Family are to be found; the family includes about 900 species in about 65 genera. These may be annual or perennial herbs, or shrubs, or, rarely, trees. Leaves are opposite or alternate, often rather harsh, rarely fleshy, simple, often entire. Some species develop spines at each node. The flowers of the Amaranth Family are very like those of the **Chenopodiaceae** but generally are less succulent and usually are imbricated with three dry, scale-like bracts which commonly are colored. Invariably the flowers occur in clustered axillary cymes which form a raceme, which may resemble a terminal panicle. Some horticultural forms are fasciated as the crested coxcombs, *Celosia cristata* cultivars. Flowers may be perfect or unisexual; the perianth is a single whorl (no petals), sepals 3 to 5, regular, free or slightly united at the base. Stamens the same number as the perianth segments, or fewer, and opposite them, filaments free or united at the base to form a tube round ovary; staminoids sometimes present. The 1-celled ovary is superior, with one style or none, stigmas various, often capitate or 2− or 3−lobed. Fruit is a capsule-like structure that opens cap-like (circumscissile), or sometimes more nearly nutlike or even berry-like. The fruit may be surrounded by the perianth but usually is not tightly enclosed as is common in many of the species of **Chenopodiaceae.**

The Amaranths and the Chenopods are generally similar in flower form, being apetalous, and with regular perianths, stamens usually opposite to and equalling the perianth lobes (sepals). But the inflorescences of the Amaranths are far more tightly clustered and with usually colored bracts, often three in number, tightly imbricate round each tiny flower. This is an important point of difference between the two families. The spines (not always present) on the Amaranths are another specific difference, as is the fruit character of each species. Most of the members of this family are tropical and not encountered in temperate zones but there are important ornamental genera and others which are notable weeds.

Among the **Amaranthaceae** genera commonly encountered are:

Acnida	*Deeringia*	*Pleuropetalum*
Aerva	*Froelichia*	*Pupalia*
Alternanthera	*Gomphrena*	*Trichinium*
Amaranthus	*Iresine*	
Celosia	*Pfaffia*	

Among these are the outstanding ornamentals, Joseph's coat (many cultivars), *Alternanthera* spp.; cockscombs, both plumose and crested types, *Celosia* spp.; bachelor's buttons or clover-straw-flowers, *Gomphrena* cultivars, and the several forms of *Iresine*, beloved of Victorian bedding gardeners. Among the worst of the annual garden weeds are the various species of *Amaranthus*, *Acnida*, and others, pooled under the common name of "pigweed". These come from seeds which germinate in warm garden soils and quickly grow into huge and highly competitive weeds which produces hundreds of thousands of seeds which can lie dormant in the soil for decades. It is a vast mistake ever to allow any pigweed to set seed in the garden. The cultivated species of *Amaranthus*, prince's feather or love-lies-bleeding, are just as bad.

Amaranthaceae

B.

$$Ca^{3-5} Co^0 S^{5 \text{ or } \underline{5}} P^{\underline{2-3}}$$
Cap-like Ach Ber-like

A.

Amaranth Family

A. Field sketch of pigweed, *Amaranthus*. **B.** Floral formula for the Family.

Amaryllidaceae Amaryllis Family

At least 65 genera contain more than 850 species making up the **Amaryllidaceae**; these are mostly in the tropical and sub-tropical regions of the world, but several species extend well into the temperate latitudes. Most are perennial, bulbous or rhizomatous herbs, or with leafy stems arising from rootstocks; leaves are alternate, usually narrow, entire, basal or with no petioles or stems. Flowers are complete, mostly actinomorphic (regular) but rarely zygomorphic, epigynous, usually borne singly or in clusters from a spathe-like bract; perianth 6-part, 3 petal-like sepals, and 3 petals which often are connate toward the base and sometimes with a tubular or cup-shaped crown (corona) in the throat (as in *Narcissus*), epigynous; stamens 6, but some occasionally reduced to staminoids, all separate, sometimes epipetalous, or inserted on the epigynous disc; compound pistil of 3 closely united carpels, with single style, stigma entire, lobed, or sometimes 3-part, ovary inferior, 3-celled, each cell with numerous ovules. Fruit a capsule, rarely a berry.

In the field look for lily-like plants with lily-like flowers, but with the ovary completely inferior, and with a leafy bract subtending the flower or flowers (in *Narcissus* this is the small papery structure immediately below the blossom, in *Hippeastrum* it is the usually split, papery or leafy structure which encloses all the buds as they develop, and then releases them, drooping and withering). In the garden or in a conservatory study plants of *Agave* as this is the most obvious misfit in the traditionally defined family, having thick, fleshy leaves covered with wax, and a very long spike of small, undistinguished flowers — obviously a desert modification. Today, most experts put *Agave* into its own family and further break up **Amaryllidaceae** as presented here into numerous families.

An increasing number of Amaryllids are becoming available to us on the market these days, most suitable for pot culture but some can go into the garden at least through the warm season; in addition, there are our commonly cultivated species, both tender and hardy, and a few native genera; among these are:

Agave	*Galanthus*	*Lycoris*
Alstroemeria	*Habranthus*	*Narcissus*
Amaryllis	*Haemanthus*	*Nerine*
Clivia	*Hippeastrum*	*Polianthes*
Cooperia	*Hymenocallis*	*Sprekelia*
× *Crinodonna*	*Hypoxis*	*Sternbergia*
Crinum	*Ismene*	*Tecophilaea*
Cyrtanthus	*Ixiolirion*	*Vallota*
Eucharis	*Leucojum*	*Zephyranthes*

If everyone grew just this list of plants he would have a fine array of both pot plants for winter and summer and some fine spring, summer, and fall-blooming hardy sorts. Unfortunately, many of us overlook some of the best ones, and abuse others by mis-naming them. For example, the beautiful Hippeastrums, mostly grown now in hybrid forms, are all too commonly referred to as Amaryllis, while the true *Amaryllis*, quite a different thing, is a fine ornamental in its own right. How *Polianthes* ever came to be "tuberose" is anybody's guess. As children we knew lovely little pink *Zephyranthes grandiflora*, the pink zephyr-lily, as Independence Day lily because those of our neighbor, grown in an old blue enamel wash basin, always bloomed on the Fourth of July. Now I plant mine in the open garden and they bloom every time it rains or whenever I water the border.

Amaryllidaceae

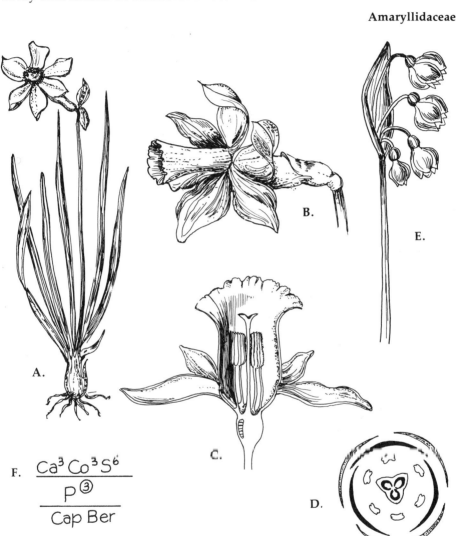

Amaryllis Family

A. Field sketch of narcissus, *Narcissus poeticus*. **B.** Sketch of a long trumpet narcissus. **C.** Longitudinal section through a narcissus flower indicating the inferior ovary and insertion of the stamens. **D.** Floral diagram for yellow star-grass, *Hypoxis*; this diagram clearly indicates the six stamens which separate Amaryllids from the Irids which have only three. **E.** Field sketch of snowflake, *Leucojum*. **F.** Floral formula for the Family.

Annonaceae Custard-apple Family

More than 2100 species distributed through about 120 genera make up this almost entirely tropical family of trees and shrubs. All have alternate, simple, entire, pinnate-vined leaves with no stipules. Dormant buds are naked (no bud scales). The flowers are usually perfect, actinomorphic (radially symmetrical) with superior ovaries. Calyx of 3 sepals, often leaf-like. Corolla of 6 petals, usually thickish, and often in 2 rows, mostly valvate in the bud, rarely imbricated. Stamens spirally arranged and numerous (polyandrous). Pistils several or many, separate or cohering in a mass; fleshy or pulpy in fruit.

The distinctive twig and leaf characters of **Annonaceae** and the systems of 3's in calyx and corolla (quite unusual in dicotyledonous plants), the numerous spiral stamens, and the usually separate simple pistils (carpels) are good field characters. Any time you happen on a tree or shrub with leaves arranged and shaped as described above, and with these key floral characters, you may be sure of your identification. Most members of this family are native to tropical regions of Asia and Africa with some few in the New World. Only *Asimina*, pawpaw, occurs in a temperate zone, both in eastern North America and also in Australia.

Among the genera encountered in cultivation are:

> *Annona*
> *Asimina*
> *Centabotrys*
> *Eupomatia* (sometimes in its own family)
> *Guatteria*
> *Monodora*
> *Uvaria*
> *Xylopia*

Many species of **Annonaceae** are important economically; in the tropics various species are used for medicine, for ointments, and for perfumes and cosmetics. Many species produce edible fruits which are staple foods in some tropical areas and which are grown in frost-free zones in this country; among them, the sweet-sop, *Annona squamosa* and the sour-sop, *A. muricata*. Country youths throughout eastern North America know of "secret" groves of pawpaws in deep, rich soils of streams and they eagerly wait for the first frost to slightly discolor the banana-like rinds of the custard-filled fruits, bringing them to mellow, full flavor.

Custard-apple (Pawpaw) Family

Field sketch of pawpaw, *Asimina triloba;* the artist presents a composite picture because in nature the purple-brown flowers emerge before the leaves expand. Pawpaw is the only frost-hardy representative of this large tropical family. Flower arrangement is simple; three sepals, three petals, numerous stamens in several whorls, and a central cluster of numerous simple pistils, all superior. The fruit is a large berry.

Apocynaceae Dogbane Family

Most of the 2000 species which make up the 200 genera of the Dogbane Family are tropical or sub-tropical but a few grow in temperate regions and some are important ornamentals. These may be trees, shrubs, creepers, or perennial herbs, mostly with opposite (few with alternate or whorled) leaves, simple, entire, very rarely with stipules. Flowers complete, regular, often showy; calyx with 5, sometimes 4 lobes, persistant, often with glands; corolla with 5, sometimes 4 lobes, with a distinct tube and salver-shaped face or funnel-form; stamens with free filaments, epipetalous on the corolla tube; the corolla may be hairy within; anthers sometimes gathered (connivent) about the stigma, sometimes lengthened into stiff spines; pistil superior; 2 carpels which may be united but in American species with separate ovaries but united at style and stigma; fruit may be berry-like, or paired follicles with many usually flat seeds, often with a crown of hairs or down (commose). These plants have acrid-poisonous juice.

Two separate carpels united at the style and stigma, pistil superior, combined with calyx and corolla characters described above provide easy identification of this group of plants; if further characteristics are needed look for paired, simple, entire leaves almost never with stipules. It is an easy family. Avoid the juice of all species; some are rubber-producing, *Carissa carandas* yields edible fruit (karaunda) in India, and *Acokanthera schimperi* in East Africa yields a devilish arrow poison. When "the Assyrian came down like a wolf on the fold" the entire host was destroyed having grilled their meat on the unfamiliar and deadly twigs of *Nerium oleander*.

Some genera in the Dogbane Family are:

Acokanthera	*Hancoria*	*Prestonia*
Adenium	*Ichnocarpus*	*Rauwolfia*
Aganosma	*Kickxia*	*Rhazya*
Allamanda	*Kopsia*	*Strophanthus*
Alstonia	*Landolphia*	*Tabernaemontana*
Alyxia	*Lyonsia*	*Tenaris*
Amsonia	*Mandevilla*	*Thenardia*
Apocynum	*Mascarenhasna*	*Trachelspermum*
Beaumontia	*Melodinus*	*Urechites*
Carissa	*Nerium*	*Vallaris*
Carpodinus	*Ochrosia*	*Vallesia*
Cervera	*Odontodenia*	*Vinca*
Chilocarpum	*Pachypodium*	*Willughbeia*
Echites	*Parsonia*	*Wrightia*
Gonioma	*Plumeria*	

$$S^{4-5}$$
$$\frac{Ca\,\widehat{(4\text{-}5)}\,Co\,\widehat{(4\text{-}5)}\,P\,\textcircled{2}\,\widehat{(1\!:\!2)}}{Bac\ Dr\ Fol}$$

C.

Dogbane Family

A. Field sketch of periwinkle, *Vinca*. **B.** Floral diagram of periwinkle, fairly characteristic for the entire family. **C.** Floral formula for **Apocynaceae.**

Aquifoliaceae Holly Family

A family of 2 to 5 genera, trees and shrubs, with about 500 species, mostly American but also in Europe and Asia. Leaves mostly alternate, rarely opposite, usually evergreen but some deciduous, simple, with small stipules. Flowers white, greenish or yellowish, small, axillary, mostly perfect but sometimes dioecious; solitary or in clusters, rarely in cymes, actinomorphic. Flower parts usually in 4's, sometimes 5's, but may be 3 to 6. Calyx commonly of 4 (or 5) more or less connate sepals; corolla of 4 (or 5) petals, free, or united at the base; stamens as many as the petals and alternating with them, often barely attached to them at the base, or else hypogynous; compound pistil of 3 to 6 closely fused carpels, but usually 4, stigma sub-sessile and lobed, ovary superior, usually 4-celled, each cell with 1 or 2 ovules. Fruit a drupe (as a holly "berry").

Field characteristics include the general appearance of the plants — refer above to leaf description and gross anatomy and location of flowers — and to details of flower structure. Note the absence of the hypogynous disc, and the commonly tetramerous (4-parted) flowers which sometimes are complete. Flowers in this family sometimes are described as polygamodioecious, which means that while flowers have both stamens and pistils, only one sex is functioning in either any given flower or in the flowers of one particular plant. For example, flowers of "female" hollies often contain rudimentary stamens, and flowers of "male" hollies often contain rudimentary pistils, but in practice, a given plant is male (non-fruiting) or female (producing "berries").

The genera of **Aquifoliaceae** which may be encountered in the wild or in cultivation in N. America are:

Ilex
Nemopanthus

We think of the **Aquifoliaceae** as a family of ornamentals, with particular reference to the hollies (*Ilex* spp.). While many of these are important garden trees and shrubs, others are of economic importance in agriculture, paticularly *I. paraguayensis* (*I. paraguariensis*) which furnishes maté, the "tea" of S. America.

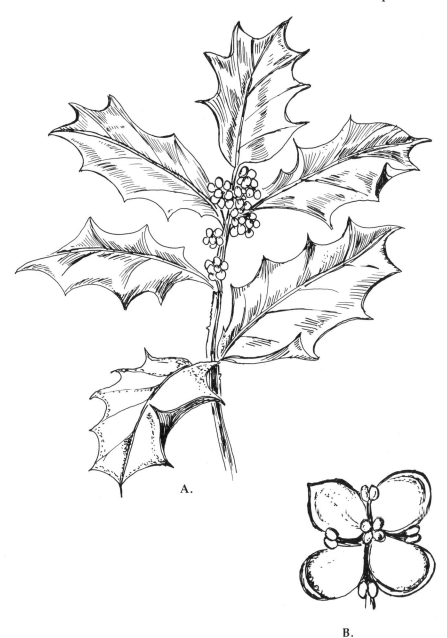

A.

B.

Holly Family

A. Field sketch of a flowering branch of American holly, *Ilex opaca*; male flowers occur in clusters, sessile or nearly so, while female flowers (on a different plant) occur singly. **B.** Functional male flower of holly, with aborted pistil in the center.

Araceae Arum Family

Only a few of the 115 genera, with about 2000 species, grow naturally in the North Temperate zone, but this is a tremendously important tropical family where some species spread for acres, and many supply economically important products. Most are perennial herbs or with more or less woody bases, and even in some cases woody stems, often with tuberous rhizomes or massive rootstocks, often climbing shrubs or epiphytes with aerial, adventitious roots. Some are water plants and many grow in marshes and bogs. Many have heart-shaped (cordate), or spear-shaped (hastate), or arrow-shaped (sagittate) simple, large leaves, but some are palmate or pinnate, and some have regular or irregular holes. Think of the various forms of ornamentals sold as *Philodendron* in the plant shops (sometimes they are other genera) and you will visualize these foliage possibilities. Often the leaf stalks (petioles) are fleshy, often rounded on the side away from the plant and flat or concave on the inner side. Veins may be pronounced in the leaves. The juice of these frequently is acrid, sometimes pungent, and some are extremely poisonous. There are rare tropical species where bodily contact with the foliage can be fatal!

The flowers of these are reduced and modified, and are crowded onto a club-shaped structure called a spadix which usually is subtended by a more or less leaf-like structure called a spathe. Visualize Jack-in-the-pulpit, calla, and an *Anthurium*; the central yellowish stalk is the spadix, the brown-striped green, or white, or red, leafy structure is the spathe. Most commonly the flowers are separate on the spadix, with staminate flowers above the pistillate ones but some species have perfect flowers. All are densely packed together, usually with no perianth at all or with 4 to 6 scales as a perianth. Stamens may be 4 to 10, or even reduced to 1, filaments very short, often united; pistil compound, mostly a 1 to 3-celled ovary with 1 to several ovules in each cell, and a condensed stigmatic surface, style usually wanting or very short. The fruit is a berry, and these usually are densely crowded on the spadix, often orange or red.

Field characteristics depend on the above listed characteristics in various combinations; usually Arums can be recognized in the vegetative stage by their characteristic leaves and stems; in a well stocked and labeled shop study the various tropical members of the family. Among our native species you should find and carefully analyze flowers of *Acorus*, calamus, *Arisaema*, Jack-in-the-pulpit; *Calla*, water-arum, *Orontium*, golden club; *Peltandra*, arrow-arum;, and *Symplocarpus* (east) or *Lysichitum* (west), skunk-cabbage. They may not be as spectacular as the tropical ones, but by and large, our native Arums have a lot more charm.

For lists of the tropical species refer to special literature such as the entry **Araceae** in Vol. 1 of *The Royal Horticultural Society Dictionary of Gardening*.

We know most of these plants as ornamentals or native wildflowers. In the tropics they supply shelter, cordage, medicine, drugs, poisons, starches, green vegetables, fruits, and much more. Among the very poisonous ones available to us is the *Dieffenbachia*, dumb-cane, so named because a drop or two of the milky juice will paralyze the vocal cords, preventing speech; a bit more paralyzes the entire throat and usually leads to agonizing suffocation and death.

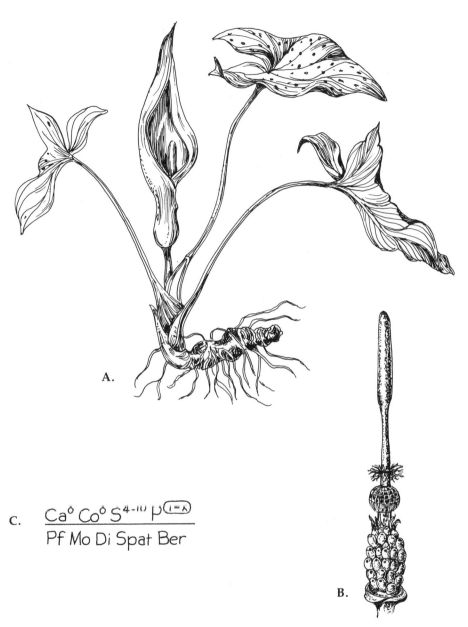

C. $\dfrac{Ca^0 \; Co^0 \; S^{4-10} \; p^{\underline{(1-\infty)}}}{Pf \; Mo \; Di \; Spat \; Ber}$

Arum Family

A. Field sketch of a cookoopint, *Arum maculatum*, with the typical inflorescence composed of an enwrapping bract, the spathe, and the more or less fleshy spadix bearing male and female flowers. **B.** The spadix (spike) of *Arum*, with an elongated cluster of pistillate flowers below and a modified cluster of staminate flowers just above. **C.** Floral formula for the **Araceae**.

Araliaceae Ginseng Family

About 70 genera with 700 species of trees, shrubs, and herbaceous plants are widely distributed through tropical and temperate regions, with centers in the Indo-Malayan area and also in tropical America. These often are prickly, some are climbing; leaves alternate, rarely opposite, simple and entire or lobed, or palmately or pinnately compound, usually exstipulate. Flowers small, greenish or white, actinomorphic (regular), perfect or staminate or pistillate (plants may be dioecious), commonly in umbels but sometimes racemose; *epigynous*; calyx greatly reduced with 4 to 5 sepals, minute or mere teeth, or none, on the rim of the epigynous disc; petals usually 5, rarely 4 to 10, free, rarely united, sometimes more or less united at the tips and falling as a unit, inserted on the rim of the epigynous disc; stamens usually 5 or twice the number of petals and alternating with them, free, inserted on the inner rim of the epigynous disc (sometimes stamen number is multiplied); compound pistil of 2 to 15 carpels, styles usually more than 2, sometimes many, usually free but sometimes connate with lobed stigmas, ovary inferior with 2 to 15 cells, each with a single ovule. Fruit a berry which rarely splits into segments (or drupaceous or dry). This family is very like **Umbelliferae** but with usually more than 2 styles and quite different in character.

Field characteristics are in the flowers as vegetative traits are shared by many other species; the epigynous structure of the flower, with a multiple celled inferior ovary with just a few seeds, the tree petals and stamens often of the same number, and the nearly lacking or quite lacking calyx brings you to **Araliaceae**. Due to the small size of the flowers it takes some experience to distinguish these features readily. Secure flowers of *Hedera*, ivy, and dissect them carefully, noting the organization of the inflorescences as well as that of the individual flowers. Probably you can locate flowers of *Aralia*, *Dizygotheca*, and *Polyscias* in a greenhouse for further study. You will need a 10X hand lens.

A great many species of the tropical **Araliaceae** make splendid house plants and these with others are grown in frost-free California and Florida gardens; and there are the introduced garden species, and our interesting natives; among them are:

Acanthopanax	× Fatshedera	Pentapanax
Aralia	Fatsia	Polyscias
Boerlagiodendron	Hedera	Pseudopanax
Brassaia	Horsfieldia	Schefflera
Brassaiopsis	Mertya	Sciadophyllum
Cussonia	Nothopanax	Tetraplasandra
Dendropanax	Oplopanax	Trevesia
Dizygotheca	Oreopanax	Tupidanthus
Echinopanax	Panax	

Primitive peoples have considered some of the **Araliaceae** to be of medicinal value, including English ivy, *Hedera helix*, and the American sarsaparilla, *Aralia nudicaulis*. The Chinese still are convinced of the efficacy of ginseng, *Panax quinquefolium*. Chinese rice-paper is prepared from the pith of *Tetrapanax papyriferum*.

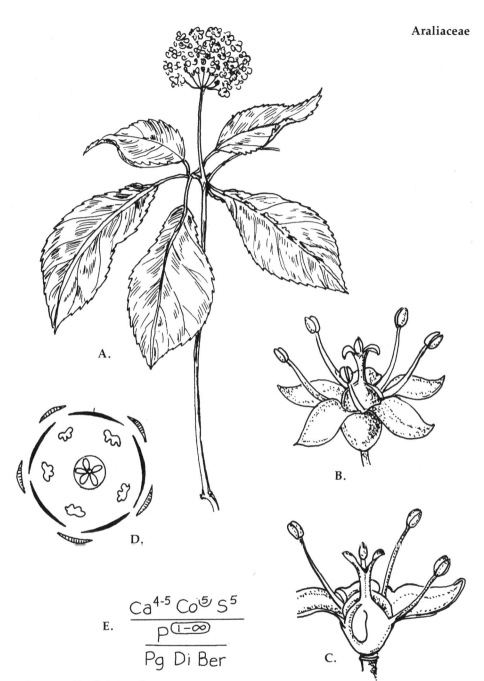

A.

B.

D,

C.

$$\frac{Ca^{4-5} \; Co^{\textcircled{5}} \; S^5}{P^{\textcircled{1-\infty}}}$$
$$\overline{Pg \; Di \; Ber}$$

E.

Ginseng (Aralia) Family

A. Field sketch of ginseng, *Panax quinquefolium*, with most of the foliage (in a whorl below the flower cluster) removed but with a typical palmately compound leaf illustrated. **B.** Entire flower of *Panax*. **C.** Longitudinal section through a *Panax* flower. **D.** Floral diagram of ginseng. **E.** Floral formula for **Araliaceae.**

75

Aristolochiaceae Birthwort Family

Dutchman's Pipe Family is a less used but more descriptive common name for this group of plants; Birthwort alludes to the supposed medicinal value of the plants in aiding child-birth (due to the bent form of the flowers). About 400 species in 7 genera make up the family which is distributed mostly in tropical and warm temperate areas, largely South American. These are mostly twining woody plants, or herbaceous, leaves alternate, usually broad (often cordate) and entire, with petioles. The sap is colorless, bitter or peppery, sometimes aromatic. Flowers are perfect, the calyx is conspicuous, purple to purplish-green, petals absent. The 6-celled ovary (rarely 4 or 5) is coherent, at least at the base, with the tube of the calyx (the ovary is partly or wholly inferior, rarely superior), and forms a many seeded capsule or berry when in fruit. Stamens 6 to 36, more or less united with the style. The flowers of all members of this family are bi-sexual (perfect) epigynous, and regular or irregular, with perianth lobes usually in 3's or none.

Field characteristics are easy as only a few genera are to be encountered; the *Asarums* (wild-gingers) with their kidney-shaped leaves rising on stiff petioles from stout, creeping rhizomes which bear regular, axillary flowers, small, nearly sessile, with three brown or reddish reflexed, pointed lobed, and with or without dense hairs. Certain of the wild-gingers now are included in the genus *Haxastyis*. The Aristolochias are the Dutchman's pipes, Virginia snakeroots, and pipe-vines. All are more or less woody twining plants or upright, slender herbs (*A. serpentaria*) with bold, usually cordate, leaves; the calyx includes an elongated, somewhat inflated tube, usually curved, which expands abruptly into a one-sided (oblique) rather heart-shaped limb. Some of these emit a disagreeable odor. About 180 species are listed for the genus *Aristolochia* with perhaps 7 or 8 occurring in the milder parts of the U.S.

Commonly encountered genera in the **Aristolochiaceae** are:

> *Asarum*
> *Hexastylis*
> *Aristolochia*

Birthwort Family

A. Field sketch of *Aristolochia clematitis* **B.** Longitudinal section of a flower. **C.** Floral formula for the Family.

76

A.

B.

C. $\dfrac{Ca\circled3 \ Co^0 \ S^{6+6}}{P\circled6}$

Cap

Asclepiadaceae Milkweed Family

A very large family of about 2000 species of perennial herbs and (mostly) climbing shrubs distributed through some 250 genera, the members of the Milkweed Family are largely tropical with only a few genera in the temperate zones. Africa holds the greatest concentration of these plants. Most have milky juice; leaves are mostly opposite (rarely whorled, seldom alternate), simple, entire, and without stipules; or reduced or obsolete in cactus-like species. The flowers, complete and regular, usually are in many-flowered umbels, cymes, or racemes. They mostly are small, and with flower parts in 5's; calyx of 5 separate sepals (they may be widely attached, i.e., connate) which persist; corolla 5-lobed with a very complicated structure, the corona, ascending centrally around the style in some genera; stamens epipetalous, alternating with the corolla lobes, and are involved in very strange fusion arrangements in various genera; ovary superior, 2 carpels separate but united in style and a stigma, and the anthers often fuse with the rim or lower surface of the stigma into a structure known as a gynostegium. In some genera where the petals do not form a corona that structure develops from the backs of the anthers. Whatever its origin, the corona is involved in a complicated pollination process. The pollen coheres into waxy or granular masses called pollinia. Fruit is paired follicles each filled with seeds crowned with tufts of silky hairs. Most species are fragrant, but a few of the fleshy-stemmed ones, as *Stapelia*, give off a carrion scent.

Field Characters. If the flower has 5 separate sepals and 5 at least partially fused petals with a very complicated central structure which involves petals, stamens, and the stigma, and if the leaves are simple, and stems have milky juice, it surely is a Milkweed. Beginners sometimes confuse species of **Asclepiadaceae** with members of **Apocynaceae** but the stamens have loose pollen and sepals always show some degree of fusion in the dogbanes. Both share the characteristic of two ovaries united at the style and stigma.

Some genera in the **Asclepiadaceae** are:

Ampelamus	*Echnidopsis*	*Pergularia*
Arauja	*Fischeria*	*Periploca*
Asclepias	*Gonolobus*	*Philbertia*
Asclepiodora	*Gymnema*	*Physostelma*
Brachystelma	*Hoodia*	*Piaranthus*
Calotropis	*Hoya*	*Raphistemma*
Caralluma	*Huernia*	*Sarcostemma*
Ceropegia	*Huerniopsis*	*Stapelia*
Chlorocodon	*Lachnostoma*	*Stephanotis*
Cryptostegia	*Macroscepis*	*Tavaresia*
Cynanchum	*Marsdenia*	*Trichocaulon*
Daemia	*Metaplexis*	*Trichosacme*
Dipladenia	*Microloma*	*Tylophora*
Diplocyatha	*Oxypetalum*	*Vincetoxicum*
Dischidia	*Oxystelma*	*Wattakaka*
Duvalia	*Pectinaria*	*Xysmalobium*

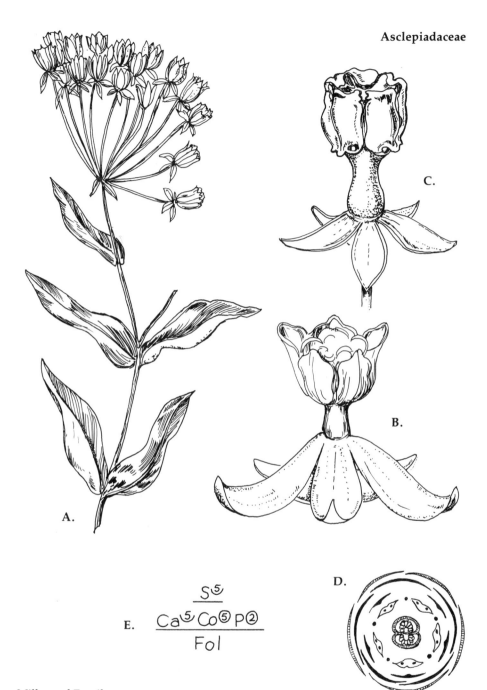

$$\frac{S^{\small⑤}}{Ca^{\small⑤}\,Co^{\small⑤}\,P^{\small②}}$$

E. $\dfrac{S^{⑤}}{Ca^{⑤}\,Co^{⑤}\,P^{②}}$ ... Fol

Milkweed Family

A. Field sketch of a milkweed, *Asclepias*. **B.** A single flower of Asclepias, with sepals below and the corona enclosed within the petals above. **C.** The same flower with petals removed. **D.** Floral diagram for *Asclepias*. **E.** Floral formula for the **Asclepiadaceae.**

Balsaminaceae Touch-me-not Family

More than 600 species in 4 genera make up this mostly tropical Old World and Asian family of herbs. All have crisp, translucent, watery stems, usually with swollen nodes. Leaves opposite or alternate, mostly simple and often toothed, without stipules; leaves of some New Guinea species (and their hybrids) often colorful. Flowers complete, zygomorphic, often nodding, and spurred; calyx of 3, 4, or 5 sepals, often unequal and petaloid, the two lateral ones usually small and greenish, but the posterior one prolonged backward into a honey-spur; corolla of 5 petals, or 4 or 2, alternating with the sepals, and rarely separate, mostly with the anterior one free and the others connate in pairs; stamens 5, filaments short and broad, anthers connate round the pistil (the growth of the ovary eventually breaks the stamens at their insertion), hypogynous; pistils compound of 5 carpels as indicated by the 5 cells of the ovary, ovary superior, with 3 to many ovules in each cell; stigmas sessile. Fruit a 5-valved capsule which, when ripe, explodes at a touch, hence the common name of this group of interesting plants.

Field characteristics are easy for these; beginning with the seedlings, easily recognizable by their very large, slightly kidney-shaped, usually lettuce-green cotyledons. Plants with glassy, water-filled, often slightly or strongly tinged (usually red or purplish) stems with enlarged nodes and simple, usually alternate leaves, are apt to be in this family, and when the irregular flowers show the characteristics describecd above, the identification is sure. Among the floral features, the spurred sepal and the connate anthers capping the stigma in combination are unique. The delightfully explosive capsule with valves which recoil tightly is a further characteristic.

Most plantsmen know **Balsaminaceae** through the various native N. American and garden species and hybrids of the genus *Impatiens*; in conservatories one sometimes encounters members of the other genus, *Hydrocera*.

Balsaminaceae probably derives its name from the ancient Arabic word for some species of *Impatiens, balassan*. Several Middle Eastern and African species of *Impatiens* yield dyes — red, yellow or black — and some have been used for medicine. One of the oldest Western World house plants probably is *Impatiens sultani*, grown by housewives everywhere, and apparently everblooming, as the "Buzzy Lizzie" of the English-speaking countries or the "Fleissige Lieschen" where German is the language.

Balsam (Touch-me-not) Family

A. Field sketch of jewelweed, *Impatiens capensis*; foolproof field characteristics include the nectariferous spur, succulent, "glassy" stems, and seed pods, also succulent, which burst violently when handled. **B.** Floral diagrams of touch-me-not. **C.** General floral formula for the Family.

A.

B.

C. $\dfrac{Caz^{3-5} Coz^{3-5} S^{\textcircled{5}} P^{\textcircled{5}}}{Cap \; Bac}$

81

Berberidaceae Barberry Family

Twelve genera with about 600 species comprises the Barberry Family, a widely scattered, Northern Hemisphere group of trees, shrubs and herbaceous plants (some of them climbers), with the Barberries extending into South America to the Straits of Magellan. A recent trend separates the 3 woody genera (marked with an asterisk, below) into **Berberdaceae** with the 9 more or less herbaceous genera included in the family **Podophyllaceae;** further splitting separates out 2 additional families. The traditional treatment presented here is in keeping with most horticultural literature. Leaves variously shaped, simple or compound, alternate, either with dilated bases or with stipules. Flowers solitary or in clusters; perfect, actinomorphic, hypogynous; sepals and petals in threes, usually in 3 whorls, rarely 2 or 4 whorls. Stamens usually as many as the petals and opposite them and ranging in number from 4 to, rarely, many, anthers usually opening by 2 lids (valves) at the top. There is a single pistil of 1 to 3 carpels with a short style or no style, stigma usually peltate. Fruit a berry or capsule, seeds few or many.

Field characteristics: Plants obviously dicots, but with flower parts, calyx and corolla, in 3's, a usually single superior ovary, free stamens opposite the petals, petals often with nectaries. Three sepals, three petals, and anthers opening by hinged lids indicate **Berberidaceae;** but the American may-apple, *Podophyllum peltatum*, has twice as many stamens as petals and with anthers opening along the sides; some of the woody species have colored inner bark or wood.

Some members of the Barberry Family:

Achlys	*Diphylleia*	*Mahonia*
Berberis	*Epimedium*	*Nandina*
Bongardia	*Jeffersonia*	*Podophyllum*
Caulophyllum	*Leontice*	*Vancouveria*

Barberry Family

A. Field sketch of barberry (*Berberis*). **B.** Floral diagram of *Berberis*. **C.** Barberry flower detail, semi-schematic. **D.** Floral formula for the Family.

A.

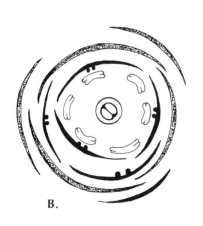

B.

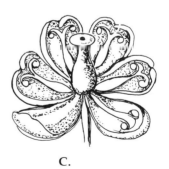

C.

D. $\dfrac{Ca^6\,Co^6\,S^{4-9}\,P^1}{Ber\ Cap}$

83

Betulaceae   Birch (or Hazel) Family

Some American authorities refer to this as the **Corylaceae**, or Hazel Family. More than 150 species of deciduous trees and shrubs are grouped into 6 genera which occur in the temperate and colder regions of the Northern Hemisphere. Leaves are alternate, with pinnate veins, usually toothed, and with stipules which fall early. Flowers are mostly of a single sex, regular, much reduced; the perianth of pistillate flowers lacking in *Alnus* and *Betula*, reduced to a crown of epigynous scales in other genera. Staminate flowers in slender catkins; 3, or by reduction 2 or 1, flowers behind each bract, perianth a single whorl, 2 to 4 lobed or absent, stamens tiny, 2 to 10, rarely more. Pistillate flowers in short spikes or clusters or rarely in catkins; perianth insignificant pistil compound, of 2 carpels, with 2 styles, ovary inferior and originally 2-celled each cell with 1 or 2 ovules, but only a single ovule develops into a seed. Fruit an indehiscent nutlet, often winged, either separating from the bract and bracteoles as *Alnus* and *Betula* or forming a sort of protective involucre as *Corylus*, or a winged or bladder-like organ as *Carpinus* and *Ostrya*.

Field characteristics are not easy, though students soon learn to combine twig, foliage, leaf-scar, and flowering or fruiting characters for a firm identification. The usually toothed, alternate leaves with early-falling stipules is a starting point. When present, the slender male catkins are a good character, and during late summer the female catkins of *Betula* and *Alnus* provide firm identification once one is familiar with their structure. With a good hand lens or better, a dissecting microscope, study the structure of the male catkins and the female inflorescences. Also, learn to know the dormant buds and their subtending leaf-scars, which provide a good means of identification.

The 6 genera of **Betulaceae** all include significant ornamental, woodlot, or horticultural species; they are:

Alnus	*Carpinus*	*Ostrya*
Betula	*Corylus*	*Ostryopsis*

Birch Family

A. Field sketch of white birch, *Betula pendula*, with terminal staminate catkins and a pistillate catkin on a lateral branchlet. **B.** Female inflorescence of birch. **C.** Male inflorescence of birch. **D.** A schematic diagram of the pistillate inflorescence of birch; note the single bract and the two bracteoles which more or less enclose the three flowers. **E.** A schematic diagram of the staminate inflorescence of birch; note that the bract and bracteoles which were separate in the female inflorescence are laterally united in the male. **F.** Floral formula for the **Betulaceae.**

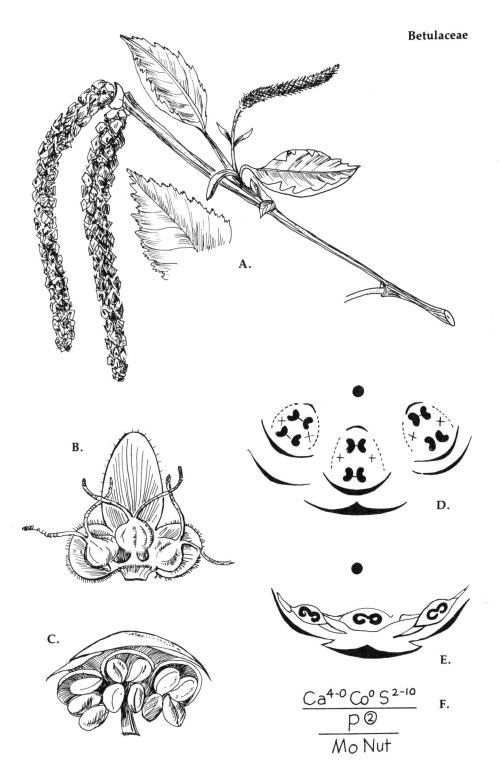

A.

B.

C.

D.

E.

$$\frac{Ca^{4-0} \, Co^0 \, S^{2-10}}{P \, ②}$$
Mo Nut

F.

Bignoniaceae Bignonia Family

Mostly trees, shrubs, and woody vines with only a few herbaceous species, the members of **Bignoniaceae** are included in some 800 species in about 120 genera. They are mostly tropical or sub-tropical with only a few temperate region species. Leaves are opposite, rarely alternate, usually compound, and without stipules (exstipulate). Flowers are mostly large and showy, in terminal or axillary racemes or panicles, hypogynous; calyx synsepalous, tubular or campanulate (bell-shaped) or rarely spathe-like, 5-lobed or 5-toothed; corolla sympetalous, 5-lobed and usually oblique or more or less 2-lipped with a bilobate upper lip and a trilobate lower lip, hypogynous, imbricated; stamens mostly 4, didynamous (2 pairs of 2 separate stamens), or only 2 with 2 or 3 stamenoids, epipetalous; compound pistil or 2 closely united carpels, 1 style, slender, with usually a 2-lobed stigma, ovary superior, on an hypogynous disc, 1 or 2-celled due to the meeting of the 2 parietal placentae or of projections from them, ovules many. Fruit mostly a dry capsule, very rarely fleshy and indehiscent.

In the field look for rather large showy flowers in sizeable racemes or panicles; flowers with definite tube in most cases and 5-lobed, either somewhat 2-lipped or oblique (limb, that is, the flat face of the corolla, at an angle to the tube), with usually 2 pairs of free stamens which are epipetalous. The usually large, woody capsules with usually winged seeds ar very characteristic. Study a plant of trumpet-vine (trumpet-creeper), *Campsis radicans*; note the large, compound leaves; the 5-lobed, nearly 2-lipped calyx and the long, tubular corolla with oblique limb as described above. Particularly, notice the very typical fruit, including an opened one where the two valves of the capsule have separated from the central septum (which derived from the ovule-bearing placentae). Such a method of opening, where the septum is freed from both valves is described as *septifragal,* a term used frequently with **Bignoniaceae.**

Among the genera encountered in tropical and sub-tropical gardens, in conservatories, and more rarely, in temperate zone gardens or in the wild in the U.S. are:

Adenocalymma	Delostoma	Phaedranthus
Amphicome	Distictis	Phyllarthron
Amphilophium	Dolichandra	Pithecoctenium
Anemopaegma	Dolichandrone	Pleonotoma
Argylia	Doxantha	Podranea
Arrabidaea	Eccremocarpus	Pyrostegia
Bignonia	Fridericia	Radermachera
Campsidium	Incaravillea	Saritaea
Campsis	Jacaranda	Spathodea
Catalpa	Kigelia	Stereospermum
Chilopsis	Macfadyena	Stizophyllum
Clytostoma	Millingtonia	Tabebuia
Colea	Newbouldia	Tecoma
Crescentia	Nyctocalox	Tecomaria
Cryista	Pandorea	Tecomella
	Parmentiera	

What country child in the U.S. has not made finger covers from the flowers of trumpet-vine, or cut the stems of cross-vine to see the Maltese cross inside, or probably, tried smoking the long pods of catalpa? Suprisingly, none of this family is truly economically important; food is prepared locally from a few sorts, some yield wood, resin, or fiber. Beauty is the forte of **Bignoniaceae.**

Bignoniaceae

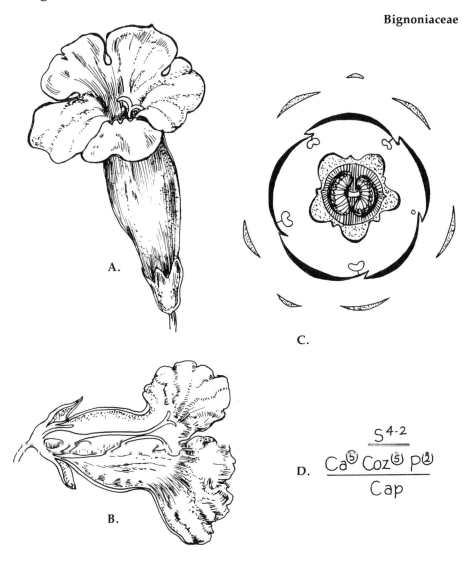

Bignonia (Trumpet-creeper) Family

A. Field sketch of a single flower of trumpet-creeper, *Campsis radicans.* **B.** Sketch of an Indian-bean, *Catalpa,* flower in longitudinal section, showing a single, dehiscent stamen below the pistil. **C.** Floral diagram of trumpet-creeper; note the 4 functional, epipetalous stamens and single staminode (which is sterile). **D.** Floral formula for the **Bignoniaceae.**

Boraginaceae Forget-me-not Family

A family of about 100 genera and 2000 species, the **Boraginaceae** are mostly coarse-leaved herbs and a few trees and shrubs, dispersed throughout the temperate and tropical regions of the world with the greatest concentration in the Mediterranean basin. Leaves usually are alternate, large, coarsely hairy, simple and mostly entire, without stipules. Flowers are mostly in a simple or forked scorpioid cyme; that is, the flower stalk is rolled, snail shell fashion, with buds more or less along just one side and, as blossoms open the cyme uncurls. Flowers, often blue or white, are complete, regular or sometimes slightly oblique. Calyx synsepalous, but often so deeply divided to appear separate, hairy, and persistent. Corolla usually 5-lobed, often with appendages in the throat. Stamens 5, inserted on the corolla tube (epipetalous) and alternating with the corolla lobes. Pistil superior, of 2 carpels, often deeply 2-lobed, a single style and either 1 or 2 stigmas. Due to the lobes of the carpels the fruits usually are 4 seed-like, 1-seeded, nutlets, or the fruit separates into two 2-seeded nutlets. The species often contain a non-poisonous, mucilaginous, slightly bitter juice and the roots of some species yield a red dye.

Field Characters. Look for the scorpioid cyme, the coarse, rough-hairy leaves, and the 4 nutlets deeply embedded, usually in the hairy persistent calyx. Members of the Mint Family also have the 4 nutlets, but their zygomorphic flowers make the distinction. The ovary of *Helotropium* is not lobed, the corolla of *Echium* is funnel-form, oblique (with a slanting face), and the stamens are of unequal length. This is an easy family when you become familiar with its harsh character and strange cyme.

Some genera in the Borage Family are:

Adelocaryum	*Eritrichium*	*Omphalodes*
Alkanna	*Hackelia*	*Onosma*
Amsinchia	*Heliotropium*	*Onosmodium*
Anchusa	*Lindelofia*	*Paracaryum*
Arnebia	*Lithospermum*	*Patagonula*
Borago	*Lobostemon*	*Plagiobothrys*
Brunnera	*Macromeria*	*Pulmonaria*
Caccinia	*Mattiastrum*	*Rindera*
Cerinthe	*Megacaryon*	*Soleanthus*
Cordia	*Mertensia*	*Symphytum*
Cryptantha	*Moltkia*	*Tournefortia*
Cynoglossum	*Myosotidium*	*Trachystemon*
Echium	*Myosotis*	*Trichodesma*
Ehretia	*Nonnea*	

Forget-me-not (Borage) Family

A. Field sketch of borage, *Borago officinalis*, showing flower parts in 5's, and actinomorphic, which distinguishes this family from the Verbenas. **B.** Field sketch of viper's bugloss, *Echium vulgare*; note the scorpioid inflorescence, characteristic of this family. **C.** Enlarged sketch of a borage flower. **D.** Floral diagram of a borage flower. **E.** Floral formula for the **Boraginaceae**.

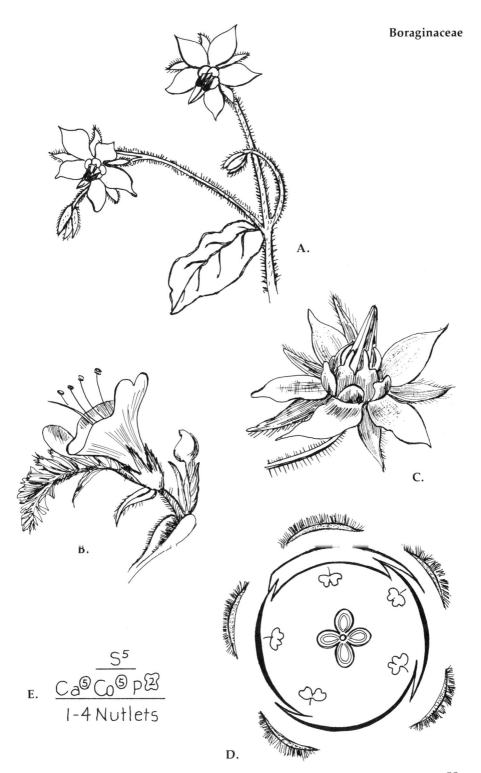

A.

B.

C.

D.

E. $\dfrac{S^5}{Ca^{\circledS}Co^{\circledS}P\circled{2}}$

1-4 Nutlets

Bromeliaceae Pineapple Family

About 51 genera include the 2000 or more species of the Pineapple Family; most are stemless or short-stemmed plants with coarse, rigid, channelled, and usually spiny leaves which are basal, alternate, and sheathing. Flowers in spikes, racemes, panicles, or heads, often in the axils of highly colored bracts; usually perfect or very rarely staminate or pistillate, regular, epigynous or less commonly hypogynous, with both calyx and corolla, each 3-part, and the lobes of both may be free or united; stamens 6, often epipetalous; compound pistil of 3 closely united carpels, with a single style with 3 branching stigmas, ovary inferior or superior. The fruit is a berry (if fleshy) or a capsule (if dry), and mostly surrounded by the persistent perianth.

This family is included largely because most gardeners are familiar with at least some of the Bromeliads; everybody knows what a pineapple is, and most know Spanish-moss from the trees in the south, though not everyone is aware that it is a flowering plant, cousin to the Bromeliads and pineapples. With the notable exception of Spanish-moss, these can be recognized by the large tough, thickened leaves (which may be covered in part or over all with scale-like hairs or with glands), combined with their epiphytic habit in most cases, and by the rather typical characteristics of the inflorescences, and certainly by flower parts in 3's (contrasted to the vaguely similar cacti and euphorbs with flower parts in 4's and 5's) even though there is great variation in the perianth structure and the ovary position.

Dissect flowers of several substantially different Bromeliads to observe the flower construction and study the plant structure carefully. Also, sever the leafy top of a pineapple retaining a core of the fleshy fruit, let it dry in shade for a few days, plant it in very sandy soil to root, and in two years or so when it blooms, study the flowers. You may happen on Spanish-moss flowering during a visit to the south, too, and the tiny blossoms are worth dissecting.

For lists of genera of these see references in encyclopedic works such as the L.H. Bailey *Encyclopedia of Horticulture,* A.B. Graf's *Exotica III,* or *The Royal Horticultural Society Dictionary of Gardening.* Also, there are special books on Bromeliads and their relatives, but only monographic works by scientists are of merit; usually the lavishly illustrated ones by amateur enthusiasts are replete with taxonomic misinformation.

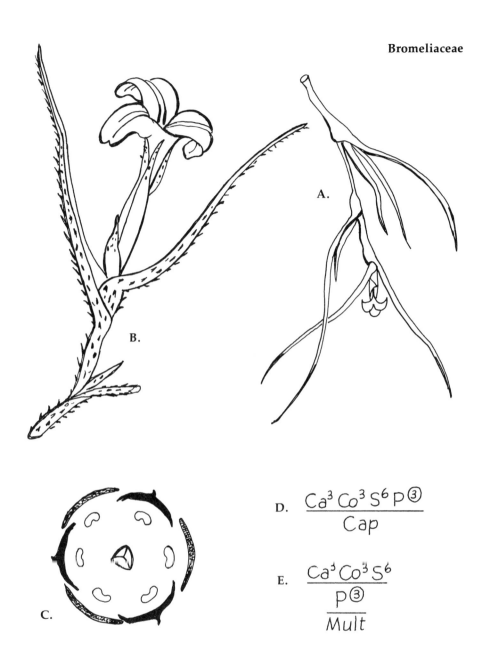

A.

B.

C.

D. $\dfrac{Ca^3 Co^3 S^6 P\textcircled{3}}{Cap}$

E. $\dfrac{Ca^3 Co^3 S^6}{\dfrac{P\textcircled{3}}{Mult}}$

Pineapple (Bromeliad) Family

A. Field sketch of a branch of Spanish-moss, *Tillandsia usneoides*. **B.** Enlargement of the flower of Spanish-moss. **C.** Floral diagram of Spanish-moss. **D.** Floral formula for the Bromeliads with a superior ovary. **E.** Floral formula for the Pineapple, which has an inferior ovary; the flowers are close set on a spike and the pineapple of commerce is known as a multiple fruit because it is composed of massed fruits of numerous flowers.

Buxaceae Box Family

A family of more than 60 species in 6 genera, the **Buxaceae** are found throughout the tropical and sub-tropical regions (one from southeastern U.S.). These are evergreen herbs, sub-shrubs, shrubs, and small trees, with simple, opposite or alternate leaves without stipules. Flowers one sex only, very rarely perfect, small, and with no corolla (apetalous). Staminate flowers with 4-parted calyx, sepals imbricated, stamens opposite the sepals and 4 to many; pistillate flower with calyx 4 to 12-parted or none, compound pistil with 3-celled superior ovary, ovules 2 or rarely 1 in each locule, styles commonly 3, simple. Fruit a capsule or fleshy, seeds few.

Field characteristics for this family are few, including the usually entire, simple, exstipulate evergreen leaves with no milky juice, and the greatly reduced perianth, flowers monoecious, and the 3-celled ovary. Similar to the **Euphorbiaceae** but in *Buxaceae* there is no hypogynous disc and no milky juice. Botanists, with dissecting microscopes, confirm their classification by the collateral suspended seeds within the 3-celled ovary and the axially directed micropyle of the seeds, but this is beyond the average field taxonomist. Structurally, the flowers of **Buxaceae** show similarities not only to the Euphorbs, but also to **Celastraceae** and to **Empetraceae.**

Horticulturists are apt to encounter only three genera of **Buxaceae** but species of all are very important in landscape work:

Buxus
Pachysandra
Sarcococca

Calycanthaceae Calycanthus Family

Two genera and 5 or 6 species in North America and in East Asia make up this shrubby family. The refined, woody plants have aromatic bark; short-petioled, simple, entire leaves arranged two at each node (oppsite), without stipules. Flowers are short-stalked, perfect, regular, perigynous, with spiral insertion of parts. Perianth segments are numerous, petaloid, not clearly defined into sepals and petals (most botanists concede that both are present). Stamens 5 to 30, perigynous. Carpels (simple pistils) numerous in an urn-like receptacle which ultimately develops into a fruit rather like a rose-hip.

There is little chance of missing members of this family in the field. Opposite-leaved shrubs are few — the viburnums, dogwoods, maples, wahoos and spindles, and a few others, *and* Calycanthus Family members. These latter are the only ones which also bear solitary flowers terminally on short, often lateral branches, flowers with spirally arranged parts as described above.

Two species of the genus *Calycanthus* occur in the eastern United States and *C. floridus* is common in cultivation. At least three more, rather insignificant, species occur in the west. Three species of *Chimonanthus* occur in China, all are in cultivation, mostly rather tender. The latter have 5 or 6 stamens per flower, *Calycanthus* flowers have 10 to 30 stamens.

Cactaceae   Cactus Family

At least 125 genera including a very large number of species (2,000+) make up the **Cactaceae** which commonly is divided into sub-families or tribes, usually 3, at least 1 of which is further divided into sub-tribes. The **Cactaceae** have succulent stems; the leaves, except in the genus *Pereskia*, much reduced or absent; on the stems a special organ, the areole, bears spines and varying amounts of wool, hair, or bristles (or combinations); new growth always occurs from the areoles; stems may be cylindrical, globular, flattened, or fluted, sometimes constricted or jointed, and the spines (not always present) usually in bundles, and usually of two kinds, long and stout, and minute and needle-like. The juice of cacti is mostly thin and watery. Flowers actinomorphic (regular), sessile or with the base of the ovary prolonged, solitary (but often in close groups or in rings near the summit of the plant), and complete (with sepals, petals, stamens, pistil). The perianth is composed of numerous, petal-like segments; there is no clear distinction between sepals and petals in most cases. The perianth is epigynous, developing round the long style with 3 or several stigmas; stamens many, spirally arranged or in clusters inside the floral cup, often epigynous; compound pistil of 3 to several carpels, ovary inferior, 1-celled, with 3 to many parietal placentae, ovules numerous. The fruit is a berry, often rather leathery outside.

The field characteristics of cacti are relatively well known; fleshy, spiny plants, more or less leafless, usually with watery juice. To separate out other succulents with a cactus-like appearance look for the areoles which are characteristic *only* of cacti. The perianth of several to many segments, sepals and petals not distinct, the numerous stamens, and especially, the inferior ovary all are characteristic of **Cactaceae.**

The list of genera in cultivation is almost endless; furthermore, classification of **Cactaceae** is far from stable, with changes and new introductions made frequently. For a reasonable summary see pp. 340-342 in Vol. 1 of the 2nd Ed. of *The Royal Horticultural Society Dictionary of Gardening*, and for details of recent classification and for further listings see the periodical of *The American Cactus Society*.

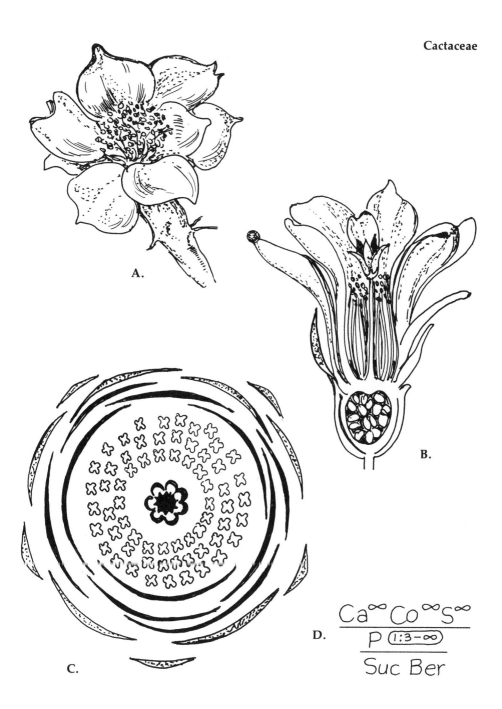

A.

B.

C.

D. $\dfrac{Ca^{\infty}\ Co^{\infty}\ S^{\infty}}{P\ \boxed{1{:}3-\infty}}$

Suc Ber

Cactus Family

A. Field sketch of a prickly-pear flower, *Opuntia.* **B.** Longitudinal section of a cactus flower. **C.** Floral diagram of a prickly-pear flower. **D.** Floral formula for the Family.

Campanulaceae Bellflower Family

About 70 genera include some 2,000 species of annual, biennial or mostly perennial herbs, with a few shrubs and trees; this is a cosmopolitan family, with representatives found throughout subtropical and temperate regions of the world, extending into cold areas and on high mountains. Most species have milky, non-toxic juice. Leaves usually alternate, rarely opposite, mostly simple but rarely lobed or divided, exstipulate. Flowers usually in racemes but sometimes in cymes or with several flowers in axils of bracts on a raceme; usually complete, actinomorphic or zygomorphic, with flower parts in 5's, epigynous; calyx 5-lobed, rarely 3 to 4, lobes inserted on the outer rim of the floral-cup which closely adheres to the ovary; corolla sympetalous, 5-parted, mostly bell-shaped (campanulate) or rotate, sometimes tubular, sometimes irregular (as *Heterotoma* and *Lobelia*), usually showy, often blue or white; stamens 5, inserted on the inner rim of the epigynous disc or at the base of the corolla, filaments often dilated, mostly free but sometimes connate, anthers sometimes more or less connate; pistil of 2, 3, or 5 closely united carpels, the single style often with a dense brush of hairs toward the stigma, stigmas 2 or more, ovary inferior, 2 to 5-celled, rarely 1-celled and often 3-celled, with many ovules. Fruit a capsule.

Often the blue, more or less bell-shaped corolla is a clue leading toward **Campanulaceae** in the field; continue through a check of flower characteristics, especially the inferior ovary with many ovules, the style with a brushy apex, and the connate anthers. If the plant has alternate, simple leaves and milky juice, the identification is confirmed. In the garden dissect flowers of any Campanulas handy — there is considerable variation in corolla and stamen structure among these — and proceed further with flowers of *Codonopis, Lobelia, Platycodon, Wahlenbergia* and any others which may be available. A study of half a dozen genera should make anyone competent to handle Bellflowers — until he first encounters those woody ones in Hawaii!

Among the genera of **Campanulaceae** encountered in gardens, botanical collections, conservatories, rock gardens, and in the wild, are:

Adenophora	*Githopsis*	*Phyteuma*
Asyneuma	*Haynaldia*	*Platycodon*
Campanula	*Heteroma*	*Pratia*
Campanumoea	*Jasione*	*Prismatocarpus*
Canarina	*Laurentia*	*Poella*
Centropogon	*Leptocodon*	*Siphocampylus*
Codonopsis	*Lightfootia*	*Specularia*
Colensoa	*Lobelia*	*Symphyandra*
Cyananthus	*Michauxia*	*Trachelium*
Downingia	*Monopsis*	*Wahlenbergia*
Edraianthus	*Ostrowskia*	

The Lobelias, especially the American sorts, are more or less narcotic, with poisonous roots; most of the rest of the plants are of no great economic importance outside their considerable value as ornamentals. It seems a shame that American gardeners stick largely to a few members of the genus

Campanula, ignoring the many other fine ornamental genera in this family which could easily supply the hard to get blue color to their gardens. Most of these are not difficult to grow from seed.

Campanulaceae

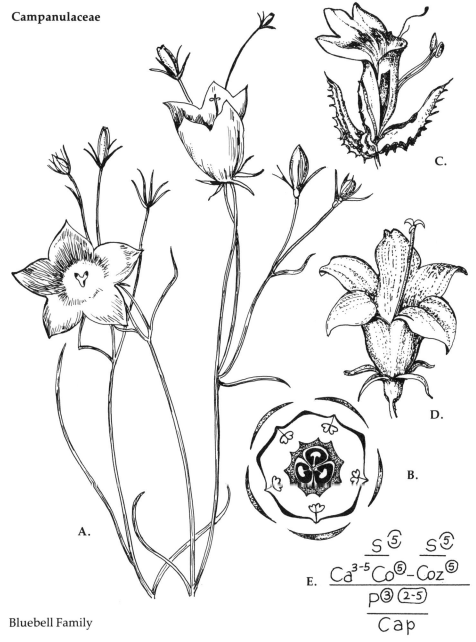

Bluebell Family

$$\frac{Ca^{3-5} \; Co^{⑤}\text{-}Coz^{⑤}}{P^{③} \; \boxed{2\text{-}5}}$$
$$\overline{Cap}$$

E. $s^{⑤}$ $s^{⑤}$

A. Field sketch of harebell, *Campanula rotundifolia* (the round leaves are in a basal rosette). **B.** Floral diagram for *Campanula.* **C.** The extremely zygomorphic flower of *Lobelia.* **D.** Another species of *Campanula.* **E.** Flower formula for **Campanulaceae** accounting for both actinomorphic and zygomorphic forms.

Cannabinaceae Hemp Family

Taxonomists inclined to erect new units of classification for every variation of plant form (splitters) regard the **Cannabinaceae** as a small family of economically important plants in the genera *Cannabis*, hemp, and *Humulus*, hops. A typical description of the family is:

Herbs with palmately veined and usually lobed or divided opposite leaves, stipules persistent. Monoecious; pistillate flowers densely clustered, the cup-shaped, fused calyx closely enclosing the 1-celled ovary, style 2-part to the base. Staminate flowers loosely clustered in racemes or panicles, with 5 sepals (free or mostly free) and 5 stamens. Fruit of these species usually is a glandular nutlet. The plants have aromatic, watery juice. Plants are harsh to the touch.

Traditionally, most botanists and horticulturists included the genera of this family in the larger Mulberry Family, **Moracaeae**. Refer to **Moraceae** for further details of plant and floral anatomy.

Students of taxonomy would do well to take note of such an instance of basic disagreement among experts on plant classification. It reminds us that we are far from knowing all there is to know about plant relationships, about the derivation of species, even about the systematic development of the plant kingdom.

Hemp Family

A. Flowering branch of a male plant of hops (*Humulus*). **B.** Flowering branch of a female plant of hops. **C.** Two female flowers in the axil of a bract of hops.

A.

B.

C.

Capparidaceae Caper Family

Mostly Tropical or Warm Temperate, this family includes about 800 species in 46 genera of herbs, shrubs, or rarely, trees. Plants usually with alternate, simple or palmate leaves, stipules present or absent. Sap is watery and may be pungent or acrid. A few species indigenous to dry regions with inrolled or much-reduced leaves. The flowers are borne solitarily or in racemes, perfect, regular, similar to those of **Cruciferae.** Flowers are regular or zygomorphic, hypogynous; sepals commonly 4, rarely 8, free or slightly united. Petals free, 4 rarely 8 (rarely lacking), showy. Stamens very rarely 4, sometimes 6 (but not 4 + 2 as in **Cruciferae**), often many, often long-exserted. Pistil with two carpels but without the partition typical of **Cruciferae.** Ovary often seated on a short or elongated stalk (gynophore), or sessile, with two to many parietal placentae; ovules few to many. Flower structure often is complicated by presence of a hard disc between petals and stamens, or by the gynophore below the ovary, or by both. Fruit is a capsule, a berry, or a drupe.

Field characteristics are not simple in this family which is easily confused with **Cruciferae**, the Mustard Family. Both have superior ovaries, calyx and corolla in 4's; but in the Caper Family stamens commonly are 6 or more and never 4 long, 2 short as in the Mustards. In the Capers the ovary commonly is unilocular without a transverse partition and in the Mustards the partition is present. Often leaves of the Caper Family have stipules and the inflorescence has bracts; stipules and bracts usually are lacking in the Mustard Family.

Some experts separate out another Family, **Cleomaceae**. There is a trend to spell this Family **Capparaceae.**

Some members of the Caper Family are:

> *Capparis*
> *Cleome*
> *Crataeva*
> *Cristatella*
> *Euadenia*
> *Gynandropsis*
> *Isomeris*
> *Maerua*
> *Morisonia*
> *Polanisia*
> *Ritchiea*
> *Roydsia*
> *Steriphoma*

Caper Family

A. Field sketch of caper (*Capparis*) shrub branch in flower. **B.** Floral formula for **Capparidaceae.**

B.

$$\frac{Ca^{4-8} Co^{4-8} S^{6-\infty} P \boxed{1:2-\infty}}{Cap\ Ber}$$

A.

Caprifoliaceae Honeysuckle Family

The Honeysuckle Family, with about 15 genera and more than 400 species, is distributed largely in the temperate regions of N. and S. America but also occurs in Europe and Asia. Mostly shrubs, some small trees, some herbs, these mostly have opposite, simple or pinnately divided leaves which rarely are with stipules. Flowers epigynous, complete, mostly zygomorphic but some actinomorphic, axillary or in terminal clusters, often showy; calyx of 4 or usually 5 lobes on the rim of the floral-cup which completely encloses the ovary; corolla sympetalous, 4 or usually 5-lobed, tubular or sometimes rotate, sometimes bi-labiate; stamens as many as the lobes of the corolla (1 fewer in *Linnaea*) and epipetalous, filaments short as in *Symphoricarpos* or very long, as in *Lonicera*, anthers usually small; compound pistil of 2 to 5 (rarely to 8) carpels, style 1 or none, stigma 1 to 5, generally small, ovary inferior, 2 to 5 (or to 8) -celled with 1 to many ovules in each cell. Fruit a berry, drupe, or capsule.

These are very like members of the **Rubiaceae**, but exstipulate, and generally with larger, showier flowers. In some cases the perfoliate leaves (sessile, with bases of the blades connate round the stem) and the much extruded stamens help with field identification, but by and large all the floral characteristics have to be used for accurate identification. Look especially at the usually several-celled inferior ovary with a small or no style and small, often lobed stigma. Flower parts in **Rubiaceae** mostly are even-numbered, 4 to 6, while in the **Caprifoliaceae** they often are in 5's. In the temperate zone most hardy members of **Caprifoliaceae** are woody while a great many hardy members of **Rubiaceae** are herbaceous or suffruticose, except *Cephalanthus*. In the garden dissect flowers of various honeysuckles, beauty-bush, *Abelia* and *Viburnum* to see variations within this family.

Among the **Caprifoliaceae** genera encountered in gardens or in the wild in N. America are:

Abelia	*Leycesteria*	*Triosteum*
Alseuosmia	*Linnaea*	*Viburnum*
Diervilla	*Lonicera*	*Weigela*
Dipelta	*Sambucus*	
Kolkwitzia	*Symphoricarpos*	

A few of the honeysuckles have been used in medicine and at one time the European elder was held in high esteem as virtually a cure-all, but today elder is scarcely important but sometimes the flowers are eaten and the fruits are made into wine or the dried flowers used for tea. Most members of the family today are famous only for their ornamental value and some of the Loniceras and Viburnums are intensely fragrant, especially at dusk and dawn.

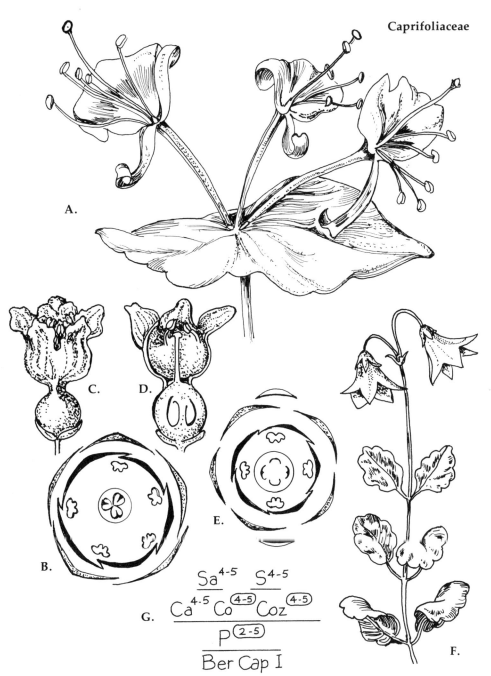

G. $$\frac{\underset{}{\overset{}{Sa^{4\text{-}5}\quad S^{4\text{-}5}}}}{\cfrac{Ca^{4\text{-}5}\ Co^{\boxed{4\text{-}5}}\ Coz^{\boxed{4\text{-}5}}}{P^{\boxed{2\text{-}5}}}}$$

$$\overline{Ber\ Cap\ I}$$

Honeysuckle Family

A. Field sketch of honeysuckle, *Lonicera*. **B.** Floral diagram of honeysuckle. **C.** Sketch of buckbrush (Indian-current), *Symphoricarpos*, flower. **D.** Longitudinal section of buckbrush flower. **E.** Floral diagram of buckbrush. **F.** Field sketch of twinflower, **Linnaea**. **G.** General formula for **Caprifoliaceae**.

Caryophyllaceae Pink Family

More than 2000 species (many with varieties, forms, and cultivars) in about 80 genera make up this North Temperate and alpine family of herbaceous annuals and perennials, a few with a more or less woody (suffruticose) base. Leaves are opposite and entire (not lobed or toothed), but on some species leaves toward the summit of flower stems may be alternate, leaves often connate at the base, with or without stipules. Stems usually with swollen nodes. Flowers mostly perfect, regular, with or without petals, sometimes strongly perfumed, usually in cymes. Calyx of 4, usually 5, separate or united sepals; corolla of 4 or 5 separate petals or rarely absent. Stamens as many or twice as many as sepals, either hypogynous or perigynous. Pistil of 3 to 5 (rarely 2) united carpels, styles 2 to 5 (rarely united into 1) usually stigmatic on the inner surfaces; ovary superior, mostly 1-celled with free-central or basal placenta, ovules usually many, rarely 1. Fruit a many-seeded capsule opening by valves or more or less indediscent, or rarely a single-seeded utricle.

Field charcteristics of the Pink Family depend on combinations of the above characteristics; look especially for the swollen joints with opposite, entire leaves, for the persistent calyx, for styles with stigmas on inner surfaces, and for special characteristics which easily identify species or genera within the group, as the clove scent of many Pinks as well as the bract below the flower and the viscid "feel" of the Catch-flies. Petals of many of the chickweeds are deeply to very deeply notched. This is an easy family, recommended for beginning taxonomists because many species in several genera are easily found in the wild.

Among the genera of **Caryophyllaceae** commonly encountered as garden ornamentals, wild plants, or lawn and garden weeds (many of these are naturalized from Europe) are:

		Petrocoptis
Acanthophyllum	*Heliosperma*	*Sagina*
Agrostemma	*Herniaria*	*Saponaria*
Arenaria	*Holosteum*	*Scleranthus*
Cerastium	*Illecebrum*	*Silene*
Corrigiola	*Lychnis*	*Spergula*
Dianthus	*Melandrium*	*Spergularia*
Drymaria	*Minuartia*	*Stellaria*
Drypis	*Moehringia*	*Tunica*
Geocarpon	*Myosoton*	*Vaccaria*
Gypsophila	*Paronychia*	*Viscaria*

From the English common names of plants in this family it is obvious that these have been associated with mankind since those distant days when men earned their daily bread and cheese literally with their noses to the ground. Catchfly, Campion, Corn Cockle, Chickweed, Pearlwort, Pink, Sandwort, Soapwort, Spurrey, and Whitlow-wort are some of the old names which tell of long forgotten associations and uses for these plants. The Pink, or Carnation, has religious and household significance reaching back beyond the Dark Ages; the saponin in rootstocks of *Saponaria*, once produced, when beaten in water, a detergent useful for washing; today we are more aware of the dermatitis causing quality.

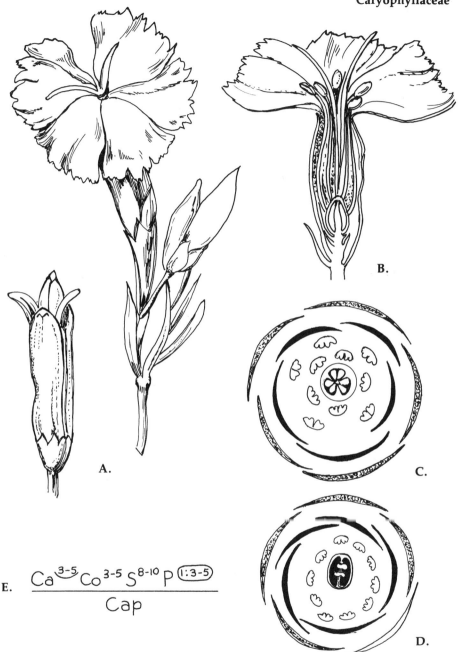

A. Field sketch of *Dianthus* branch in flower, with a mature fruit at the left. B. *Dianthus* flower in longitudinal section. C. Floral diagram of chickweed (*Stellaria*). D. Floral diagram of *Dianthus*. E. Floral formula for the Family.

Pink Family

A. Field sketch of *Dianthus* branch in flower, with a mature fruit at the left. **B.** *Dianthus* flower in longitudinal section. **C.** Floral diagram of chickweed (*Stellaria*). **D.** Floral diagram of *Dianthus*. **E.** Floral formula for the Family.

105

Celastraceae Staff-tree Family

A family of about 850 species in 60 genera of shrubs and trees (often woody climbers), these occur in temperate and warm regions. Leaves simple, not lobed, membranous or leathery, deciduous or evergreen, mostly alternate but some opposite, and with usually tiny, fugaceous stipules. Flowers small, greenish or white or rarely purplish, actinomorphic, perfect or monoecious, axillary or in terminal cymes or racemes, or solitary; both sepals and petals are imbricated in the bud. Calyx of 3 to 5 sepals, free and persistent; corolla of 3 or 5 separate petals which often are inserted upon or below a more or less conspicuous glandular disc variously shaped; stamens commonly 3 or 5, rarely 10, alternating with the petals, free, usually inserted on the glandular disc; compound pistil, ovary superior, 2— to 5-celled, and buried in the disc or distinct when the disc is reduced, style short or very short, stigma 2— to 5-lobed or capitate, ovules usually 2 in each cell. Fruit a capsule, drupe, or rarely a samara. Seeds usually with a pulpy aril.

Field identification depends on selecting as many of the various characteristics listed above as possible; generally, the small, greenish flowers, stamens alternating with the petals and the same number or twice the number of petals, *and the glandular disc beneath or more or less surrounding the ovary,* serves for identification. The aril on the seeds, usually brightly colored and contrasting to the often leathery capsule (as in *Euonymus* and *Celastrus*) is typical of this family.

While a great many species of **Celastraceae** are common in horticulture, most belong to either *Euonymus* or *Celastrus*; other genera are encountered in warm conservatories or in tropical gardens; the most common genera are:

Catha	*Glossopetalon*	*Ptilidium*
Celastrus	*Hartogia*	*Putterlickia*
Gymnosporia	*Maytenus*	*Schaefferia*
Elaeodendron	*Paxistima*	*Tripterygium*
Euonymus	*(formerly Pachystima)*	

The bittersweets, wahoos, spindles, burning-bushes and evergreen forms of *Euonymus* are sufficient to distinguish any family from a horticultural standpoint; *Catha edulis* furnishes the *khat* which stimulates the Arabs and is said to be effective against plague, and the fruit of *Elaeodendron* is eaten in S. Africa.

Ceratophyllaceae Hornwort Family

This family is included because it is commonly encountered in quiet waters throughout much of the United States and adjacent Canada and Mexico. There is only one genus, *Ceratophyllum*, with perhaps only 10 species. The plants all grow under water, and are vaguely reminiscent of some of the tropical water plants sold by dealers in aquarium supplies.

Stems are round, limp when out of water. Leaves are sessile, whorled, and finely divided into thrice-forked narrow divisions which give rise to the Greek name, *ceras*, a horn, and *phyllon*, a leaf. Flowers are minute, either male or female (monoecious), axillary, and enclosed in an 8- to 12-lobed involucre which replaces a calyx. There are no true sepals or petals. The female flowers have a simple, 1-celled superior ovary with a single ovule; male flowers bear only 10 to 20 stamens with large, sessile anthers. Fruits are achenes, beaked with the slender persistent style.

Field characteristics are easy; this is the quiet water, "ferny" looking plant with extremely reduced flowers. It is a valuable oxygenator for all water, and a hiding place for baby fishes. It propagates readily from broken pieces inserted in the bottom sand or mud. With the approach of winter plant masses sink to the bottom in nature, rising again in the spring.

Learn to know the single genus:*Ceratophyllum*, and its two American species, *C. demersum*, and *C. echinatum*.

Chenopodiaceae Goosefoot Family

The 1,500 species distributed among 102 genera in the Goosefoot Family are distributed throughout the world and gardeners are aware of only a handful of them. Most are succulent annual or perennial herbs, some are shrubs or even trees (rarely). Many of them thrive on salty (seashore) or alkaline soils where they become the dominent vegetation. Leaves usually are simple, alternate, often fleshy, sometimes reduced to scales, and without stipules. Leaves and stems sometimes are mealy or scurfy (thus, the name "goosefoot"), the sap is colorless or red, non-aromatic, neutural-tasting. Flowers are minute, greenish, in axillary clusters or cymes. Sepals 1 to 5, mostly united, rarely separate, rarely lacking, the lobes imbricated in the bud. Petals are absent. Flowers almost always unisexual. Stamens as many as or fewer than the lobes of the perianth, filaments inserted opposite the lobe at the base of the perianth. The superior pistil is of 2 or 3 carpels, rarely 5, ovary 1-celled, styles or stigmas usually 2, rarely 3 to 5. In *Beta* the ovary is half inferior. The fruit is a nutlet (achene) more or less enclosed in the perianth which may become hard, or fleshy, or thorny, or hooked. Thus a "seed", as in the common table beet, may produce several seedlings because it actually is a cluster of tightly adhering, horny calices, each containing a nutlet.

Because of the diverse character of the vegetative body of these plants field identification is not simple. The "salt-bushes" of the seashore are characteristically scurfy-stemmed, brittle, fleshy, with reduced leaves. But compare this with the beets, chards, mangel-wurzels, and spinach of the garden! In the field, look for the alternate, simple leaves which may be rather elongated or scale-like, for the tassels of tiny greenish flowers in the axils of the leaves, and for the rather "soft" or, in the case of the salt-bushes, brittle, character of the entire plant which separates it from the harsh, often stickerish feel of the allied Amaranths.

Some genera of **Chenopodiaceae** which commonly are encountered are:

Anredera	*Eurotia*	*Salicornia*
Atriplex	*Grayia*	*Salsola*
Beta	*Hablitzia*	*Sarcobatus*
Camphorosma	*Khagodia*	*Spinacia*
Chenopodium	*Kochia*	

Of the above, spinach, beet and its varieties chard, mangel-wurzel, and sugar beet, and good king henry are recognizable as kitchen garden plants. Some people use shoots of various chenopodiums, atriplexes and salicornias as pot-herbs. *Salicornia* has been used (ashed) in the manufacture of glass and soap because of its soda content. Peruvians make flour of *Chenopodium quinoa*, another species is in general use as a primitive vermifuge, still another produces a saponin. Orach (*Atriplex*) leaves are edible and the plant yields an indigo dye. *Kochia scoparia* apparently is in the only widely used ornamental though some other species in various genera grow in some herb gardens.

B.

A.

$$\text{D.} \quad \frac{Ca^{2-5} \; Co^{0} \; S^{2-5} \; P^{1}}{Pf \; Mo \; Di \; Nut \; Ach}$$

C.

Goosefoot Family

A. Field sketch of lamb's quarters (*Chenopodium*). **B.** Flower of *Chenopodium*. **C.** Beet (*Beta*) flower in longitudinal section. **D.** Floral formula for the Family.

Cistaceae Rock-rose Family

Eight genera (and at least one hybrid genus) with about 200 species make up the **Cistaceae**. These are low shrubs or herbs of the drier, sandy or alkaline soils of the Mediterranean basin and of North America, with mostly opposite often small simple leaves which are furnished with stellate and glandular hairs, the latter producing an ethereal oil. Flowers regular or mostly so, mostly colorful, some quite showy, and complete; sepals 3 or mostly 5, the external 2 much smaller and bract-like or lacking, free; corolla of 3 or mostly 5 petals, convolute in the opposite direction from the calyx in bud, separate (sometimes none), and quickly falling; stamens distinct, hypogynous, numerous, of indefinite number, filaments slender, anthers short; compound pistil with ovary superior, style single or none, stigma often discoid, sessile or nearly so, with 5 or 10 (rarely 3) parietal placentae. Fruit a 3 to 5-valved capsule.

Field characters for **Cistaceae** include the quickly falling convolute petals, many hypogynous stamens and the 1-celled, many seeded superior ovary. When present, the stellate and glandular hairs on the leaves are characteristic; it takes a hand lens to define these.

Genera encountered in gardens and in the wild include:

> *Cistus*
> *Fumana*
> × *Halimiocistus*
> *Halimium*
> *Helianthemum*
> *Hudsonia*
> *Lechea*

Several of these genera include species of great ornamental value, especially for rock gardens and seaside plantings. *Helianthemum canadense* is called, in the literature, frostweed, and by local folks "possum-ice plant" because under certain conditions (late, warm fall, and a sudden ground frost, when there is plenty of moisture in the soil) during night in autumn ice forms in the basal tissues of the plant and bursts out through splits in the squarish stem, making paper-thin, long curls like those from the plane of a master carpenter. You have to be up before the sun to see possum ice.

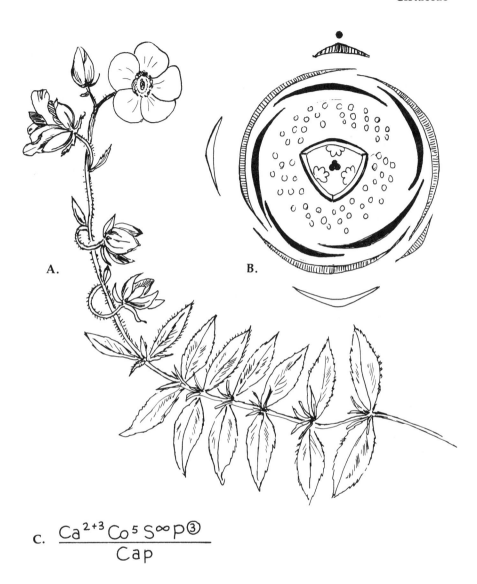

A.

B.

C. $\dfrac{Ca^{2+3} Co^5 S^{\infty} P③}{Cap}$

Rock-rose Family

A. Field sketch of sun-rose, *Helianthemum nummalurium*. **B.** Floral diagram of sun-rose; note the calyx,, with two small sepals lying outside the whorl of three. Two bracts appear exterior to the outer sepals. **C.** Floral formula for the Family; though three carpels is common in this family (a good field character when combined with numerous stamens, five free petals, and the rather unusual grouping of sepals) some members have five carpels.

Commelinaceae Spiderwort Family

About 600 species distributed through at least 40 genera make up the *Commelinaceae*. These are chiefly tropical, circumglobal, but a number of species in at least three genera of annual and perennial herbs occur naturally in the north temperate portion of the U.S. All are herbs with usually crisp, watery stems and knotted nodes; alternate leaves are somewhat sheathing at the base and with more or less linear blades with strongly parallel veins, leaf blades flat or channeled; often branching occurs freely at the nodes. Flowers usually in a cyme often somewhat enclosed in leaves which form a kind of spathe, or in axillary clusters; flowers usually complete, rarely staminate or pistillate, often (not always) actinomorphic, hypogynous, and often showy, with cyanic colors — blue, violet, lavender, pink, rose, or white; perianth of 6 parts, calyx of 3 sepals, free, usually green; corolla hypogynous, of 3 mostly ephemeral separate or rarely somewhat united petals (these often dissolve into a viscid liquid); stamens 6 or reduced to 3 with or without staminoids, hypogynous, in some genera the filament hairs are mere chains of ovoid cells, nearly transparent, but with beautifully colored cell sap surrounded by the protoplasm which can be observed in movement under a dissecting microscope; compound pistil usually of 3, rarely 2 closely united carpels, with a single style, stigma capitate or slightly 2 or 3-lobed; ovary superior, mostly 2 or 3-celled, with several to many ovules in each cell. Fruit a capsule.

In the field use the leaf and flower characteristics described above to confirm your identification of these. If you study the organization of the flowers and the plant characteristics of some common sorts such as the native Tradescantias, Commelinas, and the tropical sorts in several genera sold as "wandering jew" you note particularly the 3-part flowers, often quite triangular face-on, with extruded stamens and pistil, and the special leaves which subtend the flower cluster, and also, the mucilaginous juice which flows freely from broken stems of many of these.

Among the native and exotic genera commonly encountered are:

Aneilema	*Forrestia*	*Tradescantia*
Cochliostema	*Gibasis*	*Tripogandra*
Commelina	*Palisota*	*Weldenia*
Cuthbertia	*Rhoeo*	*Zebrina*
Cyanotis	*Spironema*	
Dichorisandra	*Tinantia*	

Though many species of these and other genera are involved in medical preparations or used for minor sources of foodstuffs in Asia, their chief economic value is ornamental. As a point of interest, many people enjoy a tender sort as a house plant; it has wiry stems, smallish channelled leaves, olive above, purplish below, and with terminal inflorescences of charming little white flowers; this came on the market originally as *Tradescantia multiflora* but soon found itself relabelled *Tripogandra multiflora*, but very soon another change was made and now the little plant is *Gibasis geniculata*! The common name is too awful to mention, and misleading geographically.

Clethraceae White-alder Family

A single genus with perhaps 30 species and several varieties makes up this small, but taxonomically important family which introduces the sub-class of plants with petals more or less consistently united (though petals of *Clethra* are separate); a description of the family is a description of the genus *Clethra*; trees and shrubs, deciduous or evergreen, with stellate pubescence; leaves alternate, short-petioled, usually entire and serrate, exstipulate. Flowers perfect, actinomorphic, hypogynous, usually white or pink, in terminal racemes or panicles; calyx of 5 free sepals which are persistent; corolla of 5 separate petals inserted on the receptacle; stgamens 10, separate and hypogynous, anthers facing outward in the bud but turning over to face inward in flower, and opening by a basal pore (which is now uppermost); compound pistil of 3 carpels, style slender, 3-lobed, stigma 3-lobed, ovary superior, 3-celled, with central placentae and many ovules. Fruit a 3-valved capsule.

In the field the inverted anthers, 3-celled, superior ovary, 5 free petals and 5 free sepals are important characteristics; also look for stamens in 2 whorls of 5 each; confirm with foliar characteristics, especially simple, alternate, exstipulate leaves. In the garden study the panicled racemes of the Sweet Pepperbush, *Clethra alnifolia*, then dissect a few flowers for the internal structure. You will need a hand lens.

All of the Clethras are well worth growing in the garden where hardy; ours are especially useful in the wildflower garden.

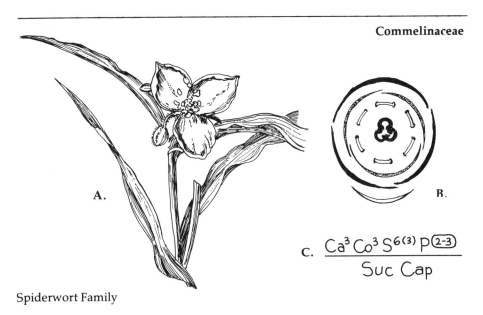

Commelinaceae

$$\frac{Ca^3\ Co^3\ S^{6(3)}\ P\underline{(2\text{-}3)}}{Suc\ Cap}$$

Spiderwort Family

A. Field sketch of spiderwort, *Tradescantia virginiana*. **B.** Floral diagram of spiderwort. **C.** Floral formula for the **Commelinaceae.**

113

Compositae Composite Family

More than 920 genera with about 19,000 – 20,000 species make up the vast family of Composites; these are world-wide in distribution, and may be annual or perennial herbs, shrubs, or in tropical areas, trees. While leaf characteristics, including shape, venation, and texture vary greatly, the leaves are mostly alternate, rarely opposite or whorled, and exstipulate. Many of the species have milky juice. The flowers of *Compositae* are mostly small to tiny, in a close head on a common receptacle, and subtended by phyllaries, a leafy involucre (which the uninitiated often mistake for the calyx). When the small flowers are pulled from the receptacle (which may be dome-shaped, conical, or discoidal) it is relatively easy to study their structure with a hand lens. Each floret is an entire flower; often each floret is accompanied by a tiny bract which generally is referred to as a "scale" or as "chaff"; the flowers may be perfect, but often are staminate or pistillate, epigynous, actinomorphic or zygomorphic; calyx, at the summit of the inferior ovary, is reduced to a fringe of hairs, bristles (awns), scales, or a minute rim, or may be lacking; when hairs or bristles are present this is commonly called the *pappus*; corolla sympetalous, either regular and tube-shaped often with rather pointed lobes, or irregular, tubular at the base, but becoming one-sided and strap-shaped (liguate), usually the corolla is 5-lobed, epigynous; stamens commonly 5 (rarely 4), epipetalous, and mostly with anthers united laterally to form a tube but with filaments free; compound pistil of 2 closely united carpels, style 1, mostly branching into 2 stigmas, ovary inferior usually with 1 cell, 1 ovule. Fruit an achene, often crowned with the persistent pappus (as dandelion "seeds").

The florets with a strap-shaped (ligulate) corolla are called ray-flowers or rays and a flower head with ray-flower at the margin or throughout is described as *radiate*; the tube-shaped florets (those with a regular corolla) are inserted on the common receptacle known as a disc, and a head with no ray-flowers is said to be *discoid*; when a flower head is composed of ray-flowers and disc flowers it is referred to as *heterogamous*, but a head of only one sort of floret is *homogamous*. The leaves of the involucre which subtends the flower head are referred to in older literature as "bracts" but now are called *phyllaries*; the small bracts or scales on the receptacle at the bases of the florets are called *chaff* or *pales*, and when not present the receptacle is said to be naked.

Hundreds of genera of **Compositae** are known to us in our gardens or in botanical collections, or among the native flora. There is little point in listing just a few of them. For fairly complete lists refer to the major horticultural encyclopedic works, to taxonomic floras, and to annotated lists in special taxonomy reference works. The family is sub-divided into a number of Tribes (varying from 10 to 14, depending on author); when you have practiced dissecting flower heads and flowers of a number of common garden sorts — *Achillea, Bellis, Centaurea, Doronicum, Echinops, Felicia, Gaillardia* . . . . on through *Zinnia*, look up one or two keys to the tribes and learn the characteritics of each group. It is a tantalizing exercise!

One would think spotting Composites in the field would be no problem, just look for florets in compact heads, on a common receptacle, and with an involucre of subtending phyllaries. Often it is just that easy. The trouble is, these things take many forms, and sometimes the flower-heads pretend to be something else (reduced or 1 or just a few florets) or something else looks, superficially, like a Composite head, as some of the clovers. Usually the specific flower structure, calyx reduced to hairs or bristles, scales, or a rim; corolla sympetalous, regular or irregular and epigynous; stamens epipetalous and mostly with anthers connected (not so in *Ambrosia* and *Xanthium*), ovary inferior, solves the problem of family. With experience you will pull apart two or three flowers (using a dissecting needle and hand lens) and accurately shove that individual not only into **Compositae**, but also into its Tribe.

Compositae

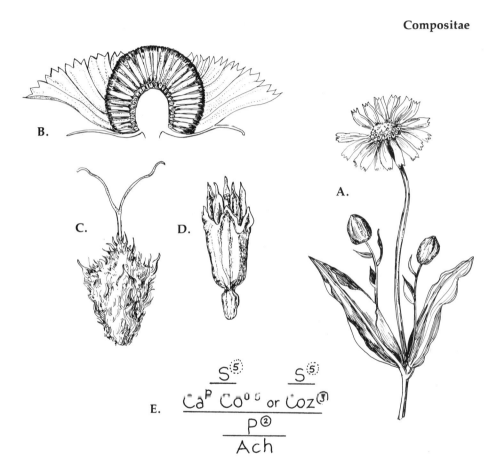

Composite (Aster) Family

A. Field sketch of *Arnica montana*, showing a typical "daisy" type head with a ring of ray flowers surrounding a cluster of disk flowers. **B.** A longitudinal section through the inflorescence of a typical Composite, with the central receptacle subtended by bracts (the involucre) and with an outer ring of ray flowers and the inner cluster of disk florets. **C.** Some Composite flowers are greatly reduced, as shown by this pistilate flower of *Ambrosia*. **D.** The staminate ragweed, Ambrosia, flower. **E.** A generalized floral formula for the **Compositae**.

Convolvulaceae Morning-glory Family

Annual or perennial herbs (many climbing by twining) and in warmer climates some woody species make up the approximately 1,400 to 1,650 species and about 50 genera of this large family. Some are thorny, woody shrubs or small trees, some yellow, leafless, twining parasites (as dodder, *Cuscuta* spp.), some nearly prostrate turf-formers as *Dichondra*; many have milky juice, some extensive tuberous roots or rhizomes. Leaves alternate, simple and entire or rarely compound, with small stipules; leaves reduced to scale in *Cuscuta*, dodder, a twining parasite. Flowers complete, actinomorphic, often quite showy, peduncles very often bi-bracteate; calyx of usually 5 sepals, separate and often overlapping, or joined, persistent; corolla of 4, usually 5 petals joined to form a funnel-shaped flower with a flaring rim or sometimes with a more tapering tube flaring to a platter-like limb, as moonflower, *Calonyction*, usually furled, umbrella-like, in the bud, (convolute) hypogynous; stamens mostly 5, epipetalous at the base of the corolla, free, alternating with the corolla lobes; compound pistil of 2, rarely 3 to 5 carpels, with 1 or 2 styles and 1 or 2 stigmas; ovary superior on a hypogynous disc, usually 2-celled or sometimes more, or sometimes with false partitions between developing seeds, ovules usually 2 in each cell. Fruit a plump, usually 2 to 6-seeded capsule or a berry which very rarely breaks into 4 1-seeded nutlets.

In the field mostly look for twining climbers, non-woody but sometimes "ropy" outside the the tropics, often with more or less heart-shaped, entire, simple, alternate leaves with small stipules, bearing more or less funnel-shaped flowers at the nodes. In addition, there are the small upright herbs with tiny morning-glory flowers as *Evolvulus*, and the nearly leafless, non-green (amber-stemmed with tiny white flowers) dodders, as well as quantities of exotics in the garden. In most cases the typical morning-glory or moonflower type of blossom with calyx and corolla in 5's, stamens more or less epipetalous and also usually 5, and the superior ovary with usually 2 carpels, will confirm your identification. You may have trouble with the small, nearly bell-shaped flower of *Dichondra*, with the rather reduced flowers of dodder, and perhaps with some species of *Quamoclit*, particularly *Q. lobata* (which used to be *Mina lobata*) with a slightly irregular corolla; it would be a good idea to look up blossoms of each of these and sketch them to commit them to memory.

Among the cultivated and native genera of *Convolvulaceae* most commonly encountered are:

Alona	*Dichondra*	*Osteocarpus*
Argyreia	*Evolvulus*	*Pharbitis*
Breweria	*Falkia*	*Porana*
Calonyction	*Hewittia*	*Quamoclit*
Calystegia	*Ipomoea*	*Rivea*
Convolvulus	*Jacquemontia*	
Cuscuta	*Lettsomia*	

The sweet-potato, *Ipomoea batatas*, and field bindweed, *Convulvulus arvensis*, are sufficient to make any plant family both famous and infamous; but beyond the many kinds that are first rate ornamentals, several supply

116

rather strong drugs; violent purgatives and cortisone are prepared from these as is oil of rhodium used to adulterate attar of roses and as a rat attractment, and more, much more. These are versatile plants, indeed. Plant moonvines to watch the flowers open in the evening.

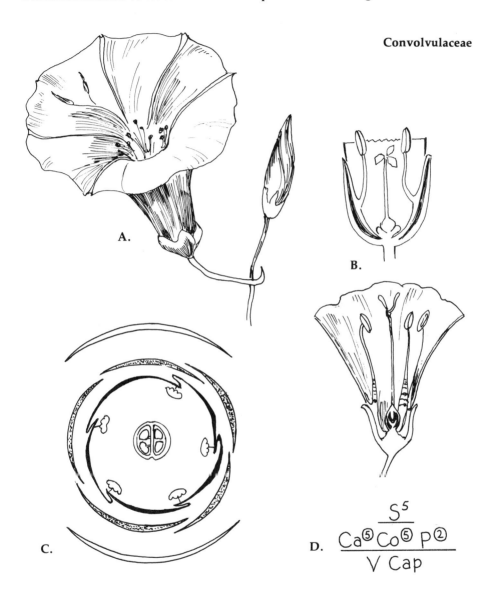

Convolvulaceae

A.

B.

C.

D. $\dfrac{S^5}{\dfrac{Ca^{\textcircled{5}} Co^{\textcircled{5}} P^{\textcircled{2}}}{V\ Cap}}$

Morning-glory Family

A. Field sketch of field bindweed, *Convolvulus arvensis.* **B.** Longitudinal sections of two members of this family, showing variations in the disc below the ovary and the epipetalous insertion of the stamens. **C.** Floral diagram of a common morning-glory. **D.** Floral formula for the Family.

Cornaceae Dogwood Family

Experts in taxonomy have whittled away at the **Cornaceae** in recent years, separating out some members, fragmenting others. Today, these tree, shrubs and very few perennial herbs fall into about 12 genera with about 100 species, mostly native to north temperate areas of N. America and Asia, but some sub-tropical and some in the southern hemisphere. Bark of these is bitter, tonic, with clear juice. Leaves opposite, a few alternate, entire, and exstipulate; veins often rather pronounced. Flowers small, greenish-yellow or whitish, in terminal umbellate clusters, corymbs, or rarely capitate with involucral bracts which often are showy, perfect or unisexual, actinomorphic, epigynous; sepals 4, rarely 5, minute or lacking, on the rim of the epigynous disc; petals 4, rarely 5 or lacking, usually valvate in the bud, inserted on the rim of the disc; stamens separate, 4 or 5, alternating with the petals and inserted on the disc; compound pistil with 2 (rarely fewer or more) carpels, usually a single style with capitate or lobed stigma; ovary inferior, 2-celled (or 1 to 4), each cell with a single ovule. Fruit a 1 to 4-celled berry or drupe.

In the field, in the U.S. and Europe, not many shrubs and trees show opposite leaves (learn to distinguish the various viburnums, euonymuses, maples, buckeyes, and so on), and none of these except the Dogwoods have showy, petal-like bracts subtending a rather tight cluster of fairly insignificant flowers; further, the tetramerous (flower parts in 3's), polypetalous, epigynous flowers are characteristic of this family, as is the fruit. The fruit, however, varies; study specimens of fruit from *Cornus florida*, *C. kousa*, and from one of the osier dogwoods such as *C. stolonifera*; compare, if handy, with fruits of *Aucuba*.

In the U.S. we see many species from the genus *Cornus* and quite a few forms of *Aucuba*, but we have to resort to our Arboreta or to European collections to see the other cultivated genera in this family, among which are:

Aucuba
Cornus
Corokia
Curtisia
Griselinia
Helwingia

Some taxonomists include the genus *Davidia* with these; more recent studies seem to indicate that it belongs with the sour gums (*Nyssa* spp.) in the **Nyssaceae.** For years these two families were considered as one. Today the genus *Cornus* is being broken up; no doubt logical, when one considers the diversity of growth habit and fruiting habit, but one wonders if such changes ever can become common in horticultural usage.

The Dogwoods have great ornamental value and most serve wildlife as a food source; their economic value has declined, though once the very hard, non-splintering wood was used for arrow shafts, for skewers, and before plastics, for shuttles in power looms. In the Orient the fruit is eaten to some extent.

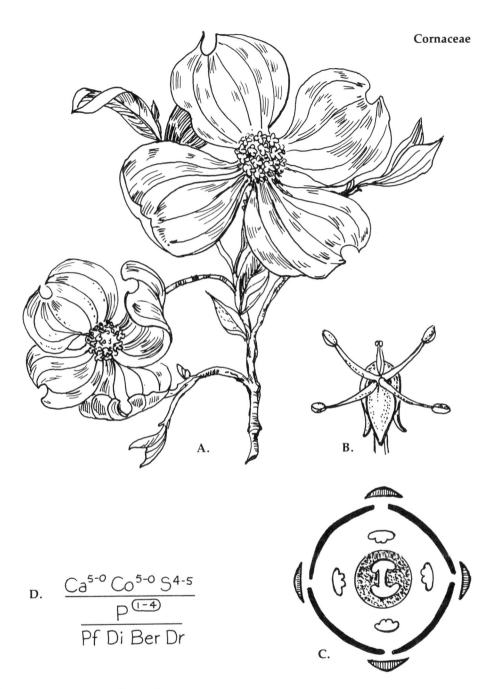

A.

B.

D. $$\frac{Ca^{5-0}\ Co^{5-0}\ S^{4-5}}{P^{\boxed{1-4}}}$$
Pf Di Ber Dr

C.

Cornel (Dogwood) Family

A. Field sketch of flowering dogwood, *Cornus florida*, showing the large, white bracts surrounding the cluster of small, yellow flowers. **B.** A single flower of *Cornus sanguinea*, a species with no corolla. **C.** A typical floral diagram for *Cornus*. **D.** Floral formula for **Cornaceae.**

Crassulaceae Orpine (Stonecrop) Family

These are succulent herbs and pliable shrubs usually with fleshy leaves and stems; often rosette-forming. The 1,400—1,550 species in 32-35 genera (depending on authority) are distributed throughout the tropical and warm Temperate zones of the world, but are concentrated in S.Africa. Most grow in dry areas; growth is "tufted", leaves closely packed, with waxy surfaces, sunken stomata, and often pale-colored. Leaves are opposite or alternate, simple or pinnate, often very succulent, stipules lacking. Flowers are perfect, regular (actinomorphic), usually small and star-like, usually in cymes; flower parts may be any number 3 to 30. Sepals 4 to 5, usually free and inserted on a tubular receptacle, petals 4, 5, or lacking, free or slightly joined. Stamens as many or twice as many as the petals, free, usually hypogynous, sometimes epipetalous, rarely perigynous. Pistils superior, 3 to several, usually carpels are free, mostly flask-shaped with a simple stigmatic surface capping a short style. Mostly a tiny scale on the receptacle lies at the base of each carpel. (This is a critical distinction from the very similar **Saxifragaceae**). Ovules numerous, rarely few or one. Fruit a group of follicles, dry and dehiscent, opening down a ventral suture.

Field characteristics of the Orpines begin with the complete symmetry of the flowers, both radially, and numerically. Generally the fleshy nature of the family and superior ovaries separates it from **Roseceae**; floral symmetry and separate carpels separates the family from the **Saxifragaceae**. Take apart a few flowers of sedums and kalanchoes, run your fingers over stems and leaves of these, bryophyllums and sempervivums, and you will quickly get the feel of **Crassulaceae.**

Some ornamental and commonly encountered genera of **Crassulaceae** are:

Adromischus	Greenovia	Sedum
Aeonium	Kalanchoe	Sempervivella
Aichryson	Monanthes	Sempervivum
Bryophyllum	Orostachys	Tillaea
Chiastophyllum	Pachyphytum	Umbilicus
Cotyledon	× Pachyveria	Vauanthes
Crassula	Pistorinia	Villadia
Dudleya	Rochea	
Escheveria	Rosularia	

Orpines, with their mucilaginous sap, are well equipped to survive drought; collected plant specimens have been known to grow for months in a plant press! The sap contains much tannin and sometimes acids, and has been used to dress wounds and burns. Many of the easily available species make good house plants as they tolerate the warm arid atmosphere. But do not try to rebloom your kalanchoe, which is a greenhouse proposition, and pronounce it correctly, ka lan KO ee.

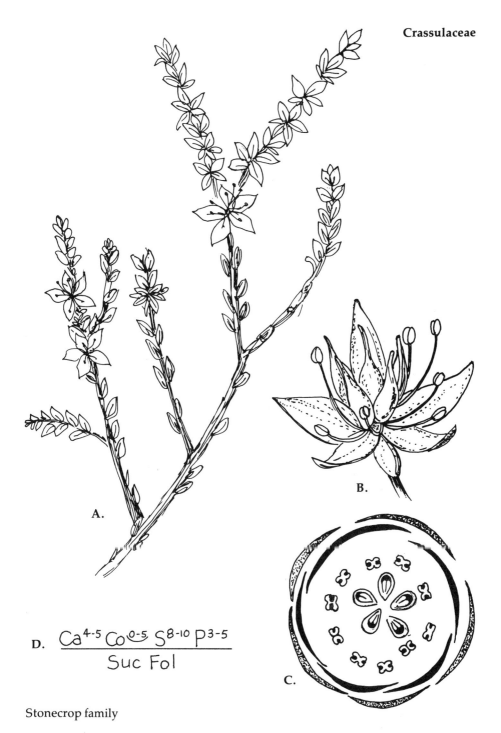

D. $$\frac{Ca^{4-5} \; Co^{0-5} \; S^{8-10} \; P^{3-5}}{Suc \; Fol}$$

A. B. C.

Stonecrop family

A. Field sketch of *Sedum* flowering branch. **B.** Semi-diagrammatic drawing of *Sedum* flower. **C.** Floral diagram of *Sedum*. **D.** Floral formula for the **Crassulaceae**.

121

Cruciferae Mustard Family

Largely of the temperate and colder regions of the world, with only a few tropical representatives, the **Cruciferae** includes about 3,200 species in more than 375 genera; plants are mostly herbaceous annuals and perennials with only a few shrubs and sub-shrubs. The leaves of these usually are alternate, some are pinnately lobed, as shepherd's purse. Flowers are quite distinctive, proving the Latin name of the family, in being truly cross-shaped. Flowers are perfect, regular, small but often showy, usually in terminal racemes. Calyx of 4, rarely 3, separate sepals (polysepalous) which are in 2 rows and fall early; corolla usually of 4 petals, often with a spreading limb; stamens usually 6, 4 long and 2 short (tetradynamous) but rarely 2 or 4; the pistil is sessile, usually elongated by not always, of two united carpels, with 2 stigmas. Fruit a dry pod usually dehiscent and often with a silvery, paper-like partition in the middle (silique). Juice is clear, acrid, as watercress.

Field characteristics here are easy. The flowers are typical, with usually fugaceous (early falling) sepals; petals 4, cross-shaped; stamens, mostly 4 + 2 or 4 or 2; pistil of 2 united carpels, with 2 stigmas. Juice with a peppery tang, never poisonous, sometimes very bitter. No other 4-petaled flower matches these characteristics.

Horticulturally, many genera are important as ornamentals or as vegetables; among them are:

Alyssoides	Draba	Matthiola	Schizopetalon
Alyssum	Erysimum	Megacarpaea	Schouwia
Anastatica	Farsetia	Moricandia	Selenia
Arabis	Heliophila	Morisia	Sinapis
Aubrieta	Hesperis	Nasturtium	Sobolewskia
Aurinia	Hutchinsia	Noccaea	Staehelina
Barbarea	Iberis	Notothlaspi	Stanleya
Berteroa	Ionopsidium	Orychophragmus	Streptanthus
Biscutella	Isatis	Parrya	Tchihatchewia
Brassica	Kernera	Peltaria	Vella
Braya	Lepidium	Petrocallis	Vesicaria
Cakile	Lesquerella	Ptilotrichum	Thlaspi
Cardamine	Lobularia	Raphanus	
Crambe	Lunaria	Ricotia	
Dentaria	Malcolmia	Schivereckia	

Among the **Cruciferae** are notable vegetable species, ornamental species, field-crop species, and weeds galore. Every gardener is acquainted with many of the Brassicas, cabbages, cauliflowers, broccolis, brussels sprouts, kohl rabi, and the like, the many kinds of radishes in the genus *Raphanus*. There are the many garden flowers, alyssums and aurinias, stock and wallflowers, candytufts and honesty with its strange Latin binomial, *Lunaria annua*, when it is an out and out biennial! There are the mustards grown for their oil, *Isatis tinctoria*, woad, once widely grown for the blue dye produced by fermenting the entire plant. The ancient Britons were said to have worn a coating of this blue dye rather than clothing and one would have thought them blue without dye in the usual British climate.

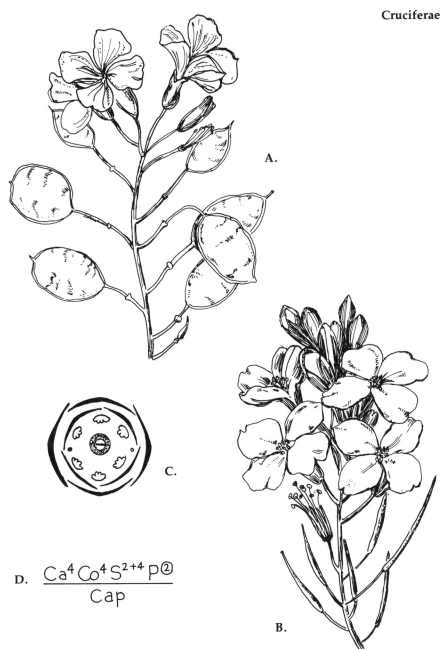

A.

C.

D. $\dfrac{Ca^4 Co^4 S^{2+4} P\textcircled{2}}{Cap}$

B.

Mustard Family

A. Field sketch of honesty, *Lunaria annua*, illustrating flowers and the flattened seed pods. On maturity, the two valves of the capsule fall away leaving the papery, transparent septum; it is this feature that accounts for the other common name, money-plant. **B.** Field sketch of a flowering and fruiting stalk of radish, *Raphanus*. **C.** Floral diagram of one of the cresses. **D.** Floral formula for the **Cruciferae**.

123

Cucurbitaceae Gourd Family

Mostly a tropical or sub-tropical family of mostly tendril-climbing, sappy, annual herbs, the **Cucurbitaceae** includes about 100 genera with more than 800 species. Several species in less than a dozen genera are native to or have naturalized in the United States. Leaves alternate, broad, with palmate veins, simple or often lobed or divided, and rarely compound, usually with harsh hairs on one or both surfaces, petioles usually hollow, crisp. Flowers axillary, solitary or in a small cluster, actinomorphic (except stamens), apparently epipetalous, mostly yellow or white, sometimes quite large and showy, very rarely perfect, more commonly staminate or pistillate (mostly both on the same plant), and often with tendrils, branched and spirally coiled, at the nodes opposite the flowers; in some, male flowers with long pedicels, female flowers on short, stout pedicels, but this is not a constant character; male flowers with calyx of 3 to 5 lobes on a cup-shaped or tubular floral cup; corolla of 3 to 5 sympetalous petals (or sometimes separate petals); stamens 1 to 5, usually appear to be 2½, that is, two with 2-locular anthers and 1 with a 1-locular anther, stamens sometimes are united by their filaments and the twisted, tortuous anthers or by just the anthers, stamens inserted inside the petals on the floral cup; female flowers commonly with limb of calyx and corolla more or less combined, each 3 to 5-part, and more or less funnel-shape or rotate, epigynous; compound pistil of 3 (rarely 1 or 2) closely united carpels with a single simple style or with 3 free style branches, often the style is pillar-like with a massive, much convoluted stigma, ovary inferior, 3− (rarely 1 to 10) celled, usually with 3 parietal placentae (or placentae corresponding to the number of cells), and with 1 to many ovules in each cell. Fruit a dry berry with thick rind (Pepo), or juicy with a leathery or hard rind, very rarely dehiscent.

In the field look for the bold leaves on long trailing or climbing stems with alternate leaves and with spiral tendrils at some of the nodes; flowers large or small, usually yellow or white, and most commonly with male and female flowers at separate nodes on the same stem. Look for the contorted, often connate anthers and for the inferior ovary. If the flower parts are more or less in 3's or 5's, with the special stamen characteristics in the male flowers and with the tricarpellate ovary in the female flowers, usually the identification may be considered confirmed. In the garden examine flowers of cucumber, different sorts of gourds (several genera are involved here) both summer and winter squashes, and one or two kinds of melons, to observe a range of structural variations.

Among the genera most commonly encountered in cultivation or in botanical collections, or in the wild are:

Abobra	*Coccinia*	*Gymnopetalum*	*Sicyos*
Alsomitra	*Cucumis*	*Lagenaria*	*Telfairea*
Anguria	*Cucurbita*	*Luffa*	*Thladiantha*
Benincasa	*Cyclanthera*	*Megarrhiza*	*Trichosanthes*
Bryonia	*Ecballium*	*Melothria*	*Zehneria*
Cayponia	*Echinocystis*	*Momordica*	
Ceratosanthes	*Fevillea*	*Sechium*	
Citrullus	*Gurania*	*Sicana*	

Quite a large number of species in a wide range of genera are important economically, especially for food, either "vegetable" or as sweet fruit. The many kinds of gourds supply primitive utensils and fabric; leaves, stems, and roots of some species contain subresinous substances which are physiologically active. Many are grown as ornaments or just for fun. Try the squirting-cucumber!

Cucurbitaceae

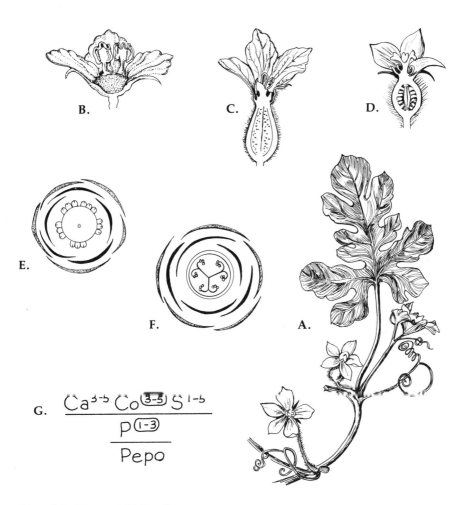

Pumpkin (Cuncurbit) Family

A. Field skech of watermelon, *Citrullus vulgaris*, showing staminate (left) and pistillate flowers. **B.** Longitudinal section of a staminate watermelon flower. **C.** Longitudinal section of a pistillate flower of cucumber. **D.** Longitudinal section of a pistillate flower of watermelon. **E.** Floral diagram for a generalized staminate cucurbit flower. **F.** Floral diagram for a generalized pistillate cucurbit flower. **G.** Floral formula for the **Cucurbitaceae.**

125

Cyperaceae Sedge Family

The sedges fall into about 90 genera which include more than 4,000 species; these are grass-like or rush-like, and usually quite easy to put into the proper family. The technical characteristics also are those used for field identification and so are joined for this discussion. Herbaceous plants in tufted clumps or with rhizomatous rootstocks, roots very fibrous; upright stems (culms) are mostly solid (as contrasted to the hollow internodes of grass culms), and culms are mostly 3-sided (triangular in cross-section — your fingers can distinguish this characteristic if you twirl a stem) as contrasted to the round stems of grass; leaves, when present, are in 3 ranks (2 in grass), and the sheath is closed (usually only overlapping in grass). Flowers usually without perianth, inclosed in bracts rather like the glumes of grass (but not so organized), and these are in spikelets which in turn are in spikes or panicles. Stamens 3 (rarely 1 or 6), carpels 3 or 2, style 2-cleft, with a 1-celled ovary containing 1 ovule, the fruit is a very characteristic achene (nutlet). In some genera the male and female flowers are in different parts of the same spike (above and below).

Only a few of the sedges are involved in ornamental horticulture, among them:

Carex	*Gahnia*	*Mariscus*
Cyperus	*Hypolytrum*	*Scirpus*
Eriophorum	*Mapania*	

These mostly appear in water-garden plantings or sometimes in wild gardens. Many, many more genera are found in the wild, mostly in damp places or at water margins, some standing in the water (but some are to be found in quite dry sites, too). As classification of these is easy and good experience, plan to don your waders and take to the mud for some aquatic taxonomy. Technical keys are available in local area floras such as *Gray's Manual of Botany*, but easier, more or less vegetative keys are found in general texts such as Norman Fassett's *Manual of Aquatic Plants* which is easy to use and most informative.

Several of the Sedges supply economic materials; the nutlets of some furnish food for primitive peoples and for waterfowl, the root-stocks of some are considered edible, papyrus (in *Cyperus*) is important enough historically to make any family famous, and the culms of some of the aquatic genera have been used for thatching though usually that job is left to the reeds.

Sedge Family

A. Field sketch of sedge, *Carex*. **B.** Pistillate (female) flower of a species of *Carex*. **C.** Staminate (male) flower of a species of *Carex*. **D.** Perfect flower of *Scirpus*. **E.** Staminate flower of another species of *Carex*. **F.** Perfect flower of *Cyperus*. **G.** Floral diagram of a staminate flower of *Carex*. **H.** The female flower in diagram. **I.** Floral formula for **Cyperaceae**.

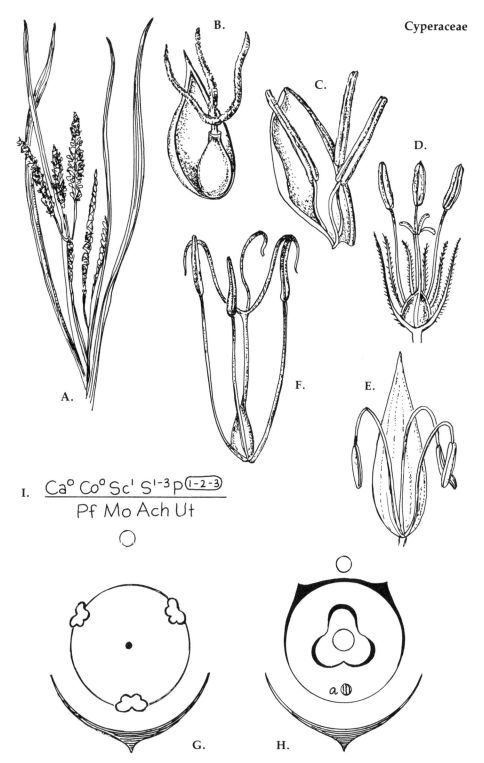

A. B. C. D. E. F.

I. $\dfrac{Ca^0\ Co^0\ Sc^1\ S^{1-3}\ P\boxed{1-2-3}}{Pf\ Mo\ Ach\ Ut}$

G. H.

127

Dioscoreaceae   Yam Family

Eleven genera with about 650 species of climbing herbaceous plants all with tuberous or rhizomatous rootstocks make up the Yam Family whose members are mostly distributed in the tropics and sub-tropics, but extending sparingly into the North Temperate zone. Leaves are alternate, strongly ribbed and net-veined, with petioles, mostly arrow-shaped. Some species produce aerial tubers at the nodes. The juice is mostly milky. Flowers small, in racemes or spikes, usually dioecious, actinomorphic, epipetalous; perianth tubular, of 6 segments in two quite similar whorls, stamens 6 but sometimes 3 are reduced to staminoids; compound pistil of 3 closely united carpels, with 3 distinct styles, stigmas simple on each style, ovary inferior, 3-celled or rarely with a single cell, ovules mostly 2 in each cell. Fruit a winged capsule or a berry.

This family is easy to distinguish in the wild; the climbing annual habit of the shoot, peculiar leaves as described above, definite stamen number, and inferior, 3-celled ovary with 2 ovules in each cell, serve for identification.

Only a few species of *Dioscorea* occur natively or as naturalized exotics in temperate North America, but sometimes other genera are encountered in botanic gardens, including:

Bordera
Dioscorea
Rajania
Tamus

Around old homesteads (sometimes where no buildings have survived for decades) occasionally are found plants of *Dioscorea batatas*, the Chinese yam, or cinnamon vine, once grown as an ornamental for its handsome leaves and cinnamon-scented spikes of small flowers. Gather a few aerial tubers and start your own plant. It is a treasure!

A.

B.

C. $\dfrac{Ca^{③} Co^{③} S^{⑥\,or\,③} P^{③}}{Cap\ Mo}$

Yam Famiy

A. Field sketch of wild yam, *Dioscorea villosa;* the heart-shaped, strongly ribbed leaves and, especially, the three winged, tough papery capsules make excellent field characters. **B.** Floral diagram of *Dioscorea*, generalized to include all species. **C.** Floral formula for **Dioscoreaceae**.

Dipsacaceae Teasel Family

Eight to 10 genera include about 275 species of annual, biennial, or perennial herbs and some sub-shrubs are mostly native to the Mediterranean basin and adjacent countries but some kinds have been widely naturalized throughout the temperate zones. Leaves opposite or rarely whorled, usually lobed, toothed or deeply cleft, or entire, often very rough, exstipulate. Flowers in cymes or crowded into involucrate heads, mostly small, perfect, usually zygomorphic, epigynous, each small flower surrounded by a cup-shaped scarious involucel; calyx of 4 or 5 synsepalous segments, cup-like, or divided into bristly segments on the rim of the epigynous disc; corolla 4 or 5-lobed, sympetalous, tube-shaped; stamens 4, rarely 2 or 3, epipetalous; compound pistil of 2 closely united carpels, style thread-like, stigma simple or two-branched, ovary inferior, 1-celled, with a single ovule. Fruit an achene.

Some of these are rather thistle-like, others more like a typical Composite flower head; but in the field the involucrate small flowers in involucrate heads, the sympetalous corolla with 4 *separate* epipetalous stamens, and the 2-carpel pistil with a single cell, inferior ovary, and single ovule, are distinctive. You will need a hand lens and probably tweezers, a dissecting needle, and a single-edged razor blade to dig out all the details of flower construction. In the garden take apart flowers of one or more species of *Scabiosa* and if you have it, dig into a teasel flower. In the latter, the often connate leaf-bases (which catch and hold water) are a good field character when combined with the rather large, prickly, elongated-ovoid flower heads.

The genera of **Dipsacaceae** most often encountered in the garden or naturalized in N. America are:

> *Cephalaria*
> *Dipsacus*
> *Knautia*
> *Morina*
> *Pterocephalus*
> *Scabiosa*
> *Succisa*

The common word "tease" referred originally to treating newly woven woollen fabric to raise the nap; the hooked-spiny, dried heads of *Dipsacus fullonum* (teasel), did the job (and still does, for top quality woollens). The process is know as "fulling cloth". Some species in this family have been used in rather primitive medicines. The great value of the plants is ornamental and as a first class source of seed for song birds. Gardeners who grow only the beautiful annual sort of *Scabiosa*, overlooking the smaller sorts usually considered suitable for rock gardens, and perennial ones, are missing a bet. In fact, most of these look good in either the cultivated garden or in the wild garden. The sub-shrub, *Pterocephalus parnassi* is a charming little plant in the rock garden.

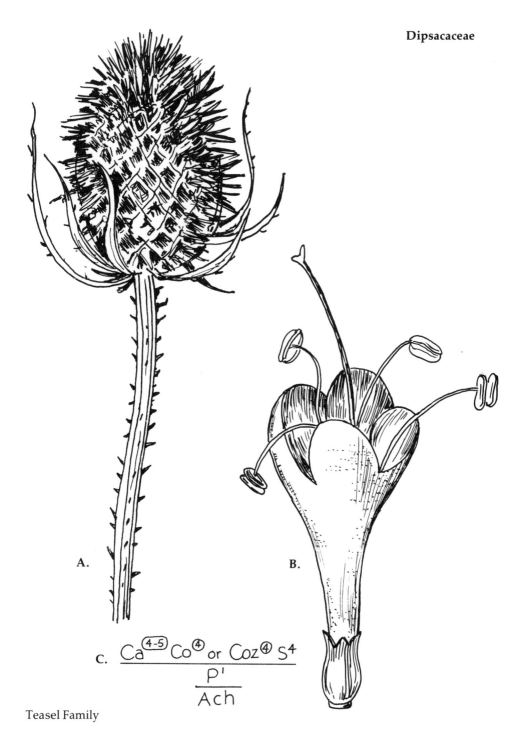

A.

B.

C. $\dfrac{Ca^{\widehat{(4\text{-}5)}} \; Co^{\textcircled{4}} \; \text{or} \; Coz^{\textcircled{4}} \; S^4}{\dfrac{P^1}{Ach}}$

Teasel Family

A. Field sketch of a teasel, *Dipsacus fullonum*, head. **B.** Sketch of a single flower from a teasel head. **C.** Floral formula for the **Dipsacaceae.**

Droseraceae Sundew Family

The tiny Sundews are found in all parts of the world where plants grow, though most of them occur in the milder, damper climates. About 105 species in 4 to 6 genera make up the **Droseraceae**. These are very glandular annual or perennial herbs or sub-shrubs, and their floral structure has much in common with **Cistaceae**, **Violaceae**, and with **Saxifragaceae**. Most species are very small, rosettes of rather spoon-shaped leaves with central scapes of flowers. The flowers solitary or more commonly in raceme-like structures, one-sided, simple or rarely forking with the freshest flower always up-permost. Flowers are perfect, regular, with parts in 5's or 4's, hypogynous, very rarely perigynous. Sepals joined (synsepalous), 4 or usually 5, im-bricated; petals free (polypetalous), usually 5, convoluted or imbricated; stamens usually 5 in 1 or more whorls, anthers attached at the middle and facing outward. Pistil superior, carpels 2 to 5, usually 1 to 3-celled, with twice as many styles or stigmas as there are parietal placentae. Fruit a dry capsule with many seeds. Often the withered calyx, corolla, and stamens persist.

In the field look for tiny rosettes with spoon-shaped leaves bearing motile tentacles which secrete terminal droplets of sticky fluid. (Some foreign sorts have leaves of other forms and with sticky, reduced leaf hairs only). Usually some small insects are trapped on at least some of the leaves. American species are found in quite damp sites. The American genus commonly seen is *Drosera*.

Genera of **Droseraceae** which may be encountered are:

Aldrovanda
Dionaea
Drosera
Drosophyllum
Roridula

Enjoy these in the wild; they are exceptionally difficult to grow but are manageable under terrarium conditions. Buy plants *only* from dealers who propagate them; our wild stock is desperately imperiled by collectors. Few of the Sundews have little value, though on the Iberian Peninsula some species are pot-grown and set about for their insect-catching habit; others contain reddish or purple dyes; the staining liquids Aqua-auri and Rosoglio are prepared largely from *Drosera rotundifolia*.

Sundew Family

A. Field sketch of *Drosera* indicating the glandular leaves. **B.** Floral diagram, some-what irregular, of *Drosera*. **C.** Floral formula for the Family.

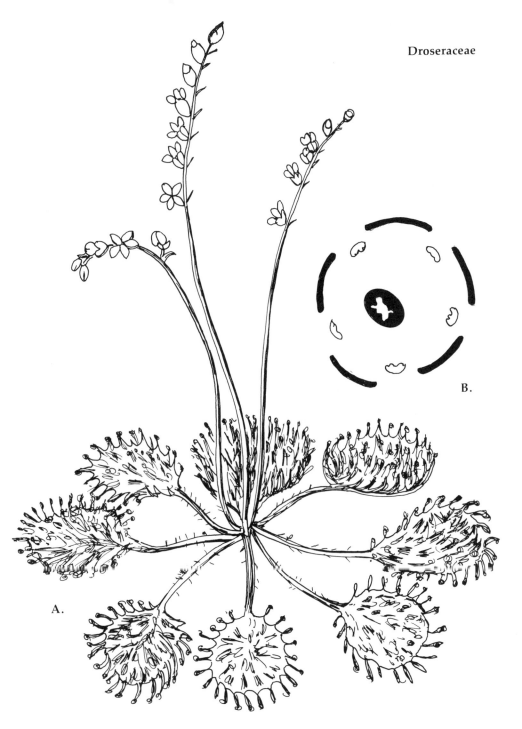

A.

B.

C. $\dfrac{Ca^5 Co^5 S^5 P\textcircled{4}}{Cap}$

133

Ebenaceae Ebony Family

Five genera with about 450 species make up this family of trees and shrubs which grow almost exclusively in the tropics with the notable exception of some specieds of *Diospyros*. All have watery juice and very hard wood; leaves usually are alternate, simple and entire, without stipules. Flowers are axillary, solitary or in few-flowered cymes, flowers usually staminate or pistillate (sexes may be on different plants = dioecious) or with some perfect flowers on the plant mingled with flowers of one sex, actinomorphic; calyx of 3 to 7 sepals, connate but with free lobes, persistent, corolla of 3 to 7 petals, joined but with free lobes and often urceolate (urn-shaped) hypogynous, commonly coriaceous (leathery); stamens short, usually double the number of corolla lobes but sometimes as many or numerous, separate or united in pairs, usually epipetalous (inserted on the petals) or rarely hypogynous; compound pistil with 2 to 8 carpels, with 2 to 8 styles distinct or united at the base, ovary superior, several-celled usually with 2 ovules in each cell. Fruit a several seeded berry.

Among the important field characteristics are the superior, several-celled ovary, flowers of single sex (mostly), and the absence of milky juice. Also look for the epipetalous stamens and joined petals and sepals. These characteristics joined with the foliar characters usually confirms **Ebenaceae.** *Some tropical species cause severe dermatitis.*

The genera sometimes seen in sub-tropical and tropical gardens are:

> *Diospyros*
> *Euclea*
> *Maba*
> *Royena*

One species, *Diospyros virginiana*, persimmon, is hardy well northward into temperate N. America. It makes a poor garden tree as root sprouts form freely and are virtually indestructible. *D. kaki*, from China and Japan, is more tender, with larger, handsome fruits which are a favored fruit in some places. It is easily grown and worthwhile where hardy. Ebony wood comes from large tropical species of *Diospyros*.

D. $\dfrac{Ca^{3-7} \ Co^{3-7} \ S^{6-20} \ P^{3-\infty}}{Pg \ Di \ Ber}$

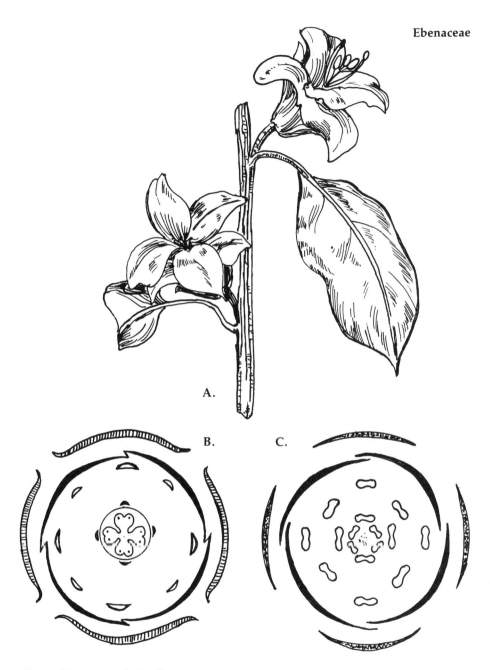

A. B. C.

Ebony (Persimmon) Family

A. Field sketch of a twig of persimmon, *Diospyros*, showing staminate and pistillate flowers. **B.** Floral diagram of a pistillate flower of persimmon. **C.** Floral diagram of a staminate flower of persimmon. **D.** Floral formula for **Ebenaceae;** the sub-tropical and tropical species and genera of this family vary considerably from the familiar North American and Japanese persimmons.

135

Elaeagnaceae Oleaster Family

Three genera include about 50 species of shrubs and trees which occur in the temperate and sub-tropical regions of the northern hemisphere. Leaves opposite or alternate, mostly simple, mostly entire, without stipules. *The outstanding vegetative characteristic of this family lies in the minute silvery or golden-brown peltate or stellate scales which usually thickly cover the leaves and soft twigs.* Flowers axillary, solitary or clustered (often densely clustered below the 1-year shoots), or cymose, white or yellow, often fragrant, perfect or monoecious, actinomorphic, and apetalous; calyx lobes 4 at the rim of the floral cup which is more or less tube-shaped in the perfect and female flowers, or cup-shaped and flattened in the male flowers; stamens as many or twice as many (4 or 8) as sepals and alternating with them, inserted in the throat of the tube (usual in perfect flowers) or on the rim (more common in male flowers), the filaments are short, free; compound pistil, with a single style which often is thread-like and stigmatic on one side, the ovary is 1-celled with a single ovule, and often is so invested by the base of the floral-cup as to look truly buried, and hence, inferior, but this is said by experts to be extremely close perigyny, and the ovary is mostly classed as superior; certainly, there is room for argument. Fruit pulpy or meaty, berry-like, inclosing a large, hard achene.

The silvery or golden-brown scales on leaves and young twigs, and also the punctate character of the leaves, often suffices in the field to identify members of this family; the usually 4-cleft perianth, mostly tubular or at least deeply cup-shaped, with small, mostly included stamens on the throat or inner rim, and the single celled ovary with a single ovule confirms the identification. These are very like members of the **Thymelaeaceae**, but differ especially in the pulpy fruit which encloses the single nutlet.

The three genera of the **Elaeagnaceae**, all with species valuable for ornamental plantings, are:

Elaeagnus
Hippophae
Shepherdia

By and large, these are steppe plants, nearly xerophytic, growing on dry, sandy or gravelly barrens and alkaline plains, but also on dry seashores. But they are tolerant of most garden conditions except shade. One of the most useful is *Elaeagnus pungens*, with several fine cultivars, especially those with silver-white or lemon yellow variegations; these may be grown as free standing shrubs or sheared into tight, thorny hedges. The fruits of several of the species — in all genera — are more or less used in food products.

$$E. \quad \frac{Ca^{2-4} \ Co^{0} \ S^{2-4} \ P^{1}}{Pf \ U \ Bac \ Dr}$$

136

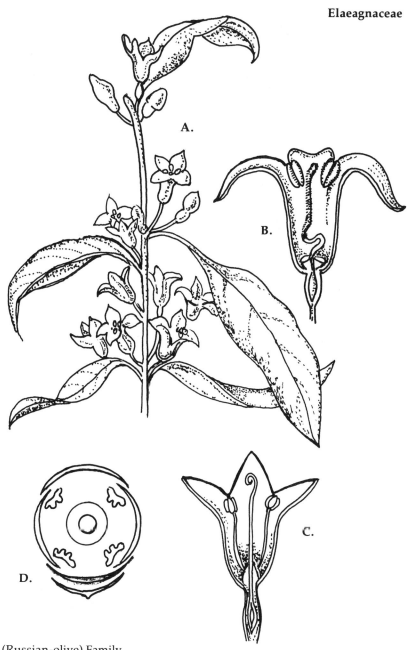

Oleaster (Russian-olive) Family

A. Field sketch of Russian-olive, *Elaeagnus angustifolia*. **B.** Sketch of a staminate flower of *Elaeagnus* in longitudinal section showing the epipetalous stamens and aborted pistil. **C.** A perfect flower of *Elaeagnus* with epigynous stamens. **D.** Floral diagram. **E.** An atypical formula for one group in the **Elaeagnaceae**; a formula showing the ovary in an epigynous or even hypogenous state would be more accurate.

137

Ericaceae Heath Family

Native to both Northern and Southern Hemispheres especially the New World and the Eurasian land mass, the Heath Family is composed of about 70 genera with more than 2,000 species in cold and temperate regions. In the tropics ericaceous species grow on high mountains. These are mostly shrubs or small trees, with usually alternate, but sometimes whorled (rarely opposite) leaves which bear no stipules. Often the leaves are evergreen, more or less leathery, sometimes needle-like. Flowers are perfect, regular or nearly regular, solitary or in terminal or axillary panicles or racemes. Sepals united to form a 4 or 5-lobed calyx which persists, the corolla is sympetalous, 4 or 5-lobed or urn-shaped, inserted below a fleshy disc. Stamens as many or twice as many as the lobes of the corolla and free from it, borne on the disc at its base. Anthers open commonly by terminal pores. The pistil with 1 style, 1 stigma, is superior or inferior; ovary with 2–5 cells and many ovules. The fruit is a capsule, rarely a berry or a drupe.

Field characteristics include combinations of characters such as evergreen leaves, needle-like or leathery, and urn-shaped flowers such as heaths, heathers, phyllodoces, vacciniums, and andromeda, or with open, funnel-shaped to flaired flowers, brightly colored and often in showy "heads" such as kalmia, and rhododendron, the latter typically with slightly irregular corolla and with greenish (or other colored) spots on two lobes. Look for the persistent calyx, stamens inserted on a disc inside the corolla, a 2—5 celled ovary and pistil with single, delicate style and stigma. Plants almost always restricted in nature to cold, cool, or cool-temperate climates and occur on high humus, acid soil. Some authors separate from this family a group of genera called **Vacciniaceae**. Originally included here were **Montropaceae** (Indian Pipes and Beechdrops) and **Pyrolacae** (Pipsissewas and Wintergreens).

Some genera in the Heath Family are:

Agapetes	Daboecia	Pentapera
Agarista	Diplocosia	Pentapterygium
Agauria	Elliottia	Pernettya
Andromeda	Enkianthus	Phyllodoce
Arbutus	Epigaea	× Phyllothamnus
Arcterica	Eremia	Pieris
Arctostaphylos	Erica	Psammisia
Befaria	Ericinella	Pterospora
Blaeria	Eurygania	Rhododendron
Bruckenthalia	Gaultheria	Rhodothamnus
Bryanthus	Gaylussacia	Sympieza
Calluna	Gonocalyx	Themistoclesia
Cassiope	Kalmia	Thibaudia
Cavendisia	Kalmiopsis	Tripetaleia
Chamaedaphne	Macleania	Tsusiophyllum
Chiogenes	Menziesia	Vaccinium
Cladothamnus	Orphanidesia	Wittsteinia
Comarostaphylos	Oxydendron	Zenobia

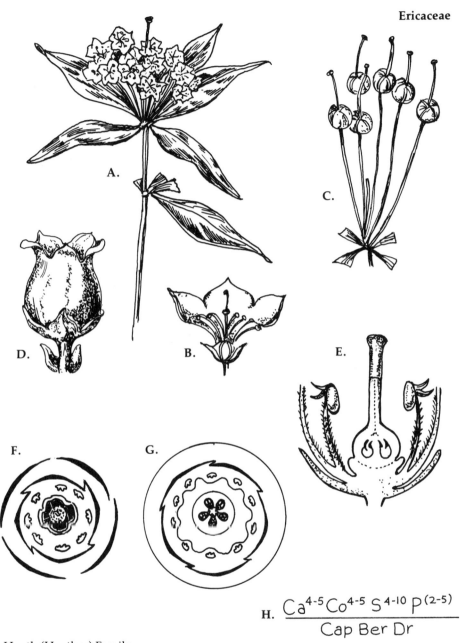

H. $$\frac{Ca^{4\text{-}5} Co^{4\text{-}5} S^{4\text{-}10} P^{(2\text{-}5)}}{Cap\ Ber\ Dr}$$

Heath (Heather) Family

A. Field sketch of a flowering branch of mountain-laurel, *Kalmia latifolia*. **B.** Detail of a *Kalmia* flower in longitudinal section. **C.** Mature seed bearing capsules of *Kalmia* with dried styles still intact. **D.** Sketch of a bear-berry, *Arctostaphylos* flower. **E.** Bear-berry flower in longitudinal section; note the fleshy disc below the ovary and the appendages on the stamens. **F.** Floral diagram for blueberry, *Vaccinium*. **G.** Floral diagram for heath, *Erica*. **H.** Floral formula for the **Ericaceae**.

Euphorbiaceae Spurge Family

More than 7,500 species distributed through about 290 genera make up the **Euphorbiaceae**, mostly shrubs or herbs, sometimes trees, found throughout the world except in the Arctic and Antarctic regions. Plant forms vary greatly in this family, from familiar, twiggy growths with rather ordinary leaves to plants which are fleshy, succulent, thorn-bearing, and in general, very like cacti. With the Euphorbs one has to regard flower structure as the most important characteristic for identification. Plants usually with acrid, milky juice, leaves mostly alternate, sometimes opposite, simple and entire, or lobed or coarsely toothed, or compound, in the succulent forms mostly reduced; flowers actinomorphic, or very rarely irregular, monoecious (staminate or pistillate), rarely perfect, hypogynous, usually subtended by bracts, or involucrate; calyx various, sepals if present few, often free but sometimes connate, sometimes absent; corolla if present usually free, but mostly absent; stamens reduced to 1 or twice as many as sepals, or many (perhaps 1,000), free or sometimes connate; compound pistil, ovary superior, usually 3-celled but sometimes 1, 2 or 4-celled, style and stigma various, ovules 1 to 2 in each locule. Often the pistil rests on a disc which may be ring-shaped, cup-shaped, or often glandular. In some species the naked pistillate flowers are surrounded by several to many staminate flowers and sterile stamens, the whole reproductive group then surrounded by a corolla-like involucre in which case the entire structure (as seen in the Christmas *Poinsettia*) is known as a *cyathium*.

Field characteristics of these vary greatly; experts on cacti and succulents spot the Euphorbs vegetatively usually because cactus spines arise from areoles while spines of the Euphorbs do not; in many cases the milky juice helps in identification, especially if the flowers are typically Spurge Family, of one sex, and greatly modified. Colorful bracts, too, often point toward this family. Because of the diversity, this is a wonderful group of plants to study if you are not allergic to their sap! From the garden bring in flowers of the various kinds; castor-bean, chenille plant, and the various hardy or annual Euphorbs such as snow-on-the-mountain and creeping-spurge. Perhaps you have a potted "devil's spine", *Euphorbia pedilanthus* (*Pedilanthus tithymaloides*) or a crown-of-thorns flower to add to the collection. Study the flower clusters or flowers in their whole form to get a feel for organization. Then begin to take them apart a bit at a time. Because all parts are hypogynous this is rather easy (but sticky). Before long in a tropical conservatory you can meet the true rubber tree, or a jatropha, or a manihot, in flower and recognize it immediately because those peculiarly assembled flowers stick in one's memory.

Of the dozens of genera of **Euphorbiaceae** in cultivation, the following (some native) may be encountered:

Acalypha	*Cnidoscolus*	*Fluggia*	*Mallotus*
Alchornea	*Codiaeum*	*Hevea*	*Manihot*
Aleutites	*Croton*	*Himalanthus*	*Mercurialis*
Andrachne	*Crotonopsis*	*Hippomane*	*Monadenium*
Breynia	*Dalechampia*	*Hura*	*Omphalia*
Bischofia	*Daphniphyllum*	*Jatropha*	*Pedilanthus*
Cluytia	*Euphorbia*	*Macaranga*	*Phyllanthus*

Poranthera	*Sapium*	*Stillingia*	*Toxicodendron*
Ricinus	*Securingea*	*Synadenium*	*Tragia*

Many species of **Euphorbiaceae** are of great economic importance; several kinds still are used in medicine, a few are used as foods by primitive peoples (also as arrow poisons); and cassava and tapioca are prepared from roots of *Manihot utilissima*. Rubber comes from the juice of *Hevea*, inks, oils, soaps, dyes (to color Edam cheese), and fats all are derived from various Euphorbs. As ornamentals many are great favorites, the woody ones being of special value in tropical areas. What would Christmas be without a poinsettia?

Euphorbiaceae

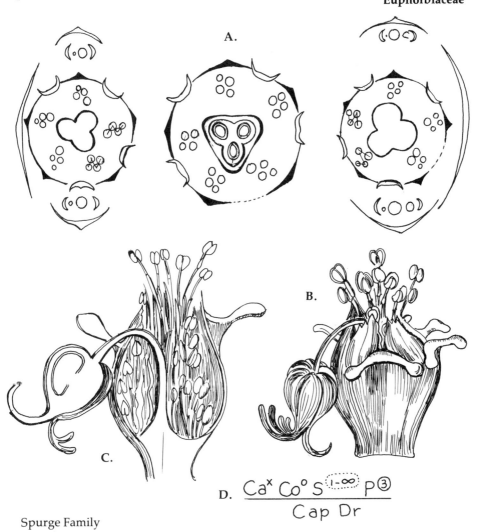

$$\underline{Ca^x\ Co^o\ S^{\overline{1-\infty}}\ P③}$$
$$Cap\ Dr$$

Spurge Family

A. Floral diagram of a *Euphorbia* flower cluster branch with three modified flowers (cyathia), only the middle one having the fertile female flower. **B.** Cyathium of *Euphorbia*. **C.** Same cyathium longitudinally sectioned showing extruded ovary and enclosed stamens. **D.** Floral formula.

141

Fagaceae Beech Family

Eight genera including about 900 species of trees and a few shrubs make up the Beech Family. Most species occur in temperate and sub-tropical regions. The leaves are alternate, simple, lobed or toothed, with straight, pinnate veins, and with stipules which usually fall early. Flowers axillary on young shoots, always of one sex; staminate ones in slender catkins (aments) or clusters, perianth 4 to 7-lobed, stamens twice as many as perianth lobes; one staminate flower occurs at each bract in the catkin; pistillate flowers solitary or in groups of 3's, perianth greatly reduced, epigynous (ovary inferior) pistil with 3 styles, ovary 3 to 7-celled, 1 or 2 ovules in each locule (usually only 1 ripens). Fruit a nut, occurring singly, or clustered 2 or 3, enclosed or partly enclosed in a cupule of consolidated bracts which become indurated (woody) through maturity. Study the caps of acorns or the "husks" of beechnuts to visualize the latter point.

In the field the fruit, if present, readily identifies members of this family. Familiarize yourself with the structure of acorns and their caps, of the burrs of chestnuts and beechnuts, and the fruits of *Nothofagus*, if possible. The leaf characteristics in this family are not distinct enough — though quite suggestive — to be absolutely reliable, but details of leaf-scars and winter buds, beyond the scope of this work, are infallible. Flower structure, while difficult for the beginner, always gives positive identification.

All of the genera in **Fagaceae** are valuable for ornamental planting and many species are of economic importance (lumber, cork, tannin, dyes, creosote, food), and are:

> *Castanea*
> *Castanopsis*
> *Fagus*
> *Lithocarpus*
> *Nothofagus*
> *Quercus*

Beech (Oak, Chestnut) Family

A. Field sketch of a staminate (male) catkin of white oak, *Quercus alba*, showing the knot-like clusters of greatly reduced flowers. **B.** Twig-end of white oak with pistillate (female) flowers. **C.** Enlarged staminate flower composed only of a few (4 to 6) sepals and several (indefinite number) of stamens. **D.** Enlarged pistillate flower showing sepals, as in the male flower, and with the 3-lobed stigma indicating 3 carpels in the compound ovary which is inferior. **E.** Floral diagram of female beech inflorescence with two flowers (as indicated by two separate ovaries each with three carpels) enclosed in an elaborate cluster of bracts and bracteoles as well as the sepals immediately exterior to the ovary. **F.** Another type of floral diagram, English oak, *Quercus robur*, which indicates the cupule in which the flower is partially submerged as well as the bract (dark bracket) and bracteoles (broken lines) exterior to the cupule. **G.** Floral formula.

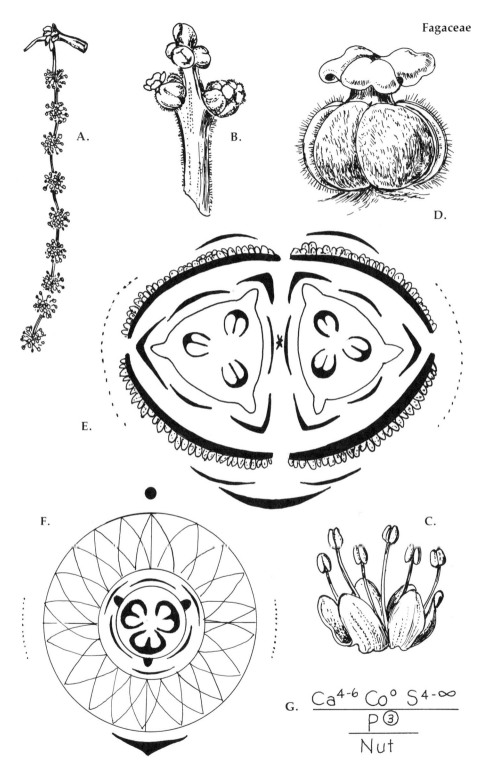

Fagaceae

A.

B.

D.

E.

F.

C.

G. $\dfrac{Ca^{4-6}\ Co^{0}\ S^{4-\infty}}{P\ \textcircled{3}}$

Nut

143

Gentianaceae Gentian Family

About 70 genera made up of some 1,100 species of annual, biennial, or perennial herbs (and a few woody kinds) make up the Gentian Family. These are distributed through mostly temperate regions, but some are arctic or sub-arctic, a few grow in marshes or salt soils, fewer are aquatic or epiphytes. Leaves are opposite (rarely alternate or whorled), entire, glabrous, without stipules, but species of *Menyanthes* alternate and trifoliate, petiolate, and *Nymophoides* alternate, petiolate, crenate. Flowers are complete and regular; calyx with 4 lobes (rarely 5 to 12) usually synsepalous forming a persistent tube. Corolla sympetalous, tube short or long, and usually 5-lobed (or 4 to rarely 12); corolla may be bell-, funnel-, or salvershaped. Stamens the same number as corolla lobes and *alternate* with them, epipetalous. Pistil superior, compound of 2 united carpels, ovary usually 1-celled, style simple, often lacking, stigma 2-lobed. Fruit a capsule with many seeds.

Field Characters include, excepting the two genera specified above, opposite, simple, glabrous leaves without stipules, persistent, bell-shaped or tubular calyx usually of 4 or 5 joined sepals; bell-shaped, funnel-form, or salver-shaped corolla commonly with 4−5 lobes *and with the same number of epipetalous stamens alternating with the corolla lobes*. The above characters, joined with the unilocular pistil of 2 united carpels easily identifies the Gentian Family.

Some genera in the Gentian Family are:

Bartonia	*Frasera*	*Nymphoides*
Cansora	*Gentiana*	*Obolaria*
Centaurium	*Halenia*	*Orphium*
Chironia	*Ixanthus*	*Sabbatia*
Chlora	*Leianthus*	*Sebaea*
Coutoubea	*Limnanthemum*	*Swertia*
Erythraea	*Lisianthus*	*Tachiadenus*
Eustoma	*Lomatogonium*	*Villarsia*
Exacum	*Menyanthes*	

Gentian Family

A. Field sketch of fringed gentian, *Gentiana crinita*. B. Field sketch of *Gentiana verna*. C. Flower of the Russell prairie-gentian, *Eustoma russellianum*. D. Floral diagram, composite, for the genus *Gentiana*. E. Floral formula for the **Gentianaceae**.

144

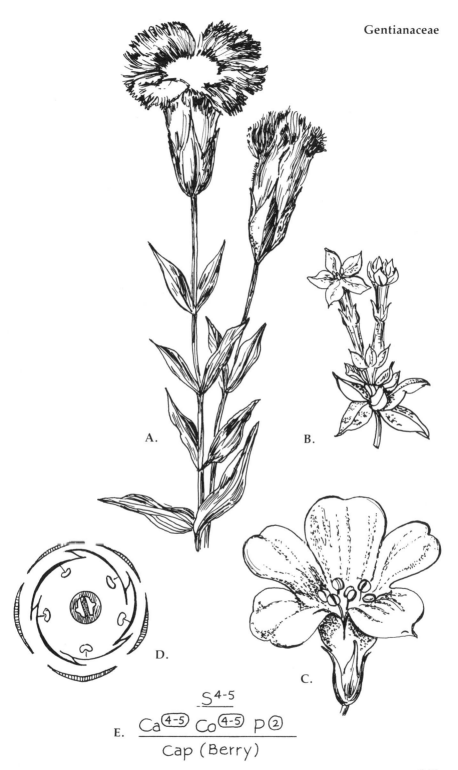

A.

B.

D.

C.

E. $\dfrac{\underline{S^{4\text{-}5}}}{Ca^{\textcircled{4\text{-}5}}\ Co^{\textcircled{4\text{-}5}}\ P\textcircled{2}}$

Cap (Berry)

Geraniaceae Geranium (Crane's-bill) Family

Eleven genera with about 750—800 species of annual and perennial herbs, a few sub-shrubs, and still fewer larger woody species, distributed world-wide, and especially in Africa. Plant forms are very diverse, from almost rosettes to fleshy, succulent structures. Leaves opposite or alternate, of quite diverse form but often deeply lobed, with or without stipules; some with pungent scent when crushed. Flowers commonly conspicuous, complete and often regular, or somewhat zygomorphic; sepals 5, free or united somewhat in certain species, persistent, the dorsal sepals sometimes spurred in certain species; corolla of 5 petals (or rarely none) inserted at the base of the floral disc; stamens 2 or 3 times the number of petals (some may be sterile filaments), more or less connate at the base, filaments often glandular at the base; compound pistil of 3 to 5 closely united carpels, ovary superior, 3 to 5-celled, with usually 2 ovules in each cell; ovaries continue upward, elongating into a style with 5 stigmatic lobes. Fruit a schizocarp, splitting from the central persistent style.

The flower, with its crane's-bill pistil, is a sufficient field character for this family. In structure the Geraniums are very like the Wood-sorrels (they once were included together) but the fruit provides the distinction.

Among the **Geraniaceae** encountered in the wild or in cultivation are the following genera:

> *Balbigia*
> *Biedersteinia*
> *Erodium*
> *Geranium*
> *Monsonia*
> *Pelargonium*
> *Sarcocaulon*

The **Geraniaceae** are astringent, especially the roots, most species containing various resins and other free acids. From time immemorial some have been used for wounds, for dysentery, as a source of musk scent or for other scents. By far their greatest use is ornamental.

Geranium (Crane's-bill Family)

A. Field sketch of *Geranium maculatum* branch. **B.** Floral diagram for the Family. **C.** Floral formula for the Family.

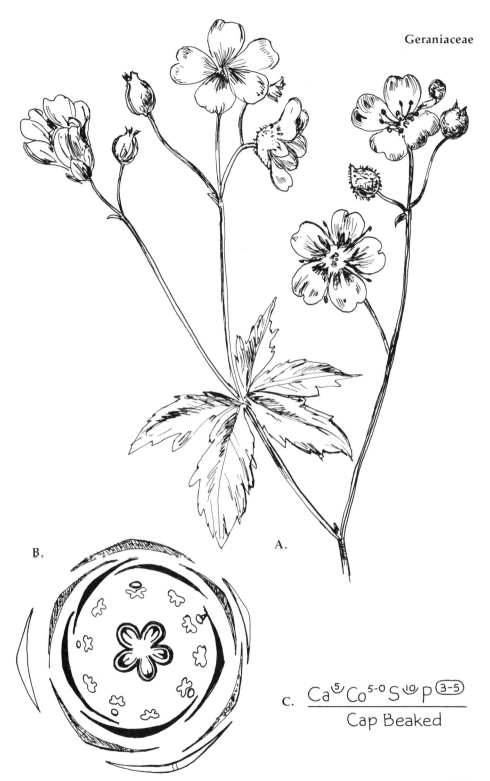

A.

B.

C. $\underline{Ca^5 Co^{5-0} S^{10} P\,\boxed{3\text{-}5}}$
Cap Beaked

Gramineae Grass Family

About 600 genera which include some 10,000 species, in world-wide distribution make up the Grass Family; by far the greatest number of these are herbaceous but a few (the bamboos) are shrubby or tree-like. The stem is round, often hollow between the nodes, and with solid, very hard nodes. There is also, in many cases, a second sort of stem, the below-ground *rhizome*, usually tough and wiry, from which the above-ground stems break at the nodes, and with adventitious roots also at the nodes. Leaves are in 2 ranks, of characteristic structure; the leaf is in two distinct parts. Where it leaves the node the leaf enwraps the stem (usually the margins overlap and are free but rarely they are joined); this portion is called the *sheath*; below the next higher node a free *blade* portion of the leaf extends away from the stem. Usually both sheath and blade are more or less linear but there is considerable variation here, especially in the case of the blade; where the blade bends away from the sheath a special structure, the *ligule*, is inserted. Like the sheath, the ligule encircles the stem and it may be papery and membranous, cartilaginous, or reduced to a mere rim or dissected into a fringe of hairs or bristles. The ligule is very important in separating the genera (and sometimes species) of grasses. The veins in grass leaves almost without exception are strongly parallel, and the margins of the leaves may be rough. Flowers of grasses may be perfect or staminate or pistillate, and the plants may be monoecious or dioecious. Flowers are arranged in small spikes called *spikelets* which are grouped in spike-like or branching panicles. The whole point of Grass Family classification boils down to identifying a spikelet and the structure of its components. The perianth of Grasses is quite missing or represented by insignificant and minute processes or scales called *lodicules*, but a series of bracts subtend the flower, and these with the reproductive organs make up the spikelet. At the base of the spikelet are 2 empty bracts called the *1st* (lower) *glume* and the *2nd glume* (either or both of these may be obsolete or missing in certain genera), the "stem" above the glumes is called the *rachilla*; above the 2nd glume is 1 (or more than one) *lemma*, and if several lemmas are present they alternate on the 2 sides of the rachilla. Each lemma subtends and partially encloses the base of an opposing bract, the *palea*. The palea encloses the flower. The actual flower consists either of stamens, or pistils, or both. Stamens usually 3 (rarely 1 or 2, and in the bamboos up to 120), the filaments usually elongated and slender, often dangling, the anther rather spear-head shaped and more or less free to move. Pistil usually of 1, or sometimes 2 or 3 fused carpels, usually 2 styles or stigmas. Fruit most often a *caryopsis*, that is, a seed inseparably enclosed in a very thin pericarp, or a naked achene, or rarely, other.

To become an expert on the grasses one must be proficient with hand lens and dissecting tools; then comes the trick of defining the structure of a spikelet. Problems arise because all parts usually are quite small, and often some are modified, missing entirely, or present in multiples. It is a rare spikelet, indeed, which proceeds 1st glume, 2nd glume, lemma, palea, inflorescence, with all parts easily recognizable. But you can spot the Grass Family easily; look for the usually hollow internodes and horny nodes of the stems, the leaves with sheathing bases and free blades with a ligule of some sort at the juncture, veins strongly parallel in the foliage; flowers reduced to stamens and pistils, enclosed in a system of small, sheathing bracts. These characteristics, easy in the field, bring you right to **Gramineae.**

Dozens of Grass genera are in cultivation either for crops or in some aspect of ornamental horticulture, and great many more are encountered in "wild" situations; some of these may well be introduced exotic species which have become naturalized. For comprehensive lists of the various Grass genera see local and area floras (such as *Gray's Manual of Botany* for the northeastern U.S.) and the larger and more complete horticultural encyclopedic reference works. Also, the U.S.D.A. handbook, *Grasses,* is a classic, as is Hitchcock's *Manual of the Grasses.*

As you work with grasses you will pick up interesting short-cuts in identification. For example, in most of the bluegrasses the lemma is rather cottony at the base and keeled (the two sides clasping like the sides of a canoe), and even easier, often the leaf blade tips also are slightly keeled, rather like the end of a canoe, but much shallower. Such characteristics make life simpler for grass taxonomists.

Gramineae

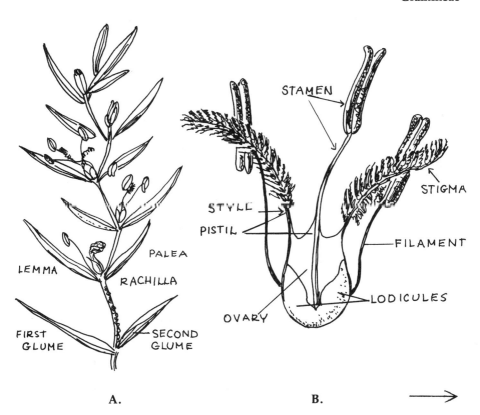

A.

B.

149

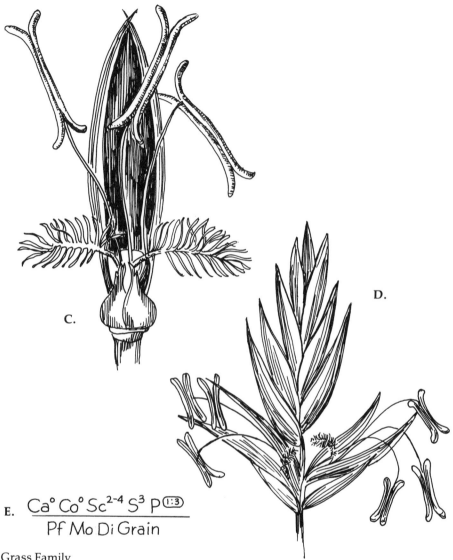

E. $\dfrac{Ca^{\circ}\,Co^{\circ}\,Sc^{2\text{-}4}\,S^3\,P\,\boxed{1\!:\!3}}{Pf\,Mo\,Di\,Grain}$

Grass Family

A. A grass spikelet; this represents no species, but shows the parts of a typical spikelet in its complete form. Two bracts, the first glume and second glume, at the base of the zig-zag rachilla, define the spikelet. Along its length in two ranks are the florets, each composed of an outer bract, the lemma, an inner bract, the palea, and innermost, the stamens and pistil. Students of grasses soon learn that this apparently easy to define spikelet structure seldom presents itself in nature. **B.** A more or less stylized grass flower; the *lodicules* represent a vestigial perianth and usually are delicate and papery when present. **C.** Flower of fescue, *Festuca*, highly enlarged, with two lodicules, the feathery stigmas and three stamens with the palea behind. **D.** Shows fescue florets in the spike. **E.** Floral formula for the Grass Family.

Guttiferae St. John's-wort Family

This family also is known as the **Guttiferaceae, Clusiaceae,** and as the **Hypericaceae,** at least in part, when it sometimes is divided. Also, the common name in some literature is Garcinia Family. The family includes 950 to 1,100 species in 40 to 45 genera; these are trees, shrubs, and a few herbs of the tropics (mostly) and temperate regions. The family name given above refers (in Latin) to the *drop-bearing* nature of the foliage of many species, that is, to the oil glands and ducts which appear as tiny pellucid dots in the leaves when they are held to the light. These have opposite or whorled, rarely alternate leaves which are simple, entire, mostly sessile, and exstipulate. Flowers mostly cymose, sometime solitary, actinomorphic, hypogynous, and mostly complete; commonly bisexual flowers and pistillate and staminate flowers are all found on the same plant; calyx of 4 or 5, rarely 2 to 6, sepals, more or less connate, which are imbricated in the bud; corolla of 4 or 5 (rarely 2 to 6) separate petals which may be imbricated or convolute, often with a claw at the base; stamens many, hypogynous, usually in 3 to 5 bundles, the members of which are more or less united by the filaments, rarely monodelphous; compound pistil of 3 to 5 carpels, styles 1 to 5, stigmatic lobes often heavy and radiate, ovary superior with 3 to 5 cells (rarely 1), with many ovules on several parietal placentae. Fruit a capsule, as in *Hypericum,* or fleshy or leathery, berry-like or drupaceous.

The simple, smooth-sided, often sessile leaves with their pellucid dots (when viewed toward a light) make a good beginning field character. Then look for a leafy calyx and a usually colorful corolla in 4's or 5's, with bundles of stamens surrounding a 5-celled superior ovary, and you have pretty well arrived at **Guttiferae.**

The genera most commonly considered in works on ornamental and horticultural plants include:

Ascyrum
Calophyllum
Clusia
Garcinia
Haronga
Hypericum

Kielmeyera
Mammea
Mesua
Ochrocarpos
Pentadesmia
Rheedia
Vismia

Most of the tropical trees and shrubs in this family yield a yellow or greenish resinous juice when tapped by making bark incisions. The product may be a pigment, as gamboge, a resin, such as hog-gum, or it may be used as a medicinal or as a dye. Some produce edible fruits. Our native temperate zone U.S. genera, *Ascyrum* and *Hypericum,* are known as St. Peter's-wort and St. John's-wort respectively. And *Ascyrum hypericoides* comes to us as St. Andrew's Cross.

Hamamelidaceae Witch-hazel Family

These warm temperate and sub-tropical trees and shrubs fall into 100 species in 25 genera. Many more are known as fossil forms. Living species are distributed through N. America, S. Africa, and Asia. Leaves alternate, very rarely opposite, simple, often toothed, generally with stipules at least early in the season. Most are deciduous. Flowers usually are rather small, in axillary or terminal clusters or racemes. Flowers perfect, rarely monoecious (of one sex), mostly perigynous, sometimes epigynous, rarely hypogynous. Sepals 4 or 5, rarely 6 or 7, usually somewhat fused, but with free lobes, petals usually 4 or 5, sometimes none, free, on the floral cup. Stamens usually as many as the petals, or twice as many (with some sterile, changed to scales), also inserted on the inner rim of the floral cup or, rarely, hypogynous. At least the base of the ovary usually is embedded in the floral cup, or sometimes epigynous, very rarely hypogynous. Compound pistil of 2 carpels, usually united below, forming a 2-beaked structure above. The ovary is 2-celled and with 1 or several ovules in each cell, but usually only 1 or very few seeds develop. Fruit is a woody or horny 2-valved capsule with separating inner layer of different texture. The capsule opens at the summit; usually the bony seeds are expelled with force. The capsules often persist, giving a good field character.

In the field look for rather soft, simple, usually toothed, alternate leaves. After spring check for stipular scars or withered stipules at the base of the petiole. Some of these bloom in late fall, during the winter, or in very early spring. The horny capsules, individual, as in *Hamamelis*, or clustered as in *Liquidambar*, are characteristic. In flower, look for the 2-beaked pistil with the ovary buried partially(or more so) in the floral cup.

Genera of ornamental value in the **Hamamelidaceae** include:

Bucklandia	*Fothergilla*	*Rhodoleia*
Corylopsis	*Hamamelis*	*Sinowilsonia*
Disanthus	*Liquidambar*	*Trichocladus*
Distylium	*Loropetalum*	
Fortunearia	*Parrotia*	

Because of their cold weather flowering habit, many species of these are of exceptional garden merit; others (as *Parrotia*) have beautifully mottled bark. Far too few species are used in American gardens.

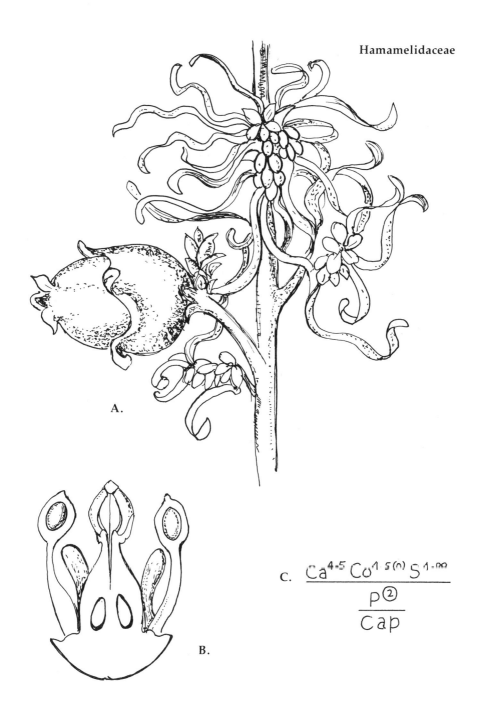

A.

B.

C. $\dfrac{Ca^{4\cdot5} Co^{1\,5(n)} S^{1\cdot\infty}}{\underline{P\textcircled{2}}}$
Cap

Witch-hazel Family

A. Field sketch of flowering twig, showing ribbon-like petals and an old seed capsule. **B.** Floral diagram. **C.** Floral formula.

153

Hippocastanaceae Horse-chestnut Family

Twenty-five or more species (with several hybrid forms) in 2 or 3 genera make up the **Hippocastanaceae** in general distribution throughout the north temperate region. These are easily recognized through their stout twigs with opposite leaves, coarse lenticels, and large, sticky or glabrous terminal buds. Leaves are palmately or digitately compound, 3 to 9 leaflets, the leaflets straight-veined; without stipules. Flowers in a terminal panicle or a thyrse, perfect or with staminate flowers intermixed, zygomorphic, usually showy; calyx of 4 or 5 sepals, separate or often connate corolla of 4 or 5 petals, white or brightly colored, unequal, clawed; 5 to 9 separate stamens often with unequal filaments, stamens inserted at the rim of or inside of an often inequilateral (lop-sided) disc; compound pistil with 1 style, 1 stigma but 3 carpels as indicated by the 3-celled superior ovary; ovules 2 in each cell. Fruit a capsule, often leathery, 3-valved, and 1 to 3-celled, with 1, 2, or 3 large seeds.

In the field the twig and leaf characteristics of the **Hippocastanaceae** often suffice for identification, but the showy panicles of white or colored flowers structured as defined above (note the disc which usually reaches beyond the insertion of the stamens) proves the identification. Also, the large fruiting capsules with the glossy seeds are unique.

Only one genus of **Hippocastanaceae** is encountered in the western world; the genus *Aesculus* includes the Old World horse-chestnuts and the New World buckeyes. A number of fine horticultural varieties as well as several species are widely planted.

Horse-chestnut Family

A. Sketch of *Aesculus*, showing typical spring flower spike and palmately compound leaves. **B.** Prickly, leathery capsule. **C.** Floral formula for the Family.

A.

B.

C. $\dfrac{Ca^{⑤} Coz^{4-5} S^{5-8} P③}{Cap}$

Hydrophyllaceae Waterleaf Family

Annual or perennial herbs or rarely sub-shrubs in 19 or 20 genera with about 275 species make up the Waterleaf Family; these are mosly from N. America, but a few in Africa, India, Japan, and the Hawaiian Islands. Leaves mostly alternate, rarely opposite, without stipules, rarely entire or mostly lobed, sometimes much divided but simple, often hairy. Flowers mostly blue, or purple or white, showy, complete, hypogynous, actinomorphic, the corolla often bell or funnel-shaped, in 1-sided cymes or false racemes, which are mostly bractless and coiled from the apex as flowers open (scorpoid); calyx 5-parted or deeply 5-cleft so that in some, sepals appear almost to be separate (they are not); corolla sympetalous, 5-lobed, lobes erect or spreading, often with scales in the throat, hypogynous; stamens 5, alternating with the corolla lobes, free, epipetalous (inserted on the corolla); compound pistil of 2 closely united carpels, style 2-cleft or 2 styles, ovary superior, entire (compare with **Boraginaceae**), 1-celled with 2 parietal placentae bearing 4 to many ovules (or rarely ovary falsely 2-celled due to complete intrusion of the parietal placentae). Fruit a many-seeded capsule.

Three families, **Polemoniaceae**, **Hydrophyllaceae**, and **Boraginaceae**, have much in common; while **Hydrophyllaceae** typically has an entire, 1-celled ovary with one or two styles, the **Polemoniaceae** ovary is typically 3-celled and rests on a definite disc, while in **Boraginaceae** the ovary either is deeply 4-lobed with the style basal or more rarely 2-lobed, with the style terminal. In the garden, study flowers of *Phlox*, *Phacelia*, and one of the forget-me-nots to get these distinctions clear. Other floral characteristics such as the 5-cleft calyx, the usually rotate (wheel-shaped) sympetalous corolla with 5 lobes, and the 5 epipetalous free stamens confirm the identification. Once you come to recognize the lobed and sometimes "water-marked" foliage of these, as *Hydrophyllum*, *Nemophila* and *Phacelia* you will get a feel for it, and will even see the connection with the more remote sorts such as *Elisia*.

Among the genera useful in the garden as ornamentals or found in the wild in the U.S. are:

Decemium	*Hydrolea*	*Phacelia*
Elisia	*Hydrophyllum*	*Romanzoffia*
Emmenanthe	*Nama*	*Wigandia*
Hesperochiron	*Nemophila*	

While *Elisia* is an out-and-out introduced weed and one or two of the other genera are somewhat invasive at least under optimum conditions, several genera include species of considerable ornamental merit — the Nemophilas and Phacelias are hard to beat — and most fit very well into the wild garden, some in sun, others in shade. Many of these are beloved of bee-keepers as they are prime honey plants.

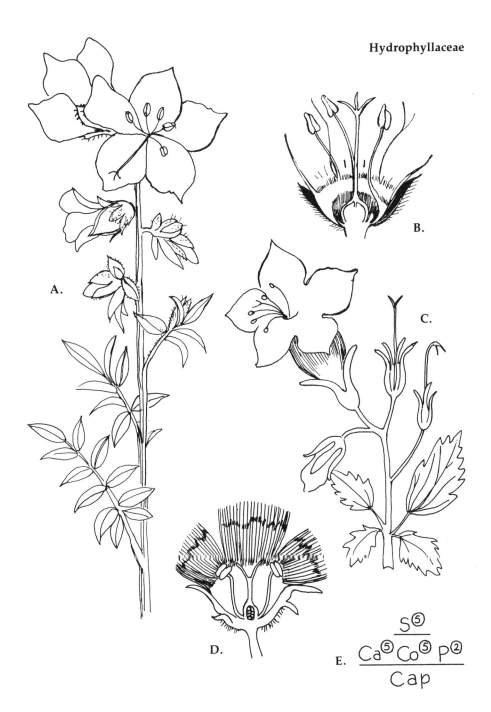

A.

B.

C.

D.

E. $\dfrac{\dfrac{S\circledS}{Ca\circledS\ Co\circledS\ P\circled2}}{Cap}$

Waterleaf Family

A. Field sketch of Virginia waterleaf, *Hydrophyllum virginianum*. **B.** Longitudinal section, petals cut away, of a waterleaf flower. **C.** Field sketch of *Phacelia*. **D.** Longitudinal section, petals cut away, of *Phacelia*. **E.** Floral formula for the Family.

157

Iridaceae   Iris Family

About 70 genera with more than 1,500 species make up the Iris Family which centers near the Cape of Good Hope and in sub-tropical America, with many sorts extending the range into temperate zones. Most are rhizomatous or tuberous-rooted herbs (many springing from corms) with basal leaves in two ranks and enfolding one another (equitant), linear or sword-shaped; often the juice of these is acrid. Flowers usually terminal or in panicles, usually showy, complete, actinomorphic or somewhat zygomorphic, epigynous, each with 2 spathe-like bracts; perianth with both calyx and corolla, all more or less petaloid; sepals 3, inserted on the rim of the floral cup closely adherant to the ovary, free; petals 3, inserted as sepals, and alternating with them; stamens 3, separate or sometimes connate, alternating with the petals, and epigynous; compound pistil of 3 closely united carpels, the single style usually is 3-cleft, bearing 3 stigmas, or sometimes 6 by branching, ovary inferior, 3-celled or rarely 1-celled, ovules few to many in each cell. Fruit a capsule, papery, leathery, or nearly woody.

In the field these are easy to recognize; look for the 2-ranked leaves springing from a rhizome, a tuber or tuberous root, or a corm; the 6-parted, showy perianth with 3 epigynous stamens, and the 3-celled inferior ovary are jointly characteristic of the family; look for the 2 bracts below each flower, usually papery or dried when flowers are fully expanded, a unique characteristic for this family. In the garden dissect and study the structure of several kinds of irises, but also of other Irids such as *Acidanthera, Belamcanda, Crocus, Sisyrinchium,* and *Tigridia,* to see variations in symmetry and relationship of flower parts.

Several beautiful genera of Irids are native to the U.S., and at least one (*Belamcanda*) has become naturalized; in addition, many are grown as hardy garden perennials or as tender perennials to be lifted through cold weather, or as house and conservatory plants; among them are:

Acidanthera	*Dierama*	*Nemastylis*
Antholyza	*Freesia*	*Neomarica*
Babiana	*Gladiolus*	*Schizostylis*
Belamcanda	*Iris*	*Sisyrinchium*
Crocosmia	*Ixia*	*Sparaxis*
Crocus	*Lapeyrousia*	*Tigridia*
Curtonus	*Moraea*	*Watsonia*

This is just a sampling of the commoner sorts which ought to be in everybody's garden or plant room. Some genera are rather limited as to species and varietal forms, but the lists of Crocuses, Gladioluses, Irises and a few others are overwhelming. By all means take advantage of these fine, reliable ornamentals. Some have been used in the past in medicinals, for dyes and pigments, as condiments or as food (the seeds of *Iris pseudacorus* once were a substitute for coffee), some few are poisonous. An interesting note has to do with the painter's iris-green, prepared by adding lime to purple iris flowers.

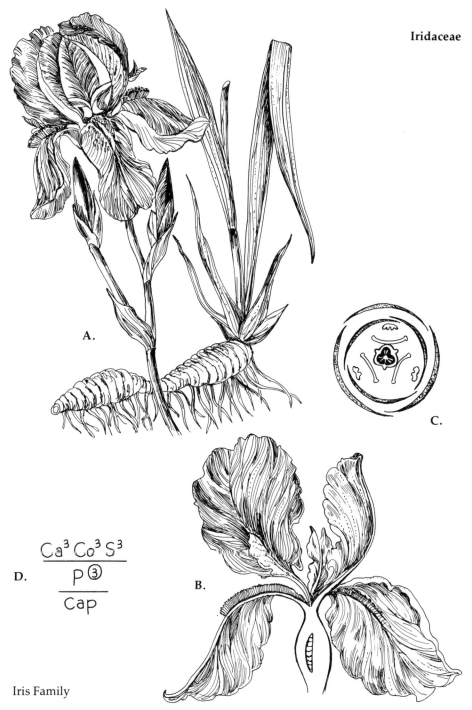

A.

C.

$$\text{D.} \quad \frac{\dfrac{Ca^3\ Co^3\ S^3}{P\ ③}}{Cap}$$

B.

Iris Family

A. Field sketch of the bearded iris of gardens, *Iris germanica.* **B.** Longitudinal section through a bearded iris flower indicating the inferior ovary (which distinguishes the Irids from members of the **Liliaceae**). **C.** Floral diagram of *Iris.* **D.** Floral formula of the Family.

Juglandaceae Walnut Family

Members of the Walnut Family number about 50 species in 7 genera, mostly trees, a few shrubs, native to the North Temperate zone. Branches are round, some with chambered pith, usually the buds are grouped at the leaf-scars, one above the other. Leaves are alternate, odd pinnate, in most cases without stipules, leaflets with glandular dots below. Flowers of one sex (monoecious); staminate flowers in long, drooping catkins, flower unit consists of a bract, two bractlets, and the flower with a reduced perianth 4-lobed, (rarely 3-6) or none, stamens small, 3 to many; pistillate flowers 2 or 3 together, or solitary, or in small racemes or spikes, each with a bract and two bractlets, 4-lobed (rarely 3–5) perianth (or none), compound pistil, inferior, styles 2, ovary 2 to 4-celled, but only 1 with an ovule. The ovary is buried completely in a mass of perianth tissue. Fruit a drupe or nut. Sap is clear and strongly aromatic.

As with other species with flowers in catkins, members of the Walnut Family are difficult for the novice to key through flower identification in most cases. Fortunately, the twig and leaf characters are sufficiently distinctive to be dependable most of the time. The combination of stout, round branches with bold leaf-scars or with pinnate leaves, and with several buds in a row at each node usually puts a specimen in **Juglandaceae**. Glandular dots on the leaf undersides, the characteristic scent of crushed twigs, leaves, or green fruits, and the indehiscent (usually) 1-seeded fruits with cotyledons enclosed in a hard, horny "nut" further clinches the identification.

Only 4 genera figure in horticulture or agriculture; they are:

Carya
Juglans
Platycarya
Pterocarya

Walnut Family

A. Field sketch of Carpathian walnut, *Juglans regia*, showing pendulous male catkins and female flowers at twig tips. **B.** Pistillate (female) flower. **C.** Staminate flowers on a portion of a catkin. **D.** Floral formula for the Family.

A.

B.

C.

D. $\dfrac{Ca^{3-6}\,Co^{0}\,S^{3-40}}{P\,\boxed{2\text{-}4}}$

Mo Nut Dr

Labiatae Mint Family

About 3,500 species in 180 genera of mostly herbs, sub-shrubs, and shrubs (and a few trees) with centers of distribution in the Mediterranean basin and in the Orient, but also abundant in the mountains of the sub-tropics and more or less general elsewhere, make up the Mint Family which is at once the joy of gardeners and the despair of students of plant tax-onomy. These mostly contain a volatile oil; stems usually 4-angled, leaves opposite or whorled, pinnately veined and without stipules, often dotted with small glands containing volatile oils; flowers complete, zygomorphic (mostly bi-labiate, hence the family name), but very rarely almost regular, hypogynous, usually in the axils of leaves or bracts, solitary, twin, or in clusters, or scattered, or often crowded into spikes or sometimes racemes; calyx synsepalous, 5-lobed or 5-cleft, regular or 2-lipped, usually green but sometimes colored; corolla sympetalous, 5-lobed, rarely 4-lobed, usually 2-lipped (one lip sometimes obsolete) with the upper lip 2-lobed or entire, the lower 3-lobed, hypogynous; stamens 4 in 2 sets (didynamous) or only 2, epipetalous (inserted on the tube of the corolla); compound pistil of 2 closely united carpels with the single style basal, stigma 2-lobed, ovary superior, 2-celled, each carpel deeply 2-lobed with a single ovule in each lobe. Fruit more or less separate 1-seeded bony nutlets which, due to the basal charac-ter of the style and the 2-lobed character of the 2 carpels, surround the base of the more or less persistent style.

This family keys out easily due to the familiar vegetative characteristics — square stem bearing minute oil gland-dotted opposite leaves usually with at least some flowers or spikelets in the axils, all warmly scented — and the flower characteristics, especially the bi-labiate characteristic, the di-dynamous stamens (which distinguishes these from **Boraginaceae**) *and the usually 4-lobed superior ovary with the basal style.* For some reason beginners sometimes tangle Labiates with the Borages, but the scorpoid inflo-rescences and 5 stamens of the latter — and flowers mostly regular (rotate) — allows for easy separation. The Verbenas, which sometimes are superfi-cially like Labiates, are separated by their terminal style.

Tremendously long lists of **Labiatae** genera are familiar to us; these are the many involved in food preparation, especially the culinary herbs; there are those grown for their aromatic oils and more which are involved in medicinal preparations. A long list of genera can be assembled in most any U.S. flower garden, and among our wildflowers the Labiates probably are second in number only to the Composites. Most garden encyclopedias devote considerable space to lengthy lists of these; see also, **Labiatae** in the *Royal Horticultural Society Dictionary of Gardening* as well as Alfred Rehder's *Manual of Cultivated Trees and Shrubs* for woody kinds.

We all grow a *Salvia* or two, usually the annual red sort and *S. officinalis*, kitchen sage; with more than 500 species of *Salvia* available perhaps we should branch out. Catmint, *Nepeta cataria*, is in most gardens as a herb, a rock garden plant, or edging for the perennial border — but there are 149 more species to try! Most of the Labiates are easy to grow; it is worth the time to seek out unfamiliar sorts and try them in the garden.

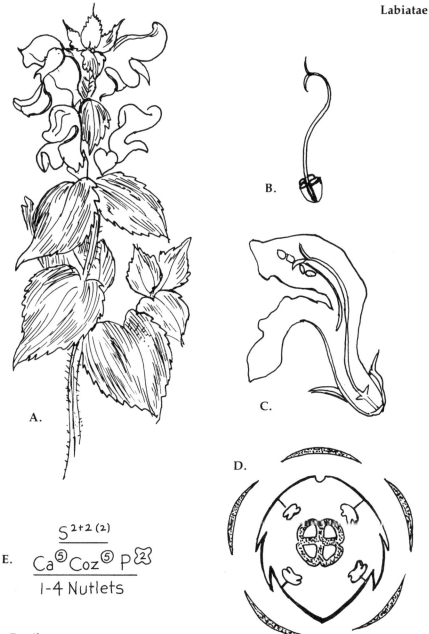

A.

B.

C.

D.

$$\frac{S^{2+2\,(2)}}{Ca^{⑤}\,Coz^{⑤}\,P^{②②}}$$

E.

$$\overline{1\text{-}4 \text{ Nutlets}}$$

Mint Family

A. Field sketch of Betony, *Stachys*. **B.** Typical Labiate pistil showing the deeply lobed 2-carpel ovary (giving the appearance of four nearly separate units) with the stigma two lobed and the style inserting deeply. **C.** Longitudinal section of a *Salvia* flower indicating relationships. **D.** Floral diagram of *Lamium*; note the stamens inserted on the corolla in two pairs, a condition described as epipetalous and diadelphous. **E.** Floral formula for the Family.

163

Lauraceae Laurel Family

About 30−35 genera including some 2,500 species make up this family of trees and shrubs, with a few parasitic herbaceous creepers. Almost exclusively tropical, a few members of the family are sub-tropical or grow in temperate climates. All are extremely aromatic.

Leaves are alternate (rarely opposite) usually without stipules, leathery, simple, mostly marked with minute pellucid dots, and in tropical species evergreen, but thin and deciduous in most temperate climate species. Flowers apparently without petals, inconspicuous, yellow or green, clustered. Flowers are radially symmetrical, perfect, or of 1 sex. Calyx of 6 (rarely 4) colored sepals in two whorls; stamens 3 to 4 whorls of 3 each, anthers opening by 2 or 4 uplifted flaps (valves); ovary superior, one-celled, one-ovuled, style filiform or short. The fruit is a berry or drupe, indehiscent, in some cases edible.

Two familiar members of the **Lauraceae** in eastern North America are sassafras, *Sassafras albidum* and spicebush, *Lindera benzoin*. In the west California-laurel, *Umbellularia californica*, is commonly encountered. Exotics commonly encountered in horticulture include the bay tree, *Laurus nobilis*, the camphor tree *Camphora officinarum*, cinnamon tree, *Cinnamomum zeylanicum*, and members of the genus *Persea* including both old and new world species as *P. borbonia*, red bay, now naturalized from the Gulf to Delaware, and *P. gratissima*, the avocado.

Field characteristics include the almost always present aromatic quality of the twigs, simple, usually alternate leaves with pellucid dots, petalless, insignificant flowers with numerous stamens, a single superior pistil, and anthers opening by uplifted flaps.

Some members of the Laurel Family:

> *Cinnamomum*
> *Laurus*
> *Lindera*
> *Litsea*
> *Neolitsea*
> *Ocotea*
> *Persea*
> *Ravensara*
> *Sassafras*
> *Umbellularia*

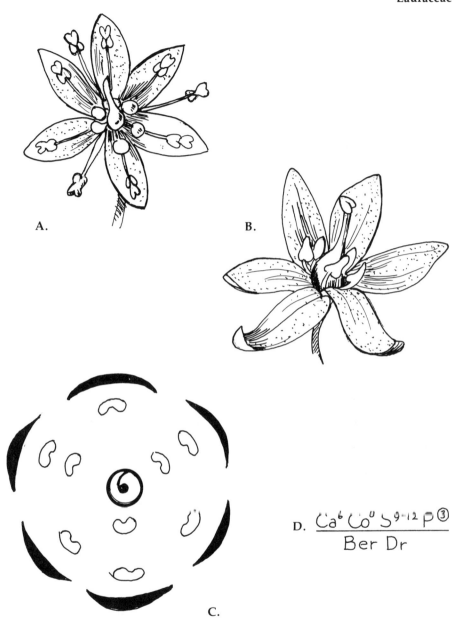

A.

B.

C.

D. $\dfrac{Ca^6\,Co^0\,S^{9\text{-}12}\,P\,③}{Ber\ Dr}$

Laurel Family

A. Semi-diagrammatic drawings of male *Sassafras* flower showing functional stamens and vestigial pistil. **B.** Female *Sassafras* flower showing vestigial stamens and functional pistil. **C.** Floral diagram of *Sassafras*. **D.** General flora formula for the Laurel Family.

Leguminosae Pulse (= Pea) Family

This huge family of annual and perennial herbs, shrubs, and trees with representatives throughout the world includes some 13,000 species in about 600 genera. Leaves are alternate, mostly compound, pinnate, tri-foliate, or digitate, or rarely simple; with stipules (which may be fugaceous). Flowers often papilionaceous (literally, butterfly-like, referring to flowers with the general structure of a sweet pea) or sometimes regular; usually in spikes, heads, racemes, or panicles. It is best to learn the floral characteristics of each of the three traditional subfamilies.

Subfamily **Mimosoideae.**

Flowers regular, small, in dense heads, with stamens overtopping the perianth; sepals reduced, 5; petals 4 to 5 often united into a hypogynous cup. Numerous stamens, filaments very long, anthers small, also hypogynous. In this subfamily the stamens always protrude far beyond the perianth. Pistil a 1-celled legume with several ovules. Leaves of these are twice pinnate. To become familiar with this subfamily study a flower head of the Japanese silk tree, *Albizia*, or of the sensitive briar, *Schrankia*.

Subfamily **Caesalpinioideae.**

Corolla sometimes nearly regular, but mostly imperfectly papilionaceous. Calyx of 5 free sepals which may be quite small; petals 5, the upper, or odd, petal inside and inclosed by the other four; often perigynous; stamens 10 or fewer, commonly free, and often inserted on the floral cup. Pistil superior, a 1-celled legume. To become familiar with this subfamily study flowers of the redbud, *Cercis*, honey-locust, *Gleditsia*, and Kentucky Coffee-tree, *Gymnocladus*, which will show a range of forms.

Subfamily **Papilionoideae.**

Calyx of 5 sepals, more or less united and often unequally so. Corolla inserted into the base of the calyx; petals 5, rarely fewer, irregular, or more commonly 2+2+1, with the upper (odd) petal larger than the others and enclosing them in the bud. The two lateral petals are oblique to and exterior to the two lower petals which commonly are closely touching or more commonly coherent by their anterior edges to form a *keel* which encloses the stamens and pistil. Stamens rarely 5, usually 10, and often 9+1, with the 9 fused by the filaments into a tube which is open on the upper side, and the 10th stamen overlays the opening. The pistil is a typical legume, with 1 cell or sometimes bilocular by an intrusion of one of the sutures, or transversely 2 to many locular by cross division into *articles*, as in seed pods of beggar's-ticks, *Desmodium*. The style is simple. Common garden peas and beans are examples.

A constant character among all these various species is the 1-celled, superior ovary with 1 to many ovules on a single parietal placenta (as the common table pea pod, which you should examine during the blooming stage). There are dozens of field characteristics, but none except the above work equally well for all members of the family. Sometimes tri-foliate leaves give a clue; often the papilionaceous flowers point the way; sometimes it is the pinnately compound leaves combined with sweetly scented flowers in balled heads which look "fuzzy" due to the greatly exerted stamens. If you find 5 sepals, free or more or less united, 5 petals, often free and often epigynous, 5, 10 (including 9+1) or many stamens, also epigynous, and the legume-type pistil you are headed into the **Leguminosae.** It really is an easy family, just quite large, and more than usually diverse.

Of the hundreds of genera of **Leguminosae** in cultivation, American plantsmen are most likely to encounter the following:

Abrus	*Hedysarum*
Acacia	*Hovea*
Albizia	*Indigofera*
Amorpha	*Isotropis*
Anthyllis	*Laburnocytisus*
Apios	*Laburnum*
Arachis	*Lens*
Astragalus	*Lespedeza*
Baptisia	*Lotus*
Bauhinia	*Lupinus*
Borbonia	*Maackia*
Caesalpinia	*Medicago*
Calliandra	*Mimosa*
Caragana	*Notospartium*
Cassia	*Onobrychis*
Centrosema	*Ononis*
Ceratonia	*Oxylobium*
Cercis	*Oxytropis*
Chordospartium	*Parkinsonia*
Chorizema	*Parochetus*
Cladrastis	*Peltophorum*
Clianthus	*Phaseolus*
Clitoria	*Pisum*
Colutea	*Pithecolobium*
Coronilla	*Platylobium*
Crotalaria	*Poinsiana*
Cytisus	*Psoralea*
Dalea	*Robinia*
Derris	*Schrankia*
Desmanthus	*Sesbanium*
Desmodium	*Sophora*
Dolichos	*Spartium*
Dorycnium	*Swainsonia*
Erythrina	*Tamarindus*
Galega	*Tephrosia*
Genista	*Thermopsis*
Gleditsia	*Trifolium*
Glycine	*Trigonella*
Glycyrrhiza	*Ulex*
Gymnocladus	*Vicia*
Haematoxylon	*Vigna*
Halimodendron	*Wisteria*

$\longrightarrow$

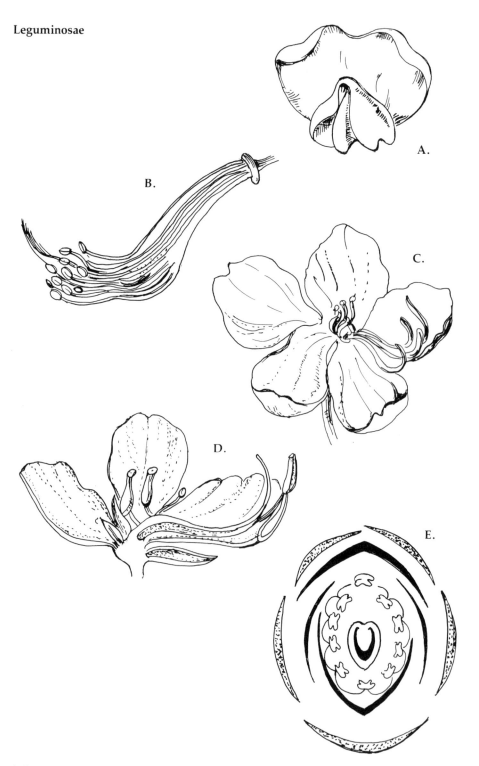

A.

B.

C.

D.

E.

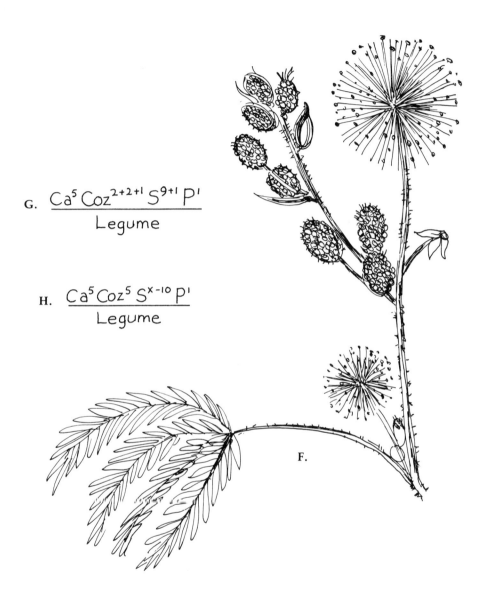

G. $$\frac{Ca^5 Coz^{2+2+1} S^{9+1} P^1}{Legume}$$

H. $$\frac{Ca^5 Coz^5 S^{x-10} P^1}{Legume}$$

F.

Pulse (= Pea) Family

A. Papilionaceous (butterfly-like) flower of *Pisum*. **B.** Pistil and stamens of *Pisum*, showing nine fused and one free stamen. **C.** Nearly regular flower of *Cassia*. **D.** Section of *Cassia* flower. **E.** Floral diagram of Sweet Pea, *Lathyrus*, typical of a papilionaceous flower. **F.** Field sketch of *Mimosa*, illustrating typical flower head of the Mimosa-type **Leguminosae. G.** Floral formula, generalized, for the Family. **H.** Formula for the non-papilionaceous members.

Liliaceae Lily Family

More than 6,500 species in at least 200 genera make up this very cosmopolitan family, world-wide in distribution, mostly in sub-tropical and temperate regions. Plants mostly are herbaceous, but some are shrubs or trees, or climbers; many of the perennial herbaceous sorts develop from bulbs or bulb-like organs, or from fleshy rhizomes or rootstocks. Most of the woody ones are in the genera *Dracaena*, *Yucca*, and *Smilax*. Leaves usually are basal in rosettes, or alternate on a stem, mostly simple and sessile, but some with a petiole and blade, leaves may be fleshy or dry and leathery, rigid and with acute tips, delicate and falling, or evergreen, veins strongly parallel. Flowers often showy but sometimes small and inconspicuous, single, or in spikes, racemes, or panicles, axillary or terminal, usually complete but rarely unisexual, mostly hypogynous but rarely with the ovary at least partly submerged in the floral-cup, actinomorphic, inflorescence subtended by a spathe-like bract in *Allium* and *Nothoscordum*; calyx of 3 separate sepals, mostly colored or white, petal-like, but sometimes green; corolla of 3 separate or sometimes sympetalous petals without or with a corona (cup), both perianth whorls mostly colored similarly except in *Trillium*; stamens mostly 6, sometimes 3 when a single whorl opposite the petals, or when 6 the outer whorl of stamens opposes the sepals, the inner 3 oppose the petals; compound pistil of 3 closely united carpels, styles and stigmas various, usually 1 to 3, ovary mostly superior, sometimes partially inferior, 3-celled, each cell with few to many ovules. Fruit a 3-valved capsule. Often taxonomists break the Lily family, as here presented, into some 78 families.

In the field look for flowers. Begin with gross structure, as perianth with two whorls of very similar segments, stamens 6, rarely 3, with a 3-celled superior ovary, often elongate and triangular in cross-section. Look for the strong parallel venation in the leaves, and if possible, for a fleshy or bulb-like rootstock or rhizome. If the plant seems to meet these criteria, proceed through the more detailed characteristics as defined in the first paragraph above. Actually, few other families can be confused with **Liliaceae**; in the superficially similar **Amaryllidaceae** the flowers mostly are subtended by a spathe-like bract (as the early shrivelling leaf-like structure which falls back when *Hippeastrum* buds break from the sheath), and the ovary always is inferior; **Iridaceae** also has a bract or bracts subtending the inflorescences and usually the two whorls of the perianth are at least somewhat dissimilar, roots usually are fibrous where Lily roots are fleshy, and corms take the place of bulbs.

A tremendously long list of **Liliaceae** genera includes species which are commonplace with us; vegetables including onion, asparagus, leeks, and the like; fiber plants as New Zealand-flax, and *Yucca*, medicinals, dyes, resins, gums, starches, and other economically significant materials come from various tropical species. Our greatest use of **Liliaceae**, other than for foodstuffs, is ornamental. Refer to the lengthy list under **Liliaceae** in Vol. 3 of the 2nd Edition of *The Royal Horticultural Society Dictionary of Gardening* to get an idea of the diversity of the family; you will encounter not only all the familiar bulbs, but other lilies as Lily-of-the-valley, aloes of various sorts, shrubs as *Danae* and *Ruscus*, *Liriope*, *Veratrum*, and *Sansevieria*, and similar sorts which do not fit into our too stereotyped idea of what a lily should be.

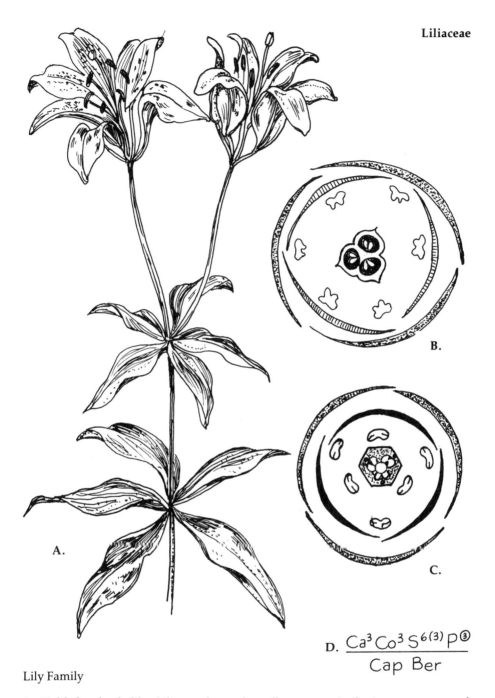

B.

C.

A.

D. $\dfrac{Ca^3 Co^3 S^{6(3)} P^{③}}{Cap\ Ber}$

Lily Family

A. Field sketch of a lily, *Lilium*; calyx and corolla are very similar in appearance and commonly are grouped together as the perianth. **B.** Floral diagram of hyacinth. **C.** Floral diagram of *Asparagus*; this is a composite diagram because asparagus commonly is monoecious, with staminate flowers on one plant and pistillate flowers on another. **D.** Floral formula for **Liliaceae.**

171

Linaceae Flax Family

The **Linaceae** always surprises North Temperate zone gardeners due to the nature of the plants. Many of the 290 species, distributed through 12 genera, are shrubs or trees! Usually these have alternate, rarely opposite or whorled leaves which are simple, entire, and with stipules or glands replacing stipules. Flowers of the Flax Family usually are terminal, and single or in corymbs or panicles. Flowers perfect, regular, hypogynous with parts in 4's or 5's; calyx of 5 or 4 persistent, free sepals, imbricated; sepals may be divided into lobes; corolla of 5 or 4 separate petals which may be clawed, the claw sometimes crested; petals are convolute and fugaceous; stamens 5, alternating with the petals, or 10, 15, or 20, often filaments with no anthers (staminoids) are present, stamens commonly united (connate) at the often glandular base, hypogynous; pistil with superior ovary which is 2, 3, or 5-celled, often with additional partitions from the midribs of the carpels, ovules few, styles the same number as carpels. Fruit usually a several-seeded capsule, seeds flat, shining. The structure of flowers of **Linaceae** has points in common with the **Geraniaceae** and **Oxalidaceae**, but also there is a suggestion of other groups such as the Silenes in **Caryophyllaceae.**

Early botanists looked on the flax flower as a "pattern" flower because of its organization in 5's. Certainly, the horticultural genera all are easy to spot with their alternate, rather glaucous, simple, rather linear leaves and with flowers in 5's and multiples of 5's, especially when the identification is rather clinched by the ring of hypogynous stamens connate at their bases surrounding the superior ovary with 5 styles and 5 or 10 cells with only a few ovules.

Only two genera of **Linaceae** ever are commonly encountered; they are *Linum*, the flaxes of agriculture (for fiber used in making linen and for seed used for linseed oil and other purposes), of horticulture — the scarlet, blue, and yellow flaxes of the garden — and our beautiful native species; and *Reinwardtia*, a sub-shrub from India which makes quite a nice conservatory plant.

Flax Family

A. Field sketch of *Linum*. **B.** Longitudinal section of *Linum* flower. **C.** Floral diagram of *Linum*. **D.** Floral formula for the Family.

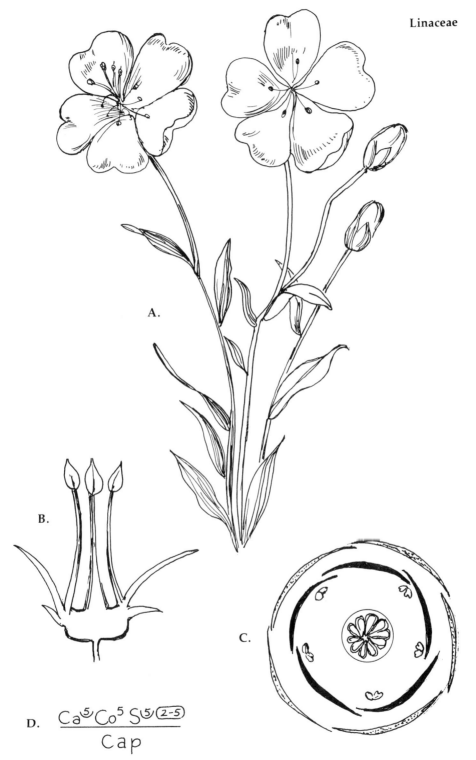

A.

B.

C.

D. $\dfrac{Ca^5 Co^5 S^{5} \boxed{2\text{-}5}}{Cap}$

Lythraceae Loosestrife Family

Twenty-five genera of herbs, shrubs, and trees include the 550 species of **Lythraceae**. These are world-wide in distribution except in the coldest areas, but most are in the tropics, especially in America. Leaves usually opposite (or whorled), simple, entire, and usually without stipules, often on branches which are 4-angled. Flowers solitary, or in racemes, panicles, or cymes; usually complete and actinomorphic (sometimes irregular), perigynous, with a more or less deep, tube-shaped floral-cup; sepals 4 (or 5, 6, or 8), sometimes petal-like; petals of the same number as the sepals or none, and inserted on the rim of the tube; stamens very low in the tube and usually twice the number of sepals, but sometimes very many, sometimes 1 or 2, free, with filaments quite variable in length (you will find filament variation in different flowers on the same plant in many cases); compound pistil, usually 2 to 6 carpels, with a single style, stigma capitate or rarely 2-lobed; ovary superior (but sometimes seems to be buried in the base of the floral-cup), 2 to 6 cells, very rarely 1-celled, ovules usually many, (style length, like stamens, variable among flowers on the same plant or on different plants of the same species). Fruit a usually dehiscent capsule.

In the field look for a more or less woody plant with quantities of rather small flowers with petals that often are quite delicate and crepe-like (as *Lagerstroemia*, crape-myrtle), on woody twigs often 4-angled, with shredding bark. The tube-shaped flowers with 2 to 6-celled *superior* ovary, and with free stamens within the tube, is generally indicative of **Lythraceae**. Sometimes it is necessary to search out all the flower characteristics (as defined above), with especial reference to the varying lengths of stamens and styles. These are very like members of the **Onagraceae** which differs in its inferior ovary, and to the **Melastomaceae** which differs in its strange stamen organization.

Many genera of **Lythraceae** include good garden and greenhouse ornamentals, and there are also some fine native American sorts, including:

Ammannia	Lafoensia	Lythrum
Cuphea	Lagerstroemia	Peplis
Decodon	Latua	Rotala
Heimia	Lawsonia	Woodfordia

Several species in different genera have been used in the past in medical preparations and for perfumery; *Lawsonia inermis* supplies not only a notable perfume but also the red-orange dye, henna. *Woodfordia floribunda* yields the red dye of India, *dhak*; other species have been used as pot herbs. *Lagerstroemia* is an important lumber tree in the tropics, and a superior ornamental small tree or large shrub in many gardens.

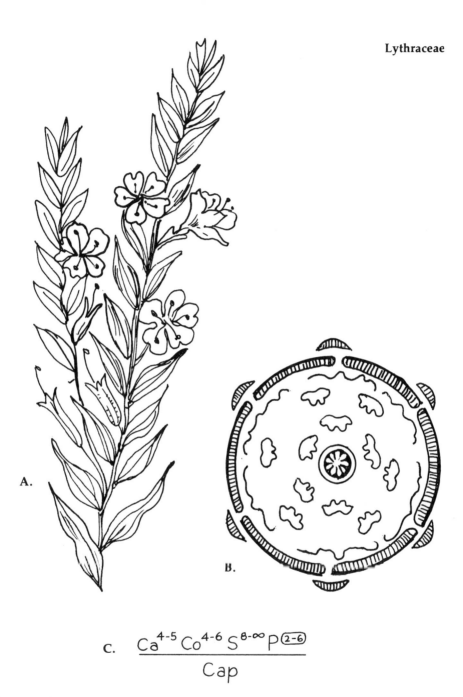

A.

B.

C. $\dfrac{Ca^{4\text{-}5} Co^{4\text{-}6} S^{8\text{-}\infty} P^{\boxed{2\text{-}6}}}{Cap}$

Loosestrife Family

A. Field sketch of loosestrife, *Lythrum*. **B.** Floral diagram for *Lythrum*, drawn to show, from the outside, a whorl of 6 sepals, 6 petals, the crepe paper-like petal appendages, the numerous stamens, and a central pistil. **C.** A generalized floral formula for **Lythraceae.**

175

Magnoliaceae Magnolia Family

The Magnolia Family includes about 12 genera and some 230 species of woody plants, trees, shrubs and creepers, distributed through temperate but mostly sub-tropical or tropical portions of eastern North America and Asia.

Leaf-buds are covered with membranous stipules, which serve as bud scales; leaves commonly are alternate, large, simple, often more or less leathery, often persistent (evergreen); stipules are deciduous; usually large. Solitary flowers are often large and showy, terminal or axillary, hypogynous, usually perfect and complete, with many stamens and carpels; the calyx and corolla are often colored alike in three or more rows of three, imbricated (rarely convolute) in the bud. Stamens many, rarely with adnate anthers, pistils simple, many, crowded on elongated receptacle. A primitive family, **Magnoliaceae** flowers' sepals, petals, stamens, and carpels often are spirally arranged. This is easily seen in the fruit of *Magnolia grandiflora* which bears brightly colored fruits in a leathery "cone", or in the dried samara-like fruits arranged spirally on a woody axis in *Liriodendron tulipifera*.

Field characteristics include: more or less woody plants with alternate leaves, stipules deciduous, large, showy flowers with similar petals and sepals, many stamens, many carpels, all spirally arranged. Bud scales leathery but not dry, wood usually white, broken twigs commonly aromatic.

Some members of the Magnolia Family:

Drimys	*Liriodendron*	*Michelia*
Illicium	*Magnolia*	*Schisandra*
Kadsura	*Mangliettia*	*Tetracentron*

A.

B. $\dfrac{Ca^x Co^x S^\infty P^\infty}{Sam\ Fol}$

Magnolia Family

A. Field sketch of a *Magnolia* flowering branch. **B.** Floral formula for the Family.

177

Malvaceae Mallow Family

Depending on the authority, this family contains up to 85 genera with 1,500 species. These are herbs, shrubs, and trees, some found throughout the world except in the colder regions. Leaves are simple, alternate, entire or variously lobed, often palmately veined, with stipules. Flowers often showy, solitary or in compound cymes, axillary, and with a jointed pedicel, actinomorphic (regular), and complete; calyx of 5 sepals (rarely fewer), free or connate, frequently with an outer epicalyx (a group of calyx-like bracts, an involucel); corolla of 5 petals, free, but often joined to the stamen sheath or column at the base; stamens many, joined by the filaments into a more or less elongated tube (monodelphous), anthers free above, clustered beneath the stigmas, anthers 1-celled, pollen spiny; compound pistil, 5 to several (rarely 1) carpels, with usually elongated styles as many as the carpels, or one, with stigmas usually as many as the carpels; ovary superior, 2 to mostly many-celled, ovules in each cell 1 to many. Fruit commonly a dry capsule or schizocarp, or in *Malvaviscus* berry-like.

This is one of the easiest families to recognize at first glimpse. That very characteristic tassel of fused stamens, barely attached to the petals at the base and hollow with the stigma or stigmas reaching through and beyond it is purely **Malvaceae**. Such a structure inside the typically hollyhock or hibiscus type of perianth insures correct classification.

Numerous genera of **Malvaceae** are native to tropical and temperate America; these and others are important in agriculture and as ornamentals; they include:

Abutilon	Iliamna	Modiola
Althaea	Kitaibelia	Montezuma
Anoda	Kostelitzkya	Napaea
Callirhoe	Kydia	Palaua
Chorisia	Lagunaria	Pavonia
Cienfuegosia	Lavatera	Plagianthus
Decaschistea	Malachra	Sida
Goethea	Malope	Sidalcea
Gossypium	Malva	Sphaeralcea
Hibiscus	Malvastrum	Thespesia
Hoheria	Malvaviscus	Urena

Pungent and poisonous properties apparently are lacking in these plants, but the mucilaginous sap of the marsh-mallow long ago was converted into a foamy sweet confection which comes to us today as the marshmallow; the slimy sap also was useful as an emollient. Many species of **Malvaceae** are used for food, the fibers of the stems of many are valuable, and the seed fibers of species of *Gossypium* are the cotton of the weaver and medicine chest. Seeds of some yield oils, flowers of some yield dyes. Most of us appreciate them as ornamentals.

A.

C.

D.

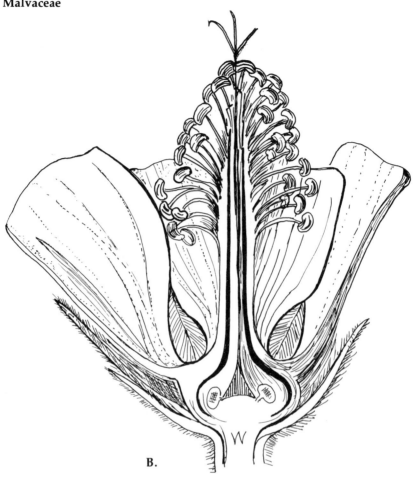

B.

E. $\dfrac{Ca^5 Co^5 S^\infty P^{5-\infty}}{Bac\text{-}Cap}$

Mallow Family

A. Field sketch of woods mallow, *Malva sylvestris*, flower. **B.** Flower of marsh-mallow, *Althaea officinalis*, in longitudinal section showing the hollow column of stamens, anthers fused below, free above, surrounding the elongated style which expands into three stigmas above the stamens. No other plant family exhibits this arrangement of stamens and pistil; it is a reliable field character for **Malvaceae**. **C.** A typically convoluted *Malva* bud. **D.** A *Malva* fruit. **E.** Floral formula for **Malvaceae**.

Marantaceae Arrow-root Family

More than 400 species in 30 genera make up the almost entirely tropical family of Arrow-roots. These closely resemble the gingers in some respects but while they are mostly American, **Zingiberaceae** are almost entirely Asiatic. The Arrow-roots are perennial with rhizomes. Leaves in 2 ranks are mostly basal, mostly more or less sheathing, with a characteristic swollen joint where leafstalk and blade join. Blades are linear to oval, pinnately parallel-veined. Flowers paired, subtended by bracts, usually on leafy shoots; complete, irregular epigynous, perianth usually of 3 sepals easily distinguished from the 3 petals. Stamens often in 2 whorls, with an inner whorl of 1 fertile stamen, petaloid, with a lateral half-anther, and several staminodea; the outer whorl when present of staminodea. Pistil with inferior ovary of 3 carpels, 3 cells or rarely 1 or 2 cells; 1 ovule in each cell. Fruit is a capsule, very rarely berry-like.

Field characteristics include the joint connecting leafstalk and blade, the unusual stamen construction and placement, and, separating **Marantaceae** from **Cannaceae**, the presence of a single ovule per ovary cell (the latter invariably has several to many). The curved embryo in the seed also is a distinguishing characteristic.

Mosty encountered as tender ornamentals for indoor growing, the following species of **Marantaceae** are relatively common:

Bamburante	Maranta	Saranthe
Calathea	Monotagma	Stachyphrynium
Ctenanthe	Phrynium	Stromanthe
Ctenophrynium	Pleiostachya	Thalia

Ranging from Florida to Texas and northward to South Carolina and southeastern Missouri, *Thalia dealbata* is a handsome native aquatic species often planted in ponds and pools as an ornamental, valued not only for its handsome, upright foliage but also for its tall spikes of blue and purple flowers produced in July and August. Rhizomes of *Maranta arundinaceae* are a source of arrowroot starch and in the tropics rhizomes of some other species are eaten.

$$\frac{Ca^3\ Coz^{\textcircled{3}}\ S^1}{P^1}$$

Bac (Petal-like Staminoids)

Marantaceae Arrowroot Family

Floral formula for the **Marantaceae**.

Moraceae Mulberry Family

A very large, mostly tropical family of a few herbs and many shrubs and trees (some species climbing or twining) in about 1,400 species in 53 to 55 genera. Perhaps 600 of the species are in the genus *Ficus*, fig; only three genera commonly are encountered natively in temperate North America. Leaves are alternate, usually simple, often quite large, often deeply lobed and with stipules which fall early (fugaceous) leaving an obvious scar. The juice of these is milky, mostly sticky, often acrid. Flowers perfect or commonly unisexual, often in dense heads or hollow receptacles, rarely in spikes; small, regular, often greatly reduced, parts in 4's, petals lacking. Thus the perianth is a single whorl, usually 4-parted (rarely 2 to 6); staminate flowers sometimes with free sepals, stamens as many as perianth lobes, *inflexed in the bud, and elastic*; pistillate flowers almost always with 4 perianth lobes, mostly united, compound pistil with mostly two styles, ovary superior or inferior, carpels 2, united and often 1 aborted; ovary 1-celled, 1-ovule. Fruit an achene (nutlet), drupe, or nut. The "fruit" of the edible fig, for example, is a *gynophore*, that is, a fleshy, inverted receptacle, hollow, bearing the true fruits, nutlets, on its inner surface. In the case of mulberry the individual fleshy segments largely are formed from the enlarged sepals which expand to cover the ripening ovary that encases the seed.

Field identification usually is no problem; native temperate N. American genera include the mulberries, and the Osage-orange, all trees, all with more or less milky juice, all with flowers staminate or pistillate, greatly reduced, and with floral structure as indicated above. A hand lens is necessary for the study of these flowers. By way of gross anatomy, look for woody plants with alternate leaves which are simple, perhaps palmately lobed, with stipules or stipular scars, and with milky juice.

Genera which may be encountered in the garden or, more commonly, in the conservatory or in a tropical planting include:

Antiaris	*Chlorophora*	*Maclura*
Artocarpus	*Coudrania*	*Morus*
Brosimum	*Coussapoa*	*Musanga*
Broussonetia	*Dorstenia*	*Treculia*
Cecropia	*Ficus*	

Outside the ornamental members of the genus *Ficus* and also the edible fig, most of these have little importance to the horticulturist. In the tropics, breadfruit and jackfruit (*Artocarpus* spp.) are important, and primitive cultures use various species as sources of dyes, spear poisons, fiber, food, and so on. The British once esteemed the insipid mulberry as a table fruit but today fruits with more flavor have largely replaced them.

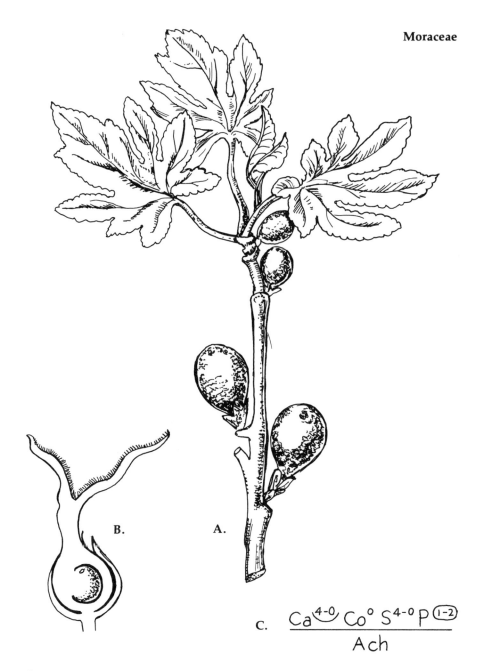

B.

A.

C. $\dfrac{Ca^{\smile 4\text{-}0} \; Co^{\circ} \; S^{4\text{-}0} \; P^{\boxed{1\text{-}2}}}{Ach}$

Mulberry Family

A. Field sketch of common fig, *Ficus carica* showing the growth habit of the strangely modified twigs which become the table figs of commerce. These are lined with tiny, greatly reduced flowers, the ovaries of which mature into small nutlets which are the true fig fruits. **B.** A female flower from the inside of the fig inflorescence. **C.** Floral formula for the Family.

Myricaceae Wax-myrtle (Sweet Gale) Family

About 40 species in 1 to 4 genera make up the **Myricaceae**; mostly shrubs, rarely small trees, these are widely distributed through temperate and sub-tropical regions. Leaves are alternate, usually simple, usually fragrant with resinous secretions in the glandular dots. Leaves of *Comptonia* pinnately lobed and with obvious stipules; those of genus *Myrica*, entire, and without stipules. Flowers of one sex or with both stamens and a pistil in catkins or spikes, a single flower at each bract; the flowers are greatly reduced, with no discernable perianth, stamens 2 to 16, usually 4 to 6; male catkins (aments) sessile and cylindrical; female flowers 1 at each bract, merely a compound pistil of 2 carpels, with 2 stigmas, 1-celled, with a single ovule. Fruit an ovoid drupe or nut generally covered with waxy or resinous grains as in bayberry, *Myrica pensylvanica*.

The **Myricaceae** are considered to be related to other amentiferous families as the Walnuts, the Beeches and the Birches. The simple, glandular-resinous, aromatic leaves and the wax-covered fruits are considered to be field characteristics of the **Myricaceae**. Indehiscent, 1-seeded fruits, and the "stripped down" flowers, just sex organs adjacent to bracts, are other reliable characteristics, particularly the ovary with 2 carpels.

Two genera are common in cultivation or the wild:

Comptonia
Myrica

A.

B.

$$S^4$$
$$\male = Br^1 \; : \; \female = Br^1 Sc^2 P^1$$

Bayberry Family

A. Field sketch of a branch of sweet gale, *Myrica gale*, with maturing female catkins.
B. Floral formulas for the male and female flowers of this Family: the male, staminate, flowers consist only of a bract with usually 4 stamens; the female, pistillate,
flowers are composed of a bract, two bracteoles (scales), and a simple pistil with a
single ovule.

185

Myrtaceae Myrtle Family

Three thousand species distributed through about 100 genera make up this largely tropical and sub-tropical family of shrubs and trees; distribution is chiefly in Australia and tropical America with 3 species in the southeast U.S. Simple, entire leaves usually opposite, glandular-punctate, exstipulate, evergreen and aromatic. Flowers actinomorphic, perfect or rarely of one sex, epigynous; calyx of 4 or 5 sepals, free or connate, often persistent on the fruit but sometimes forming a "lid" which drops from the flower; petals 4 or 5 or rarely 0, imbricated; stamens numerous, very rarely few, inserted opposite the petals in fascicles, free or connate below; pistil of 2 or 3 united carpels, ovary often inferior, one- to many-celled with one to many ovules in each cell, placentation axile or rarely parietal; style simple; fruit a capsule, berry, nut, or rarely, drupe.

Field identification begins with glandular-punctate, usually thick, evergreen opposite leaves on a woody plant; feathery-looking flowers are typical, either with showy petals and a handsome tuft of long stamens as in *Myrtus*, myrtle, or *Eucalyptus*, or else a sort of bottlebrush effect as in *Callistemon* and other genera. The usually inferior ovary with fascicled stamens surrounding a quite long style characterizes this family.

Many species in the Myrtle Family are of economic importance; most are ornamental and of use in landscape plantings from the low growing myrtle cultivars to the giant eucalypts. Lumber comes from the eucalypts and others; allspice from *Pimenta officinalis* and cloves from *Eugenia aromatica*; oil of bay rum from *Pimenta* and other aromatic oils from the eucalypts and others; the fruits of *Psidium* species yield the various guavas used in jelly-making.

Myrtle Family genera encountered in tropical or sub-tropical gardens and arboreta include:

Agonis	Comptomanesia	Micromyrtus
Angophora	Darwinia	Myrcia
Astarte	Decaspermum	Myrtus
Backhousia	Eucalyptus	Pileanthus
Baeckia	Eugenia	Pimenta
Beaufortia	Feijoa	Psidium
Blepharocalyx	Foetidia	Regelia
Callistemon	Hypocalymma	Rhodamnia
Calothamnus	Kunzea	Rhodomyrtus
Calypthrix	Leptospermum	Thryptomene
Calyptranthus	Lhotzya	Tristania
Careya	Melaleuca	Verticordia
Chamaelaucium	Metrosideros	

Gardeners with greenhouses will find that species of several of these genera make superb, if rather large, tubbed specimens of easy cultivation; many bloom beautifully under conservatory conditions. Two species of *Eucalyptus*, *E. gunnii*, cider gum, and *E. niphophila*, snow gum, are reasonably hardy, growing at least into Zone 7 in the U.S.

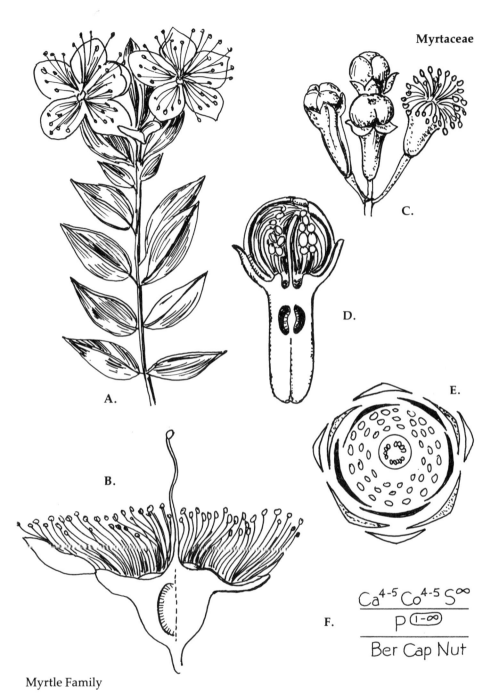

A.

B.

C.

D.

E.

$$\frac{Ca^{4-5} Co^{4-5} S^{\infty}}{P\,\overline{(1-\infty)}}$$

F.

Ber Cap Nut

Myrtle Family

A. Field sketch of myrtle, *Myrtus communis*. **B.** Flower of myrtle in longitudinal section showing the insertion of the large number of stamens inserted above the ovary. **C.** Buds and flowers of *Eugenia aromatica*, the common clove of cookery. **D.** Longitudinal section of a clove bud. **E.** Floral diagram of *Myrtus*. **F.** Floral formula for **Myrtaceae.**

Nyctaginaceae Four-o'clock Family

Mostly tropical American, this family includes some 300 species distributed through about 30 genera. These usually are herbaceous but some are shrubby; there are a few trees in the family. Leaves usually are opposite, simple, often entire, without stipules. Nodes, especially of herbaceous sorts, often swollen (tumid). Some of the woody members bear vicious spines at the nodes (as *Bougainvillea*). The flowers of these are most confusing due to mimicry; work from the inside out. The simple pistil is superior, the ovary with one cell and one ovule, and may be sessile or stalked; the style usually is long, terminating in a simple capitate stigma. Stamens usually 5, but vary from 3 to 10 and occasionally branch to give the appearance of 20 to 30 stamens united in clusters. Stamens may be free or may be slightly united at the bases of the filaments; they are hypogynous. *There are no petals.* The usually colorful, petal-like perianth consists of a tubular calyx which flairs into 4 or 5 wide-spreading lobes. Occasionally this structure is rather reduced as in the case of our native *Mirabilis* but usually it is quite showy as in the case of the cultivated Peruvian *Mirabilis*, garden four-o'clock. To further confuse the picture, external to the colorful, corolla-like calyx, is a group of persistent, often colorful bracts which is very like a calyx. This involucre may consist of separate or united bracts and most commonly is mistaken for a calyx.

No fail-safe field characters exist to insure positive, easy identification of members of the **Nyctaginaceae**. You must rely on groups of characteristics. Start with the flower; the simple, superior pistil, 1-celled, 1-ovuled, with a longish style and simple, button-like stigma is a good point. The nut-like seed, if present, is characteristic, and often this dried, ribbed or grooved achene is surrounded and enclosed by the persistent calyx. The single, colorful perianth subtended by the involucre of often enlarged and often colorful bracts is a key characteristic for botanists but sometimes confuses beginners. In herbaceous sorts, the enlarged nodes are a good field character as are the simple, slender, and extremely sharp spines of the woody sorts.

Ornamental members of the **Nyctaginaceae** include:

Abronia	*Heimerliodendron*	*Pisonia*
Boerhavia	*Mirabilis*	*Tripterocalyx*
Bougainvillea	*Neea*	

We know these largely as the Abronias, sand-verbenas of the rock garden, four-o'clocks of the garden and the less showy native sorts, and the exotic Bougainvilleas of conservatories and tropical resort areas. In South America the roots of *Boerhavia* and of *Mirabilis jalapa* substitute for jalap as a purgative. In Brazil the leaves of *Neea theifera* make a black dye and are used for tea.

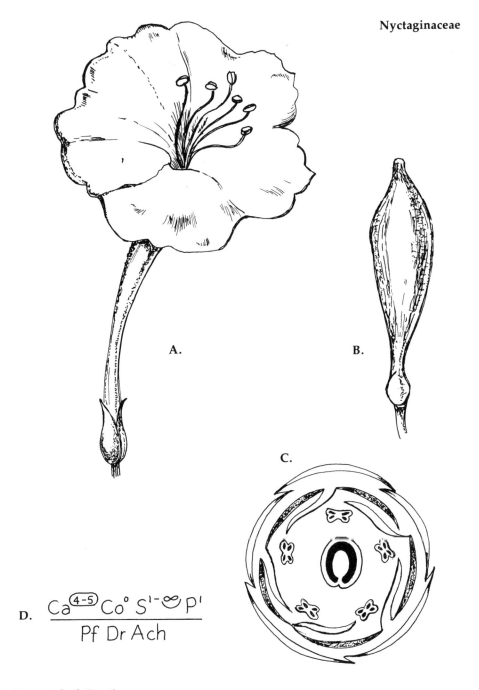

A.

B.

C.

D. $\dfrac{Ca^{\boxed{4\text{-}5}}\,Co^{0}\,S^{1\text{-}\infty}\,P^{1}}{Pf\;Dr\;Ach}$

Four-o'clock Family

A. Flower of *Mirabilis* showing tubular, corolla-like calyx with wide-spread lobes and with two bracts at the base. **B.** Fruit of *Mirabilis*. **C.** Floral diagram of *Mirabilis*. **D.** General floral formula for the Family.

Nymphaeaceae Water-lily Family

About 68 species divided among 7 genera make up the Water-lily Family; most of them occur in the tropics and in the North Temperate zone. These are marsh and open water plants with mostly large floating leaves which are simple, usually cordate or peltate, on long petioles. They arise from horizontal rhizomes (in a few instances, erect rhizomes) and are alternate in arrangement. Leaves of *Nuphar, Victoria,* and *Nymphaea* float, those of *Brasenia* are covered with slime, and most of the leaves of *Cabomba* are under water. Flowers in all cases are showy to very showy, some quite large. Flowers usually are solitary, actinomorphic (regular) and complete with sepals, petals, stamens and carpels. The carpels are hypogynous, and may be separate and free as in *Brasenia* and *Cabomba,* or united as in the remaining genera. Sepals mostly 4, sometimes 3, 5, 6, or 12, and completely free (polysepalous). Petals 3 to many, hypogynous, and usually numerous, and often showing a distinct transition between true stamens and true petals. Stamens 3 to many, usually numerous. Carpels 2 to 8 or more, usually numerous, and as indicated above, variously inserted and fused.

Field characteristics of the water-lilies vary with genus; if you find large, floating, more or less umbrella-like leaves which come from a stout rhizome buried down in the muck, chances are your plant is in the Water-lily Family. If solitary flowers on long stalks rising directly from the rhizome are present, you can be sure of the family. Lotus, *Nelumbo,* once was included in **Nymphaeaceae,** but special characteristics such as free-standing (above water) leaves, petal-like calyx, the flat-topped seed-bearing receptacle and albumin free seeds warrant a separate family, **Nelumbonaceae.**

The genera of the Water-lily Family which are encountered in horticulture or wild in North America are:

> *Brasenia*
> *Cabomba*
> *Euryale*
> *Nuphar*
> *Nymphaea*
> *Victoria*

Careful study and dissection of the flowers of this family reveal interesting relationships. The floral parts are arranged in spirals rather than concentric rings; the spiral arrangement (as visible on pine cones) is considered primitive, and is shared by other flowering families: **Ranunculaceae,** the buttercups or crowsfoots; the **Magnoliaceae,** or magnolias; and the **Dilleniaceae,** the dillenia family. The flattened disc of radiating stigmas characteristic of certain species is much like that of **Papaveraceae,** the poppies, and still other characteristics relate to the genus *Podophyllum,* mayapples, in the **Berberidaceae.** The rootstocks of many members of the Water-lily Family are rich in starch, mucilage and sugars which make them important foodstuffs in many tropical areas. Interestingly, the giant, tropical *Victoria* first flowered in artificial culture in England at Chatsworth and was named after Queen Victoria. The giant leaves will easily support a large child.

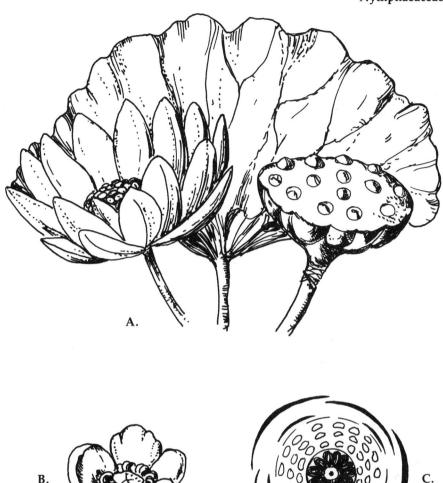

A.

B.

C.

D. $\dfrac{Ca^{3-6}\ Co^{3-\infty}\ S^{3-\infty}\ P^{2-\infty}}{Aq\ Cap\ Bac}$

Water-lily Family (including **Nelumbonaceae**)

A. Field sketch of flower, leaf, and fruit-bearing receptacle of lotus, *Nelumbium*. **B.** Sketch of spatterdock, *Nuphar*, flower. **C.** Floral diagram of spatterdock. **D.** Floral formula for the Family.

191

Nyssaceae Sour Gum Family

Two genera with about 10 species make up this very small family of deciduous trees with scaly winter buds. Leaves are alternate, simple, entire or toothed, without stipules. Flowers are perfect, or staminate or pistillate, sometimes with flowers of only one sex on a given plant, small, and in axillary or terminal heads, spikes, or umbels, actinomorphic. Calyx of 5 sepals, in male flowers minute, 5-toothed or indistinct, in pistillate flowers on the floral-cup immediately above the ovary (epigynous); petals 5 or more, or none, often very small and fleshy, deciduous, free; stamens as many or twice as many (or more) as petals, inserted (in staminate flowers) on the outside of a convex disc usually in 2 whorls or (in perfect flowers) inserted on the inner rim of the floral-cup; ovary inferior, 1-celled or 6 to 10-celled; ovules 1 in each cell, style usually elongated with simple or divided stigma. Fruit a drupe.

Field characteristics for this family of woody plants are not easy; look for the simple, alternate, exstipulate leaves. Then proceed to the often axillary flower clusters, flowers small, greenish, with sexes separate in some cases, or when both sexes are present, often with two large, white, petaloid bracts subtending the cluster. There has been considerable discussion about the proper location of the two genera in this family, and they have been (and still are) shifted by various authors.

The two genera are: *Nyssa*, the sour gums or tupelos, of S.E. U.S. and Asia, and *Davidia*, dove tree, of China. The latter is included in **Cornaceae**, the dogwoods, by some authors.

Oleaceae Olive Family

Mostly trees and shrubs, but a few herbs, about 600 species growing in sub-tropical or temperate climates make up the 29 genera in the Olive Family. The leaves are opposite, very rarely alternate or whorled, with no stipules, and simple or more commonly pinnately compound. Often the leaves are evergreen. The flowers are regular, mostly small and crowded but rarely large, not infrequently unisexual, mostly perfect. The calyx consists of 4 fused sepals, tubular with 4 lobes or teeth, but rarely apparently lacking (obsolete); corolla usually 4-lobed, but rarely lacking (red ash) or sometimes petals separate (not fused). Stamens 2, rarely 3 or 4, epipetalous; compound pistil of 2 carpels, superior; ovary usually 2-locular with 2, rarely more ovules, style simple with 2-lobed or simple stigma. Fruit a berry, drupe, capsule, or samara. Many members of this family are select ornamentals, several are economically important.

Field characters include the 4-lobed calyx, 4 petals or a 4-lobed corolla, 2 epipetalous stamens, and a superior 2-locule ovary with a simple style and simple or 2-lobed stigma. Combined with the above-described leaf characters, these floral characteristics point to the Olive Family.

Some of the Olive Family are:

Abeliophyllum	Jasminum	Osmanthus
Chionanthus	Ligustrum	Osmarea
Fontanesia	Noranhia	Parasyringa
Forrestiera	Notelaea	Phillyrea
Forsythia	Nyctanthes	Syringa
Fraxinus	Olea	

Oleaceae

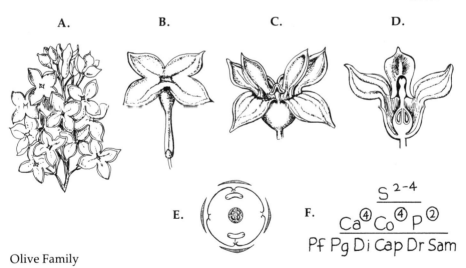

A.   B.   C.   D.

E.   F.

$$\underline{S^{2-4}}$$
$$Ca^{④} Co^{④} P^{②}$$
Pf Pg Di Cap Dr Sam

Olive Family

A. Field sketch of a lilac, *Syringa vulgaris*, a portion only of the flower head. **B.** Sketch of a single lilac flower. **C.** Flower of the olive, *Olea europea*. **D.** Olive flower in longitudinal section. **E.** Floral diagram of lilac. **F.** Floral formula for the **Oleaceae**.

193

Onagraceae Evening-primrose Family

Twenty to 36 genera include the 650 or more species of annual, biennial, or perennial herbs, or shrubs or trees (rarely) in the **Onagraceae**, depending on family limits; not uncommonly the family as presented here is separated into 3 or more families. These are found mostly in the temperate portions of the western U.S. and Mexico, but also in S. America, and some are found elsewhere in the world. Leaves usually opposite or whorled, rarely alternate, mostly simple, stipules usually lacking, or if present, often glandular. Flowers often showy, axillary, spicate or racemose, usually actinomorphic but sometimes irregular, mostly complete or rarely lacking petals; epigynous (ovary inferior), or peri-epigynous (with a floral-cup, often tube-shaped, above the inferior ovary); sepals commonly 4 (rarely 2 to 3 or 5 to 6) separate or united, inserted on the outer rim of the tube; petals commonly 4 (rarely numbered as the sepals, sometimes absent), free (polypetalous), inserted on the rim of the tube (or just above the ovary); stamens as many or twice as many as the calyx lobes and inserted on the summit of the tube (or just above the inferior ovary); compound pistil usually of 4, rarely of 2 to 6, carpels, style single, slender, stigma 4 or 2-lobed or capitate, ovary inferior, with 4 (or 2 to 6) cells, ovules numerous. Fruit a capsule (often ridged or winged) with many sometimes hairy seeds, or a berry (as in *Fuchsia*), or a nut.

In flower this is an easy family to recognize in most cases; the distinctly inferior ovary (look at some *Fuchsia* and *Oenothera* flowers), and the organization of sepals and petals in 4's definitely point to **Onagraceae**; even when the flower parts are in 2's, the long tube with the many-seeded, inferior ovary, and with stamens in the throat of the tube, make identification fairly easy.

Among the genera of **Onagraceae** to be encountered in cultivation or in the wild in the U.S. are:

Circaea	*Gaura*	*Oenothera*
Clarkia	*Godetia*	*Semeiandra*
Epilobium	*Jussiaea (or Jussieua)*	*Stenosiphon*
Eucharidium	*Lopezia*	*Zauschneria*
Fuchsia	*Ludwigia*	

Previously, the water-chestnut, *Trapa natans*, was included here, but now is in its own family, **Hydrocaryaceae**. The shoots of *Epilobium* have been used as pot-herbs and all species are grand honey plants; the roots of *Oenothera biennis* cultivars are eaten in Europe; the fruits of some fuchsias are eaten, *Jussiaea* supplies a yellow dye, and some of the woody fuchsias yield both ink and a black dye. *Fuchsia excorticata*, a shreddy-barked tree from New Zealand is most unusual; the pollen is a brilliant, royal blue! It is worth a trip to the Strybing Arboretum in Golden Gate Park, San Francisco, to see this phenomenon.

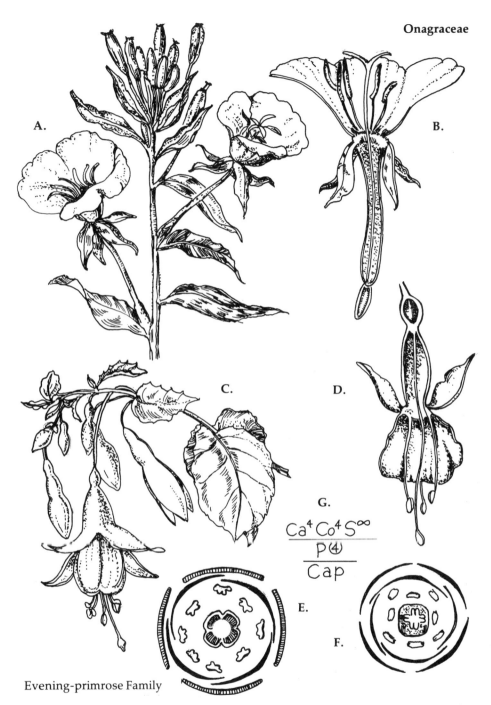

A. **A.** B.

C. **D.**

G.

$$\frac{Ca^4\, Co^4\, S^\infty}{P\,\underline{(4)}}$$
$$\overline{Cap}$$

E.

F.

Evening-primrose Family

A. Field sketch of sundrop, *Oenothera fruticosa*. **B.** Flower of evening-primrose, *Oenothera biennis*, in longitudinal section. **C.** Sketch of *Fuchsia*. **D.** *Fuchsia* flower in longitudinal section. **E.** Floral diagram of *Oenothera*. **F.** Floral diagram of willowherb, *Epilobium*. **G.** Floral formula for the Family.

195

Orchidaceae Orchis Family

The more than 20,000 species of **Orchidaceae** are distributed through more than 600 genera; while the greatest number of these are tropical (often found high in mountainous areas), several genera with numerous species are indigenous to various parts of the U.S. and a few are found in arctic regions. The majority of tropical species are epiphytic while those native to non-tropical areas are mostly terrestrial; some few of the latter group are without chlorophyll, living on decaying organic matter in the soil as saprophytes. Most orchids are perennials with bulbous, tuberous, or thickened fleshy leaves, stems and roots, but some bear more "normal" leaves; there is great variation in the vegetative character of orchids; leaves mostly are alternate, simple, entire, thin or often thick and more or less fleshy or leathery, linear, oblong, or orbicular. Flower scapes may arise from the base of the plant, from the axils of leafy stems, or from the leaves themselves, or may be terminal. Flowers are zygomorphic, sometimes bi-laterally symmetrical and attractive, but often strangely irregular and grotesque, oddly blotched, striped, or otherwise marked, or in some species, flowers are very small, even tiny, greenish, whitish, or yellowish or lurid, inconspicuous; they are complete or rarely staminate or pistillate; with a perianth of 2 whorls of 3 segments each, all petal-like, epigynous; the calyx of 3, usually separate, sepals inserted on the rim of the floral-cup, usually fairly regular; corolla epigynous, usually two petals similar and a third enlarged into a lip (labellum) and often sacchate; the central structure in an orchid flower is called the *column* composed of a single fertile stamen (or in *Cypripedium* and some other genera of 2 stamens with or without the rudiment of a 3rd) united competely with the fleshy style; the stigmatic surface usually is on the lower side of the column, and below it lies the anther with sometimes loose, granular pollen, or more commonly, waxy pollen aggregated into two masses called *pollinia* which may be free in the anther or attached by a stalk to a viscid apical or stigmatic gland. The structure of the column is quite variable but the basic components remain fairly constant; the compound pistil is composed of 3 united carpels, style and stigma are involved in the column, ovary inferior, 1 to 3-celled, with a vast number of dust-like seeds which, in most cases, consist only of a minute embryo enclosed in a few rather loose cells. Fruit is a dihiscent capsule.

While the form of orchid flowers and orchid plants varies widely, with many sorts more or less resembling non-orchidaceous species so far as plant form and flower are concerned, the column, in its many forms, and the capsule with myriads of nearly microscopic seeds, distinguishes **Orchidaceae** every time.

Even a "popular" encyclopedic horticultural reference work will list three to four hundred orchid genera, and a partial list is relatively meaningless. For local, indigenous species consult a scholarly *Flora* for your district; another way is to look for monographic works on native orchids in local botanic garden or horticutural society publications. For complete lists refer to the botanic literature or to references such as J. Hutchinson's *The Genera of Flowering Plants*. Bookshelves are replete with popular works on orchids which purport to supply accurate information on genera, species, culture, and so on, but mostly are of value only for the illustrations they contain and too often these are mislabeled.

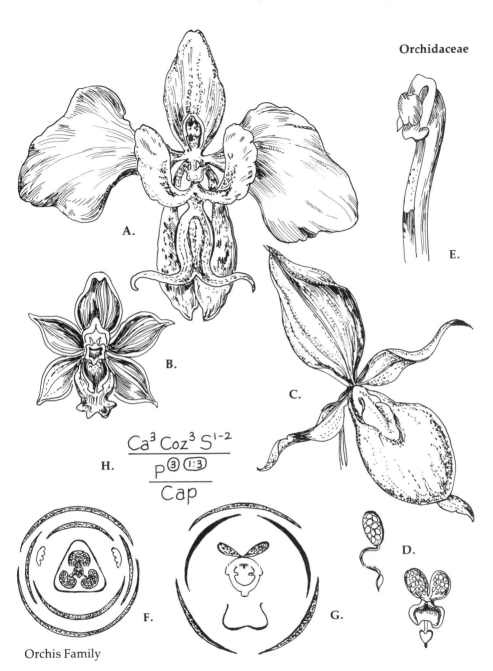

A.

B.

C.

E.

D.

$$\frac{Ca^3 \; Coz^3 \; S^{1-2}}{P^{③} ①③}$$
$$\overline{Cap}$$

H.

F.

G.

Orchis Family

A. Field sketch of the tropical moth orchid, *Phalaenopsis*. **B.** Field sketch of *Epipactis* flower. **C.** Field sketch of yellow lady's slipper, *Cypripedium pubescens*. **D.** Single pollen mass with its elastic thread (a pollinium), and a pair of pollinia united with the specialized female structure (all is known as the *gynandrium* or *column*). **E.** Another type of gynandrium, showing a single, lobed pollen mass directly above the stigmatic surface. **F.** Floral diagram of *Cypripedium*. **G.** A floral diagram for *Orchis*, simple, but showing the 3 sepals, 3 petals one bent to indicate a saccate lip, and the central column with 2 pollinia. **H.** Floral formula for the **Orchidaceae**.

197

Oxalidaceae Wood-sorrel Family

Mostly tropical or sub-tropical, some from temperate regions (most in S. America and S. Africa), 8 genera include about 950 species, mostly perennial herbs. Leaves alternate, often trifoliate, sometimes palmately or pinnately compound, without stipules. Most species with sensitive cushion (pulvinus) at the base of leaves and show sleep movements. Flowers usually large, in cymes, complete (e.g., with calyx, corolla, stamens and pistil), actinomorphic (regular = radially symmetrical), hypogynous; calyx of 5 free sepals, overlapping and persistent; corolla of 5 petals rarely united at the base, often twisted or overlapping; stamens 10, more or less connate (fused) at the base, sometimes 5 of them lack anthers; compound pistil (5 carpels), superior, with 5 styles, ovary with 5 cells with 2 to many ovules. Fruit a capsule with each cell dehiscent, or a berry. Wood-sorrels are very like the **Geraniaceae** but differ in fruit form and in the sour watery juice of many of the **Oxalidaceae.**

Most commonly encountered sorts are herbs, though the woody ones are in some botanical garden conservatories. Look for the typical digitate, trifoliate, or often palmately compound leaves rising in clusters, and especially for the regular pentamerous (five-parted), 10 to rarely 15-androus (stamened) flowers with superior ovary(s) and most commonly with a capsule seed pod. The typical "sour-grass" taste is a clincher if floral characters are confirmed. Do not be confused if stamens or styles or both are of different lengths in flowers on the same plant or on separate plants of the same species; this phenomenon is known as dimorphism (trimorphism) and is fairly common in some species of *Oxylis*.

The most commonly encountered native and cultivated genera of **Oxalidaceae** are:

> *Averrhoa*
> *Biophytum*
> *Ionoxalis*
> *Oxalis*

Many of the bulbous or tuberous species of *Oxalis* make ideal plants for growing indoors, but beginners often fail with them because they do not understand the growth cycle, especially the rest period, of these. Consult a reliable garden encyclopedia or bulb reference book for seasonal instructions for each species.

Oxalis Family

A. Field sketch of *Oxalis*. **B.** Stamens of *Oxalis*, showing varying lengths. **C.** Floral diagram for the Family. **D.** Floral formula for the Family.

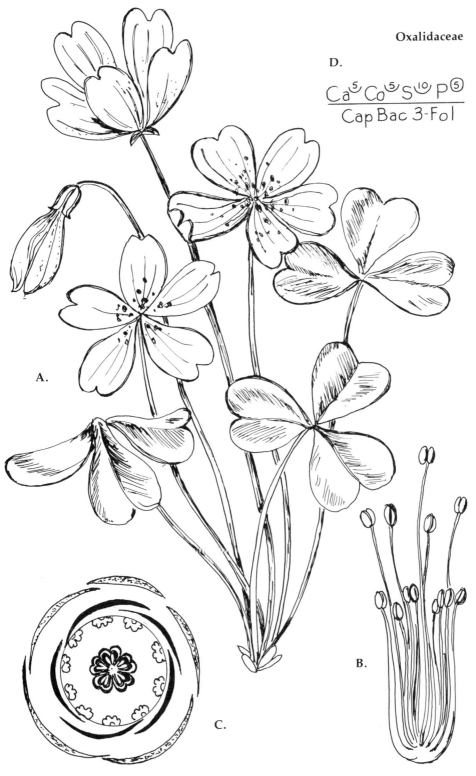

D.

$$\frac{Ca^{5} \; Co^{5} \; S^{10} \; P^{⑤}}{Cap \; Bac \; 3\text{-}Fol}$$

A.

C.

B.

Papaveraceae Poppy Family (including **Fumariaceae**)

A family of at least 32 genera and approximately 650 species, mostly North Temperate or Sub-tropical, this family includes many superior garden ornamentals as well as some choice wildflowers. Today, botanists separate this traditional group into at least two (sometimes more) distinct families, especially, **Papaveraceae** and **Fumariaceae**; note distinctions by formulas following genera list. Almost all are herbs, and most have yellow, orange, or sometimes white milky juice which often is narcotic and poisonous. Leaves with no stipules are alternate (upper sometimes whorled), simple, entire, lobed or deeply indented. Flowers perfect, regular or zygomorphic, hypogynous. The sepals, 2 rarely 3 or 4, fall as buds open; petals are imbricated and often wrinkled in the bud, 4 to 12 (often many more in "double" cultivar blossoms), and falling early. Stamens are hypogynous, free, 4−6 or many, anthers on slender filaments. Superior pistil with unilocular ovary (in *Papaver* imperfectly many locular, in *Glaucium* bilocular) containing many ovules. Fruit of this family usually is a capsule opening by pores or valves with mostly parietal placentation, or sometimes 1-seeded and indehiscent.

Field characters include colored, milky juice (not so in **Fumariaceae**), alternate leaves with no stipules on herbaceous perennials, 2 or 3 caducous sepals, 4 or more short-lived petals, and 4, 6 or a mass of stamens surrounding a bulky pistil which often has a massive often flattened stigma.

Some of the genera in this family are:

Adlumia	*Eomecon*	*Papaver*
Argemone	*Eschscholzia*	*Platystigma*
Bocconia	*Fumaria*	*Pteridophyllum*
Cathcartia	*Glaucium*	*Roemeria*
Chelidonium	*Hunnemannia*	*Romneya*
Corydalis	*Hylomecon*	*Sanguinaria*
Dendromecon	*Hypecoum*	*Sarcocapnos*
Dicentra	*Macleaya*	*Stylomecon*
Dicranostigma	*Meconopsis*	*Stylophorum*

Note: The Poppy Family is divided usually into two quite distinct families; study the differences for a clear understanding of the characteristics of these families. Family **Papaveraceae** has milky or colored juice, regular flowers with two or three sepals which fall early, and free, hypogynous petals (4 to 12), and numerous stamens, as characterized by *Sanguinaria* (blood-root) or *Papaver* (poppy). Family **Fumariaceae** includes delicate herbs with watery juice and compound, dissected leaves with flowers seemingly irregular, laterally compressed. Sepals are greatly reduced, scale-like, the corolla is laterally compressed, 4 petals in pairs with the outer petals usually with spreading tips and one or both spurred or saccate at the base. Stamens are 4, free and opposite the petals or 6, in 2 groups of 3 on either side of the pistil. Characteristic genera include *Adlumia*, climbing fumitory, *Corydalis*, *Dicentra*, bleeding-heart, Dutchman's breeches, and *Fumaria*, Fumitory.

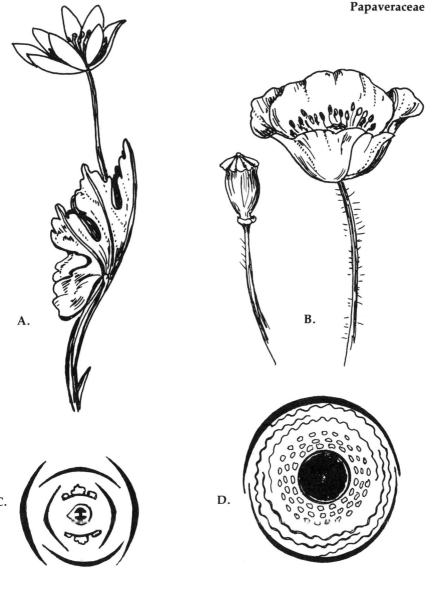

E. $$\frac{Ca^{2(3)} Co^{4-\infty} S^{\infty} P^{\underline{(2-\infty)}}}{}$$ Milky Cap

Poppy Family

A. Field sketch of bloodroot, *Sanguinaria canadensis*; note the apparent absence of sepals; these fell when the petals expanded. **B.** Sketch of a flower and capsule of the corn poppy, *Papaver rhoeas*. **C** Floral diagram of yellow fumewort, *Corydalis flavula*. **D.** Floral diagram of poppy. **E.** Floral formula for **Papaveraceae.**

Passifloraceae Passion-flower Family

Twelve genera, including about 600 species of herbaceous plants climbing by axillary tendrils, or trees or shrubs native in warm-temperature and tropical America, Asia, Australia, and Madagascar, comprise the **Passifloraceae**. Leaves of these usually are alternate and simple (often gently lobed), rarely compound, and often mottled, sometimes with stipules. Flowers are unique, with a quite complicated structure. Flowers usually perfect or unisexual, perigynous, actinomorphic (regular); calyx usually with 5 (rarely 3) sepals free or somewhat united at the base, persistent, often colored and petal-like; corolla of 5 petals (rarely 3 or lacking), separate, inserted on the rim of the floral-cup; just within the whorl of petals may be the *corona*, a fringe of usually brightly colored, usually thread-like structures; the central structure of the flower is intricate, and varies; stamens 3 to 5 or more, usually opposite the petals, inserted on the edge of the floral-cup at the base of the petals (at the base of the corona), with the filaments fused into a tube which surrounds the stalk (gynophore) of the pistil, separating above, with separate anthers, large, and attached at the middle; compound pistil of 3 carpels with 1 or more styles, free or stigmas often united, the superior ovary commonly is raised on a gynophore, 1-celled, with 3 parietal placentae, ovules numerous. Fruit a berry or a capsule.

The distinctive feature of this family is the flower structure, especially, the colorful, fringed corona overlaying the rather flat ring of petals and sepals, and the strange central structure of stamens and the elevated pistil. By all means, dissect a few flowers of *Passiflora*, passion-flower, to become familiar with their structure. In most of the **Passifloraceae** the more or less woody vine with tendrils at the nodes also is characteristic. But there is a weird African sort, *Adenia*, with a basketball-sized fleshy, woody base which supports from its upper side a swatch of thorny, sparsely branched, usually leafless woody branches. For this one you have to happen on a flower; the form, a desert adaptation, could be anything.

Among the genera of **Passifloraceae** found in cultivation or encountered wild in North America are:

Adenia	*Modecca*	*Passiflora*
Gynopleura	*Ophiocaulon*	*Smeathmannia*

The pulpy fruits of several of the tropical species of *Passiflora* are edible, at least one is narcotic, and another, *P. quadrangularis* (granadilla), with edible fruit, has a very poisonous root. Hardy sorts of these, especially *Passiflora incarnata*, but also the much smaller *P. lutea*, are well worth growing in the garden; they are hardy at least to St. Louis, but to extend the range plant them against the south foundation of a sun-drenched building.

A.

B. $\dfrac{Co^5}{Ca^{\overset{(3-5)}{\,}} S^{5-x} P^{\circledS}}$ $Cap\ Ber$

Passion-flower Family

A. Field sketch of passion flower, *Passiflora incarnata*, showing the elaborate corona — slender filaments — which grow radially from the axis of the flower. **B.** The generalized floral formula reflects that the petals, when present, are situated on the rim of the calyx.

203

Phytolaccaceae Pokeweed Family

A small family of perhaps 120 species in 17 genera, the members of the **Phytolaccaceae** are mostly tropical American with a few species in South Africa and a few more in temperate North America. They are herbaceous (always with a heavy, woody rootstock) or shrubs or trees, with alternate (rarely opposite), simple, entire leaves without stipules or with stipules greatly reduced (tubercle-like, rare); leaves usually are glabrous. Flowers are apetalous, inconspicuous, often greenish or white and usually in terminal or axillary racemes; usually bracts and perhaps two bracteoles (tiny bracts) subtend the flowers. Flowers usually are perfect, rarely unisexual. The perianth, sepals only, is regular, with 4 or 5 divisions which are succulent or leathery; the separate sepals may persist in fruit but never are modified; stamens usually are the same number as sepals and alternate with them, but may be numerous and sometimes connate at their bases. Usually filaments are inserted on a hypogynous disc, but in some few cases are perigynous; the pistil usually is superior, very rarely partially inferior, carpels one or usually several, free or more commonly united into a several-celled ovary; ovules one per locule (carpel). Styles one per carpel. Fruit a juicy berry almost always with many seeds, a drupe or an achene. Some botanists separate out genera of the family as presented here to erect other families as **Barbeuiaceae**, **Petiveriaceae**, and **Stegnospermataceae**.

In the field look for the usually drooping and slender terminal or axillary racemes of quite small greenish or white flowers. Flowers are very like those of **Chenopodiaceae** excepting the usually compound ovary of the Poke-weeds which develops into a many-seeded berry as contrasted with the 1-seeded nutlet of the Chenopods.

Another key character is the bitter, acrid sap — not recommended to taste, as often these plants are quite poisonous. While the herbaceous Chenopods and Amaranths usually have tough, stringy, and often ridged stems and rather harsh foliage, the Pokeweeds usually are more succulent in stem and leaf, with leaves glaucous and stems often delicately to strongly tinted and with a characteristic bloom.

Few of the **Phytolaccaceae** are of horticultural importance; members which may be encountered are:

Ercilla	*Peteveria*	*Rivina*
Ledenbergia	*Phytolacca*	*Trichostigma*

Rivina humilis, the rouge-plant, and *Trichostigma peruvianum* occasionally are used as greenhouse ornmentals but are not to be recomeded because of their poisonous quality. European gardeners often plant the American pokeweed, *Phytolacca americana* as an ornamental. Actually, this plant should not be grown in any horticultural situation as the plant, a long-lived perennial, acts as a virus reservoir; many highly destructive viruses survive in its tissues and piercing-sucking insects (aphids, leaf-hoppers, etc.) transmit these to susceptible plants throughout the garden. While country folk gather pokeweed shoots and young leaves in spring for greens, care must be taken to avoid the very poisonous root. American Indians used the juice of the purple berries for a rich red dye.

Pokeweed Family

Stylized field sketch of *Phytolacca* branch with flowers.

Plantaginaceae Plantain Family

A family of 3 genera with about 270 species of annual or perennial herbs (some few more or less woody species also) which occur generally in the North and South Temperate zones but with centers of distribution in the Mediterranean basin and in the central Andes of S. America, these are known to us largely as pernicious weeds and rarely, as rock garden plants. The exstipulate leaves mostly are basal, alternate or rarely opposite, mostly simple; flowers, small, perfect or rarely monoecious, in dense terminal bracteate spikes or heads on scapes which may be elongated, regular (actinomorphic), hypogynous; synsepalous calyx, 4-cleft, persistent; sympetalous corolla, 4-lobed usually dry, membranous, and veinless; stamens 4 or rarely 2, mostly epipetalous, alternating with the lobes of the corolla, inserted near the top of the tube, filaments mostly very long and slender, exserted, with mobile anthers; compound pistil of 2 closely united carpels with a single, long, slender terminal style and a small, capitate stigma, ovary superior, usually 2-celled, but sometimes 1 to 4-celled, ovules 1 to many in each cell. Fruit a circumscissile capsule (a capsule which opens by a cap = pyxis) or indehiscent nutlet invested by a dry and persistent calyx.

In the field look for plants with basal rosettes of linear-veined leaves and with slender (pencil-thick) spikes of small, nondescript papery flowers densely packed above a short or long leafless scape. Then proceed to the typically tetramerous (4-part) flowers, as described above. These are easy once you get the feel of leaves and flower spikes, but a hand lens is essential for flower structure, and a dissecting microscope is better.

While in earlier days the mucilaginous character of the wet seeds of these was of medicinal value — the mucilage still is used in India to stiffen muslin cloth — their present value lies in their use as food by songbirds, and, no doubt, in generating business for lawn service men who spray lawns for broadleaved weeds.

The commonest genus is *Plantago*, with several notably weedy species, and *Littorella*, a very similar sort which inhabits pond and stream margins, as the name indicates.

Plantain Family

A. Field sketch of *Plantago lanceolata*, the buckhorn plantain. **B.** Sketch of a flower of *Plantago major*. **C.** Floral diagram of a plantain. **D.** Floral formula for the Family; "Pyx" refers to pyxis, the term for a capsule with circumscissile dehiscence, that is splitting around, for a lid and bowl effect.

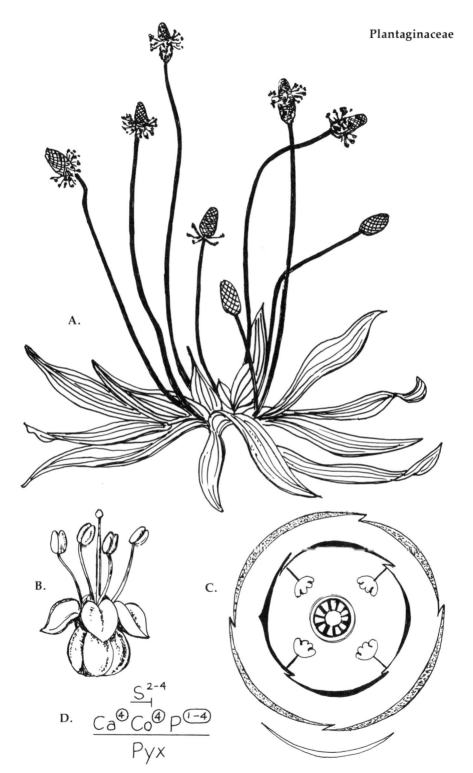

A.

B.

C.

D. $\dfrac{\overset{2-4}{\underset{\mid}{S}}}{\underset{Pyx}{Ca^{④}Co^{④}P^{①-④}}}$

Platanaceae Plane-tree (Sycamore) Family

One genus, *Platanus*, with perhaps 10 species and several horticultural hybrids, makes up this small family which is difficult to place properly in relation to other plant families. All members are large trees, various species from N. America, S. Europe, and S. Asia. They are deciduous, and with scaling bark which reveals large patches of white, cream, yellow, or lurid-yellow underbark. Leaves are simple, broadly lobed, palmate-fashion; the base of the petiole with the stipules sheathes the lateral buds — a characteristic feature. Young leaves are rusty-tomentose. Flowers are very tiny, monoecious, in dense, globular heads on rather long, dangling peduncles. Flowers perigynous, perianth inconspicuous but apparently with two whorls of 3 to 8 more or less uncertain parts; stamens 3 to 8, alternating with petals and free; simple pistils usually 3 to 8, each with 1 locule and 1 ovule. The pistillate flower clusters mature into dangling balls; the carpels remain free, but jammed together among the remains of the floral parts; each becomes a narrowly obconical, 1-seeded nutlet with a ring of bristly hairs at the base.

The characteristics in the field include the exfoliating bark, *the completely sheathed buds*, and the dangling balls of flowers or fruits. No other tree unites these characteristics.

Sycamore wood is used (with cottonwood) to make berry boxes and baskets, but it is more valuable, especially when quarter-sawed, for panelling. The grain and streaky coloring is beautiful.

A.

B. $$\frac{Ca^{3-8}\ Co^{3-8}\ S^{3-8}\ P^{3-8}}{Mo\ Nutlet}$$

Plane-tree (Sycamore) Family

A. Field sketch of *Platanus* twig with heads of fruits. **B.** Floral formula for Sycamore Family.

209

Plumbaginaceae Plumbago or Leadwort Family

A family mainly of the Mediterranean basin but found elsewhere in mild climates; the 19 genera consisting of 775 species which often grow near the sea and commonly on salty land. They are known as sea-lavenders, sea-pinks, and leadworts. Most are herbaceous, some are shrubby. The leaves are alternate, simple and entire, without stipules. Often the leaves form a basal rosette. Usually the flowers are numerous, sometimes small; they are perfect, regular, and in dry-bracted spikes, heads, or panicles that some-times are one-sided. The calyx is tubular or funnel-shaped, 5-lobed, mostly ribbed or plaited, scarious, sometimes colored, and with bracts at the base; the corolla of 5 almost free or tubular lobes, often dry and persistent; stamens 5, often inserted on the petal lobes (epipetalous); pistil with superior ovary which is 1-celled and often with 1 ovule, styles 5 usually separate, rarely united, stigmas 5 or 5-lobed. Fruit is a nutlet, capsule or other.

At first glance some Plumbago Family species resemble members of the Primrose Family but the separate styles and stigmas, and the 1-celled ovary with a single ovule make the separation. Look for the small, leaf-like bracts at the base of the calyx. Sometimes small bracts occur more or less irregu-larly at nodes, especially in *Plumbago*. Some members of this family vaguely resemble the Phlox Family, but make the separation with 5 carpels, united, and 1 ovule in **Plumbaginaceae**, 3 carpels (rarely 2) united, each with 1 or more ovules in **Polemoniaceae.**

Some genera in the Leadwort Family are:

> *Acantholimon*
> *Armeria*
> *Ceratostigma*
> *Limoniastrum*
> *Limonium*
> *Plumbago*
> *Statice*

Leadwort Family

A. Field sketch of sea-lavender, *Limonium latifolium*. **B.** Flower of sea-lavender. **C.** Flower of Cape plumbago, *Plumbago capensis*; illustrations B and C show the characteristically synsepalous calyx with free lobes, and sympetalous corolla, tubu-lar, with flaring limb, of this family. **D.** Floral diagram of sea-lavender. **E.** Floral formula for the family; the lower line indicates the straw-flower or immortelle nature of the flowers though *Cap* (capsule) for fruit identification would be more typical.

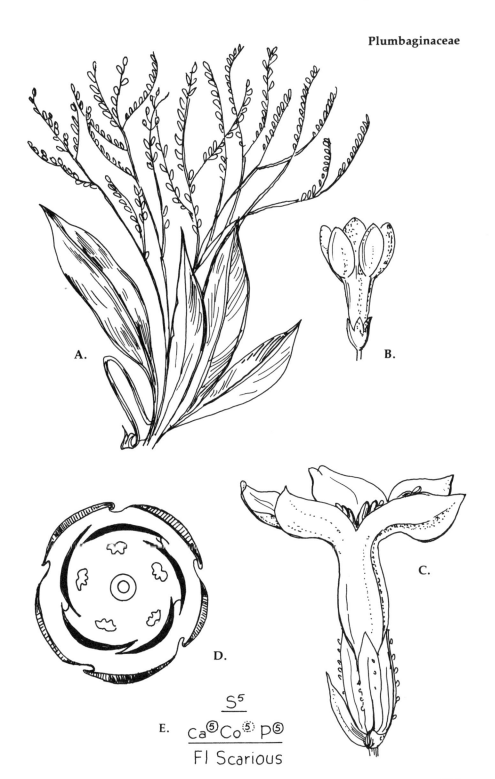

A.

B.

C.

D.

$$\frac{S^5}{Ca^{\textcircled{5}}Co^{\textcircled{5}}P^{\textcircled{5}}}$$

E.

Fl Scarious

Polemoniaceae Phlox Family

Species, about 325, of the Phlox Family usually are soft annuals or perennials, but rarely are shrubby or small trees. There are 18 genera, mostly in N. America, some in the Andes Mountains of S. America, and a few species in Europe and Asia. Leaves without stipules are alternate or opposite, usually entire, simple, pinnately compound or palmately compound. Flowers regular or nearly so, complete, and often crowded into heads or corymbs. Calyx 5-lobed or toothed, persistent; corolla 5-lobed usually with a narrow tube and with salver-form lobes; stamens 5, epipetalous, alternating with the lobes of the corolla; pistil superior, inserted on a disc but sessile, ovary with 3 (rarely 2 or 5) united carpels, and with 1 to many ovules in each cell. One often elongated style, stigmas usually 3, or 2 to 5-lobed, equalling cells in the ovary. Fruit usually a dehiscent capsule, valves usually breaking away from the three-sided central column.

Put several characters together to be sure of this rather variable family. Look first at flower characteristics, 5-lobed calyx and corolla, 5 epipetalous stamens sometimes inserted at varying levels on the corolla tube alternating with corolla lobes, and commonly a 3-celled superior ovary with a distinct style and 3 stigmas. Leaf characteristics are so variable as to be of little value, though the generally "soft" anatomy of the plant leads one to sense this family.

Some genera in the Phlox Family are:

Bonplandia	*Collomia*	*Navarretia*
Cantua	*Gilia*	*Phlox*
Cobaea	*Loeselia*	*Polemonium*

A. Field sketch of phlox.

$$\frac{S^5}{Ca^⑤ Co^⑤ P^③}$$ Cap

C.

B.

Phlox Family

A. Field sketch of phlox. **B.** Floral diagram of common garden phlox. **C.** Floral formula for the **Polemoniaceae**.

213

Polygalaceae Milkwort Family

Twelve or 13 genera including about 800 species from temperate and warm regions, world wide, make up this family of herbs, shrubs and small trees, some climbing or twining. Leaves mostly alternate, simple, entire, without stipules (exstipulate). Flowers zygomorphic (irregular), hypogynous, and perfect. Calyx of 5 sepals, imbricate, separate or more commonly slightly connate, the two inner (lateral) sepals larger, even petal-like, often winged; corolla commonly of 3 petals, rarely 5, at least the 2 upper, and sometimes all, more or less connate or coherent and sometimes coherent with the stamen tube, inner (lower) petal concave and often with a fringed crest (keel); stamens usually 8, rarely 4 or 6, connate into a tube which is split down at the back, or rarely free, stamens usually in 2 whorls; anthers commonly opening by terminal pores or slits; pistil usually with 2-celled ovary which is superior, a single style, 1 to 4 stigmas, usually a single ovule in each cell. Fruit a capsule, rarely a drupe or samara.

In the field novice taxonomists happen on a Milkwort and think they have something in the **Orchidaceae**, but as quickly as they examine the alternate, netted leaves, and the flower's 5 sepals, clustered stamens, and superior ovary, they know they have something else. Sound field characters include the distinctive perianth, the band of connate stamens surrounding the 2-celled pistil, and, of course, the rather uncommon dehiscence of the anthers which open through terminal pores or slits.

Among the genera of **Polygalaceae** which may be encountered in nature or in cultivation are:

> *Comesperma*
> *Krameria*
> *Monnina*
> *Munatia*
> *Muraltia*
> *Polygala*
> *Securidaca*

We know these mostly as rather rare wild flowers or as choice specimens for the rock garden; a few of the genera mentioned above occur in conservatory collections where the usually evergreen foliage and unusual flowers attract considerable attention. One N. American species, *Polygala senega*, senega or seneca snakeroot, has been used as an emetic or cathartic while others reputedly were antidotes for snakebite, possibly due to the bitter and astringent properties of many of this family. The old Greek name Polygala refers to the supposed stimulative action of these plants on the lactation of cattle.

Milkwort Family

A. Floral diagram. **B.** and **C.** varying forms of flower of *Polygala*. **D.** Field sketch of *Polygala*. **E.** Floral formula.

Polygalaceae

A.

B.

C.

D.

E. $\dfrac{Ca^{3+2}\ Coz^{\textcircled{3}}\ S^{\textcircled{8}}\ P^{\textcircled{2}}}{Cap}$

215

Polygonaceae Buckwheat Family

A very large family, about 40 genera with more than 750 species, with a largely North Temperate distribution, some few species are found in the tropics. Members of the **Polygonaceae** may be herbs, shrubs or trees; some species twine and climb. The stems of plants in this family usually are enlarged at the nodes, and almost always there is a papery sheath (*ochrea* or *ocrea*) which encloses the base of the petiole at the node. Leaves are alternate or very rarely opposite, simple, and almost always entire (smooth margin). Flowers are small, mostly regular, perfect or unisexual, and solitary or more commonly, clustered in spikes or racemes. The perianth of members of the Buckwheat Family is apetalous — that is, of sepals only, separate or only slightly joined; but occasionally the perianth consists of two whorls, the inner set enlarged and modified with hoods, spines, wings, or tubercles; perianth segments 2 to 6, most commonly 3, 5, or 6; ovary, compressed or 3-angled, superior, with 3 or rarely 2 to 4 carpels, 1 celled, 1 ovule present; stigmas usually 3, rarely 2 or 4; stamens 3 to 9, rarely more, filaments usually free, inserted beneath the ovary. The fruit, which forms rather early, is a 3-angled nutlet (achene) or a lens-shaped (lenticular) nut, or fruits may be winged.

Once the field plantsman becomes familiar with the swollen "joints" (nodes), paper-wrapped (the ochrea), of this family there is no further trouble with identification, but if a question arises, the flower modifications and 3-angled nutlets clinch the identification.

Some familiar genera in the Buckwheat (knotweed) Family are:

Antigonon	*Eriogonum*	*Polygonella*
Atraphaxis	*Fagopyrum*	*Polygonum*
Brunnichia	*Muehlenbeckia*	*Rheum*
Calligonum	*Oxyria*	*Rumex*
Coccoloba	*Podopterus*	

Among the above are such familiar plants as sea-grape, buckwheat, smartweeds, knotweed, lace, or silver-lace vine, prince's feather, the rhubarbs — culinary and ornamental — and the many kinds of dock.

Buckwheat (Knotweed) Family

A. Field sketch of sour dock (*Rumex*). **B.** Flower of buckwheat, *Fagopyron*. **C.** Floral diagram of *Rumex* flower. **D.** Floral diagram of *Fagopyrum* flower. **E.** Generalized floral formula for the Family.

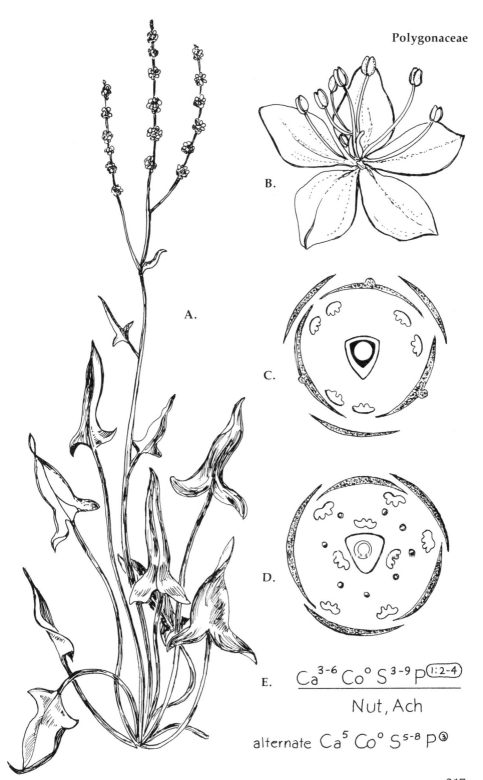

A.

B.

C.

D.

E. $\dfrac{Ca^{3-6} \ Co^{o} \ S^{3-9} \ P^{\boxed{1:2-4}}}{Nut, Ach}$

alternate $Ca^{5} \ Co^{o} \ S^{5-8} \ P^{\boxed{3}}$

217

Portulacaceae Purslane Family

The nearly 600 species in 17 to 19 genera of the **Portulacaceae** grow mostly in South America and in the Western United States, but with some species elsewhere. All are herbaceous, annual or perennial, or suffruticose, many with fleshy leaves, some with fleshy stems, plants often prostrate or caespitose, an adaptation to their desert habitat. Most have stipules which may be represented by axillary tufts of hair. Flowers are regular and perfect but often unsymmetrical due to the disparate number of sepals and petals. Usually the flowers are in cymes, but may be solitary or in racemes, and often they are showy. Calyx consists of 2 sepals, free or barely connate at the base; petals 4 to 5 (sometimes six), free or connate at the base and often fugaceous (shrivelling early); stamens in one or two whorls, hypogynous, usually 5, sometimes 10, rarely many, and inserted opposite the petals and below the pistil (hypogynous) except in *Portulaca*; pistil superior except in *Portulaca* where it is partly inferior, ovary of 2 to 8 united carpels, 1-celled usually with many ovules and basal or central placentation, styles usually several, with stigmatic surfaces on their inner faces. The fruit usually is a capsule opening along 3 seams (valves) or by a "pop-off" cap, rarely nut-like.

Key characteristics of this rather diverse family of plants include two sepals, the 1-celled ovary with many ovules and central placentation (ovules attached to a column of tissue rising through the center of the ovary), and several styles. Clinchers are fleshy stems or leaves or both, a corolla which lasts but briefly, and the herbaceous nature of the plants. Many species are mucilaginous, especially in *Portulaca*; some have a slightly bitter but harmless juice.

Many species of **Portulacaceae** are ornamental, a few are noted weeds, some few are edible:

Anacampseros	*Lewisia*	*Portulacaria*
Calandrinia	*Montia*	*Spraguea*
Claytonia	*Portulaca*	*Talinum*

Eastern North Americans know these through the rose-moss (*Portulaca grandiflora*) and Talinums of the flower garden, the spring-beauties, *Claytonia* spp., of the woodlands and open prairies, and the wretchedly invasive "pusley" or purslane, *Portulaca oleracea*, for beds and borders. Western Americans know other Claytonias, the exquisite Lewisias which include Montana's state flower and gave a name to the Bitterroot Mountains, the Calandrinias, and more Talinums. Species of Portulaca, Calandrinia, Talinum, and Claytonia have been used in the past as potherbs, and *Portulaca oleracea* was reputed to be of value not only for salads and cooked greens, but also as a source of vitamins to combat scurvy and even as a sedative!

Note: Recent largely technical research indicates that the 2 sepals of this family may be, in fact, bracts, which would require that the single perianth be considered as sepals making the corolla lacking. Bitterroot, rose-moss and spring-beauties with no petals? Such is progress.

A.

C.

$$\frac{Ca^{2} \; Co^{4-6} \; S^{4-\infty} \; P^{(2-8)}}{Cap}$$

B.

Purslane Family

A. Field sketch of rose-moss (*Portulaca grandiflora*) indicating succulent nature of the stems and leaves. **B.** Stylized longitudinal section of typical purslane flower. **C.** Typical floral formula for the Family, but note that infrequently the ovary may be partially inferior.

Primulaceae Primrose Family

   The Primrose Family includes 28 genera with more than 800 species, usually perennial (or annual) herbs but rarely sub-shrubs. Most of these are found in alpine regions but some occur in temperate zones; almost all occur north of the Equator. Leaves opposite, whorled or rarely alternate, often in basal rosettes, without stipules, and simple, rarely dissected, frequently glandular. Flowers perfect, mostly regular but rarely zygomorphic, almost always showy; calyx 5-toothed (rarely 4), persistent, sometimes becoming leaf-like; corolla mostly 5-lobed (rarely 4) commonly sympetalous but in some species petals free; corolla absent in some genera; stamens 5 (or 4 if petals are 4 and rarely 6 or 8) and often inserted on the corolla (epipetalous); pistil superior (rarely somewhat inferior), 1-celled, with 2 to 6 carpels, ovules many; pistil with a single style and stigma. Fruit is a capsule usually opening with teeth along the valves.
   In the field look for soft or somewhat fleshy leaves in a basal rosette (but some species have leafy items), one or more unbranched, leafless scapes bearing flowers in an umbel or in various sorts of bracteate clusters or rarely solitary. Commonly 5 calyx lobes, corolla with a short or long tube and rarely 4 but mostly 5 usually spreading lobes, epipetalous stamens opposite the corolla lobes, a superior ovary, pistil with a single style and stigma. Many species show heterostylism, that is, styles of different lengths in different flowers. Practice formulas and diagrams with Primula, Dodecatheon, Lysimachia, and Anagallis, all easy to find, and sharing various characteristics of the Family.
   Some genera in the Primrose Family are:

Anagallis	*Dodecatheon*	*Primula*
Androsace	*Douglasia*	*Samolus*
Centunculus	*Glaux*	*Soldanella*
Coris	*Hottonia*	*Trientalis*
Cortusa	*Lysimachia*	
Cyclamen	*Omphalogramma*	

Primrose Family

A. Field sketch of a hardy primrose, *Primula*. **B.** Enlarged flower of this primrose; note that the stigma is visible in the center of the flower, but the epipetalous stamens below it cannot be seen. **C.** Field sketch of scarlet pimpernel, *Anagallis arvensis*. **D.** Longitudinal section through a pimpernel flower. **E.** Floral diagram for *Primula*. **F.** General floral formula for the Family.

220

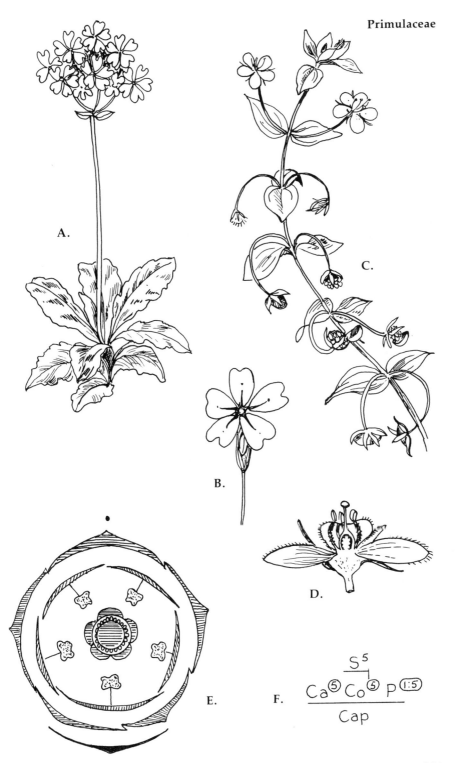

A.

B.

C.

D.

E.

F.

$$\frac{S^5}{Ca^{⑤} Co^{⑤} P^{⑴⁵}}$$

$$Cap$$

Pyrolaceae Wintergreen Family

This small family, 4–16 genera with about 75 species, delights plant lovers; all are strange-appearing, mostly difficult to grow, and thrilling to find in nature. This traditional treatment includes genera which botanists today separate into **Pyrolaceae** (evergreen foliage) and **Monotropaceae** (lacking chlorophyll). They are indigenous to the northern hemisphere. These are herbaceous or sub-shrubby, evergreen or sometimes without chlorophyll (hence, saprophytic or parasitic); leaves alternate, scattered, or basal, often thick and persistent, exstipulate. Flowers terminal and solitary, or in corymbs or racemes, perfect, actinomorphic (regular) and hypogynous; calyx of 4 or 5 more or less connate sepals (or wanting); corolla of 5 or rarely 4 (6 to 2 in *Monotropa*) separate petals (polypetalous) or petals somewhat united; stamens 10 (or 6 to 12), separate, anthers opening by apical pores or slits; compound pistil of 5, rarely 4 carpels, style slender, stigma usually capitate, ovary superior, as many cells as carpels, with central placentae and many ovules. Fruit a capsule splitting, usually, into 5 valves.

The white or amber flower stalks and flowers of the non-green genera are easily recognized; once you have seen an Indian pipe or pine-drops or sweet pinesap you never will forget; if you happen on to an unknown, non-green plant in the woods look for the highly modified flower or flowers, and carefully dissect a blossom. The usually polypetalous flowers, inverted anthers (as those of the White-alder Family), and the superior, 5-carpellate pistil with numerous ovules indicates **Pyrolaceae**. Confirm by the vegetative characteristics described above.

Only 3 genera of **Pyrolaceae** may be cultivated; wintergreen or pipsissewa, *Chimaphila* spp., one-flowered pyrola, *Moneses*, and shineleaf or wintergreen, *Pyrola* spp., make delightful plants for the wild garden. They are not easy, and should not be brought from the wild, but rather, puchased from a true propagator who raises his own stock. The parasitic and saprophytic genera, Indian pipe, *Monotropa*, pine-drops, *Pterospora*, and sweet pinesap, *Monotropsis*, cannot be cultivated due to their special nature. Often, when they appear in nature, they appear everywhere simultaneously, a flush of reproductive growth brought on by environmental conditions being just right.

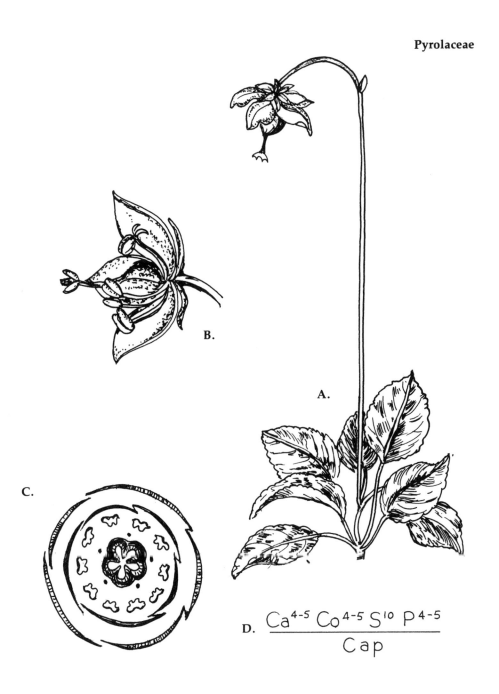

$$D. \quad \frac{Ca^{4-5} \, Co^{4-5} \, S^{10} \, P^{4-5}}{Cap}$$

Wintergreen (Pyrola) Family
(often the plants of this Family are included in **Ericaceae** in older literature)

A. Field sketch of a flowering plant of wood-nymph, *Moneses uniflora*. **B.** A single flower of *Moneses*. **C.** Floral diagram of wintergreen, *Pyrola*. **D.** Floral formula for the **Pyrolaceae**.

Ranunculaceae Buttercup or Crowfoot Family

An extremely large, diverse family; buttercup relatives exhibit widely varying characteristics. More than 2,000 species grouped in some 35–70 genera (depending on creation of new families) make up the Buttercup Family; most are herbaceous, some of these aquatic, a few are woody shrubs or climbers. A very few are annual herbs. Most occur in the Northern Hemisphere including alpine and arctic environments, a few reach into the Southern Hemisphere. Leaves alternate, rarely opposite or acaulescent, often dissected (crowfoot-like) or entire, leafstalks usually dilated sheath-like at the base and sometimes with stipule-like appendages though generally exstipulate. The sap of most **Ranunculaceae** is colorless and acrid, *often containing narcotic poisons.* Flowers are hypogynous, mostly perfect and complete, commonly actinomorphic but sometimes zygomorphic (as larkspur, *Delphinium*, and monkshood, *Aconitum*; the receptacle often is cone or dome-shaped. Calyx often colored like a corolla, sepals 3 (very rarely 2) to many, separate; corolla present or sometimes lacking, petals 3 (very rarely 2) to many, separate, often with nectaries; stamens free, usually many; pistils simple, distinct and unconnected, several to many (rarely single); ovary always superior, 1-celled, 1 to many ovules.

Field characteristics include the domed or cone-shaped receptacle supporting numerous separate simple pistils (carpels), with numerous stamens; usually these are clue enough. Quite often petals are missing and colorful sepals take their place, as in *Anemone, Anemonella, Clematis, Hepatica, Thalictrum,* and more.

The Buttercup Family is considered to be a basic primitive group of Dicotyledonous plants; probably the earliest Monocotyledonous families were derived from basic Dicots of a similar nature. The lowest Monocots share many characteristics with primitive Dicots such as **Ranunculaceae** and **Magnoliaceae.**

Some members of the Buttercup Family:

Aconitum	*Clematopsis*	*Nigella*
Actaea	*Coptis*	*Paeonia*
Adonis	*Delphinium*	*Paraquilegia*
Anemone	*Eranthis*	*Pulsatilla*
Anemonella	*Helleborus*	*Ranunculus*
Anemonopsis	*Hepatica*	*Semiaquilegia*
Aquilegia	*Hydrastis*	*Thalictrum*
Callianthemum	*Isopyrum*	*Trautvetteria*
Caltha	*Knowltonia*	*Trollius*
Cimicifuga	*Myosurus*	*Xanthorhiza*
Clematis	*Naravelia*	

Buttercup Family

A. Field sketch of marsh-marigold, *Caltha palustris*. **B.** Longitudinal section of a buttercup, *Ranunculus*, flower showing the many simple pistils surrounded by a ring of stamens, a whorl of petals and an outer whorl of sepals. **C.** Floral diagram of marsh-marigold. **D.** Floral formula for the **Ranunculaceae.**

A.

B.

C.

D. $\dfrac{Ca^{3-\infty}\ Co^{0-\infty}\ S^{\infty}\ P^{\infty}}{Ach\ Fol\ Bac}$

Resedaceae Mignonette Family

Largely of the Mediterranean basin, but also native to Europe, Africa, Asia, California, the Mignonettes include 70 species in 6 genera, mostly annual or perennial herbs, a few woody plants. It is a small family, with very few horticulturally interesting species. Leaves are alternate, simple, entire or often pinnately lobed; stipules reduced to glandular tubercles. Flowers are in racemes or terminal spikes. The flowers of **Resedaceae** are very strange. Nearly regular, they are zygomorphic due to the strange floral disc in the middle of each blossom. Calyx usually 4 to 7-lobed, polysepalous; petals separate, usually 4 to 7, entire or partially split, often small and inconspicuous, sometimes entirely lacking; the axis of the flower extends through the insertion of the petals and flares into a flattened, lop-sided disc above the petals; stamens are inserted on this disc as is the pistil; stamens 3 to 40, with slender filaments and neat, bilobed anthers; these surround the central pistil which is superior, sessile, of 2 to 6 separate or united carpels; mostly the carpels are joined into a flask-shaped pistil with a 1-locule ovary filled with many curved seeds. Strangely, the pistil usually is open at the upper end even when ovules are immature. Fruit an open capsule.

Field characteristics here are sure-fire. Study a flower of mignonette (*Reseda*) to become familiar with the above floral structures and you have it. No other family exhibits the strange disc inserted between the perianth and stamens and pistils — this structure is exserted beyond the petals even in bud. The gaping top of the ketchup-bottle pistil (which matures into a gaping capsule) is similarly unique.

Two genera of **Resedaceae** are important to horticulturists: *Reseda*, the sweetly scented mignonette of the garden, and *Astrocarpus*, garden perennials similar to the mignonettes, but with white petals and with 5 free carpels, spreading star-like, each with a single seed.

Mignonette Family

A. Field sketch of mignonette (*Reseda*) flowering stem. **B.** Sketches of single flowers of *Reseda* showing variations of structure. **C.** Floral diagram of *Reseda*. **D.** Generalized floral formula for the Family.

B.

A.

C.

D.

$$\frac{Ca\,z^{4-7}\,Co^{4-7}\,S^{3-40}\,P\,\textcircled{2-7}}{Cap}$$

227

Rhamnaceae Buckthorn Family

About 900 species, mostly tropical but widely distributed round the world, are included in 58 or 59 genera; most are shrubs, trees, some woody vines and herbs. Leaves are simple, mostly alternate but some opposite, with 3 to 5 main veins, and with small stipules. Flowers usually in axillary corymbs, small, perfect or staminate or pistillate, actinomorphic (regular) usually greenish; calyx 5, rarely 4, at the rim of a floral-cup or less commonly epigynous; petals (when present) 5, rarely 4 (or none), free, and inserted on the floral-cup or less commonly epigynous, and alternating with the sepals; stamens 5 or 4, perigynous (or epigynous), free *and opposite* the petals; a disc lines the floral-cup; compound pistil of 2 united carpels, or rarely 2−5, stigma 2 to 5-lobed; ovary superior or rarely inferior, with 2 to 5 cells with 1, rarely 2, ovules. Fruit a drupe or capsule (or winged).

Field characteristics of this family depend on the taxonomic characters defined above; the alternate, simple leaves with small stipules is suggestive; the usually cup-shaped flowers, small and greenish, in axillary clusters, with calyx and corolla in 5's, and with *stamens opposite the petals*, and with a pistil with two carpels is more definite. This family is very like **Vitaceae** and **Celastraceae** but differs from the former in that leaves of **Rhamnaceae** are small, simple, and entire, and from the latter in that the stamens are opposite the petals.

Relatively few of the genera of **Rhamnaceae** are encountered in cultivation or in the wild in the U.S.; among these are:

Berchemia	*Noltia*	*Spyridium*
Ceanothus	*Paliurus*	*Trevoa*
Colletia	*Phylica*	*Trymalium*
Discaria	*Pomaderris*	*Ventilago*
Helinos	*Rhamnella*	*Zizyphus*
Novenia	*Rhamnus*	

The berries and bark of *Rhamnus cathartica* yield a purgative medicine, and *R. purshiana* is the source of cascara segrada; others yield green and yellow dyes. Probably spiny branches of *Paliurus spina-Christi* or *Zizyphus spina-Christi* were made into the crown of thorns. Fruits of *Zizyphus jujube* make a confection in Arabic lands.

Buckthorn Family

A. Field sketch of fruiting branch of *Rhamnus*. **B.** Sketch of flowering twig to show clusters of small flowers on year-old twigs and the terminal thorn found in some species of *Rhamnus* but not in other genera of this Family. **C.** Floral diagram of *Rhamnus*. **D.** Longitudinal section of *Rhamnus* flower. **E.** Floral formula for the Family (compare with formulas for *Ceanothus* and *Zizyphus*).

A.

B.

C.

D.

E.

$$\frac{Ca^{4-5} \; Co^{4-5} \; S^{4-5} \; P\;\boxed{2-4}}{Pf \; Pg \; Di \; Cap \; Dr}$$

Rosaceae Rose Family

Some 3,000 species of herbs, shrubs, creepers, and trees are found in the approximately 100 genera of the Rose Family; representatives are found throughout the world. Because of wide variation in flower structure on occasion this family has been subdivided into **Rosaceae**, **Malaceae**, (the apple group), and **Drupaceae** (or **Amygdalaceae** or **Prunaceae**), the stone fruit group. More recently, four Sub-families, see below, have been erected. For this work, all are included in a single family. Leaves vary from simple to compound, alternate or basal (as strawberry), with stipules often adnate to the petiole, but sometimes falling early (caducous), rarely vestigial or lacking. Leaf characteristics are of very little taxonomic value in the Rose Family. Flowers terminal, in racemes or cymes, usually perfect, actinomorphic, axis (floral cup) typically cup-shaped or urn-shaped or sometimes a combination of a domed portion surrounded by a nearly flat or cupped disc as in strawberry. Calyx of 5, rarely 3 to 8, sepals (the odd ones superior) often with an epicalyx of smaller leaf-like structures; *sepals may appear to be united at the base in some cases*; corolla of 5 separate petals, imbricated in the bud; usually the petal number equals the sepal number but petals may be "doubled" in horticultural forms, or in rare cases may be lacking; petals usually inserted with stamens on the edge of a disc; stamens several to many, free, commonly inserted in several whorls of 5 on the rim of the disc just inside the petals; they are said to be *perigynous*, that is, around the ovary rather than *hypogynous* or *epigynous*. *This is a chief character separating the Rose Family from the Buttercup Family which always has hypogynous flower parts;* carpels 1, few or many, free or variously united, often with the surrounding receptacle (disc or cup); with 2 or more ovules in each ovary. Compare the many separate fruits ("seeds") each from a separate carpel on the central fleshy axis of a strawberry, several to many free fruits ("seeds") on the enclosed, fleshy hip of rose, and the united and enclosed carpels in an apple. A study of these three flowers plus one of peach or plum from the late bud stage through full blossom and on to immature fruit will give the cogent characteristics of this family.

Some members of the Rose Family are:

Acaena	Cotoneaster	Heteromeles	Parinarium
Adenostoma	Cowania	Holodiscus	Peraphyllum
Agrimonia	× Crataego-mespilus	Kageneckia	Petrophytum
Alchemilla	Crataegus	Kelseya	Photinia
Amelanchier	Cydonia	Kerria	Physocarpus
× Amelosorbus	Dalibarda	Lindleyella	Potentilla
Aronia	Dichotomanthes	Leutkea	Prinsepia
Aruncus	Docynia	Lyonothamnus	Prunus
Bencomia	Dryas	Maddenia	Purshia
Cercocarpus	Duchesnea	Malus	Pyracantha
Chaenomeles	Eriobotrya	Margyricarpus	× Pyronia
Chamaebatia	Exochorda	Mespilus	Pyrus
Chamaebatiaria	Fallugia	Moquilea	Quillaja
Chrysobalanus	Filipendula	Neillia	Raphiolepis
Cliffortia	Fragaria	Neviusia	Rhodotypos
Coluria	Geum	Osmaronia	Rosa
Comarum	Gillenia	Osteomeles	Rubus

Sanguisorba	× Sorbaronia	Spiraea	Waldsteinia
Sibbaldia	× Sorbopyrus	Stephanandra	
Sorbaria	Sorbus	Stranvaesia	

Subfamilies of **Rosaceae** are:

Rosoideae: Trees, shrubs, and herbaceous plants with stipules, flowers mostly with several to many separate carpels (apocarpous), ovaries superior, flowers perigynous, fruit an achene or drupelet, mostly an aggregate of these, as in *Rubus*.

Spiroideae: Shrubby or suffruticose plants with perigynous flowers with several (2–5, rarely 1–12) separate carpels (apocarpous), ovaries superior, mostly clustered, fruit a follicle, a capsule or rarely, an achene.

Prunoideae (= **Amygdaloideae**). Trees and shrubs with stipulate leaves, pistils mostly with one carpel (rarely 2–5), ovary superior, perigynous flowers, fruit usually a drupe, as *Prunus*.

Pomoideae (= **Maloideae, Pyroideae**). Trees and shrubs with stipulate leaves, epigynous flowers (ovary inferior), 2–5 united carpels (syncarpous), fruit a pome, as *Malus*.

Rosaceae

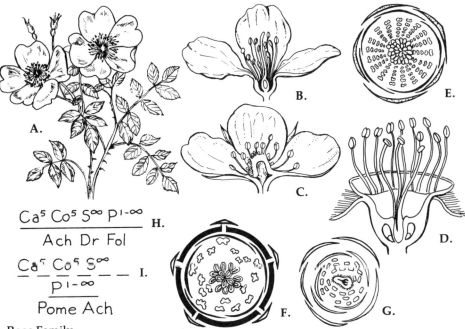

$$\frac{Ca^5 \; Co^5 \; S^\infty \; P^{1-\infty}}{Ach \; Dr \; Fol} \quad \textbf{H.}$$

$$\frac{Ca^5 \; Co^5 \; S^\infty}{P^{1-\infty}} \quad \textbf{I.}$$

Pome Ach

Rose Family

A. Field sketch of the prairie rose, *Rosa setigera*. **B.** Longitudinal section of cherry, *Prunus*, flower; note the free ovary surrounded by a floral cup. **C.** Longitudinal section of strawberry, *Fragaria*, flower; note the extruded receptacle (floral axis) supporting numerous stamens and pistils. At maturity, the enlarged and fleshy receptacle will be the "fruit" and the nutlets (each is a fruit) formed from the ovary and enclosed seed will be the "seeds". **D.** Stylized drawing of a pear, *Pyrus*, flower showing the ovary submerged in the floral cup. **E.** Floral diagram of *Rosa*. **F.** Floral diagram of *Fragaria*. **G.** Floral diagram of peach, *Amygdalus*. **H.** Floral formula for **Rosaceae** with a free ovary or ovaries as in diagrams B. and C. above. **I.** Floral formula for **Rosaceae** with an inferior ovary (epigynous insertion of flower parts), as in diagram D.

231

Rubiaceae Madder Family

A large family of tremendous economic importance, the **Rubiaceae** includes at least 6,000 species in about 500 genera; trees, shrubs, and herbs and climbers of the tropics and sub-tropical regions, a few reach into the temperate zones. Leaves mostly opposite or whorled, and mostly entire or rarely more or less toothed; opposite, entire leaves often are connected by interposed stipules, whorled leaves without stipules, or stipules may be reduced to a stipular line. Flowers actinomorphic or rarely slightly irregular, mostly complete but occasionally staminate or pistillate, solitary or in capitate clusters, cymes or panicles, terminal or axillary; sepals 2 to 6, usually 4 or 5 (or rarely none) and often one is larger than the rest and may be colored; corolla 4 to 6-parted, sympetalous, tube-shaped or campanulate, lobes often flaring, or corolla rarely rotate (wheel-shaped) epigynous; stamens 4 to 6, separate, and epipetalous; compound pistil of 1 to 8 carpels, but mostly 2, closely united, with a single slender style, stigma either capitate or else branched; ovary inferior, usually 2-celled, but may be more, with a single ovule or many ovules in each cell. Fruit a capsule, berry, or drupe.

With most of the N. American species the whorled leaves and small heads of delicate flowers with flower parts in mostly 4's or sometimes 5's, with the 2-celled, inferior ovary, make for easy classification. Some of the exotic species are not so easy, and must be keyed with all the characteristics listed in the first paragraph above. In the garden dissect (hand lens essential) a few flowers of bedstraw, sweet woodruff, some bluets, and if available, buttonbush and partridge berry to get the feel of this delightful and diverse family. Somehow the flowers of these are very restrained in design, rather like a piece of Shaker furniture, and soon you will get to recognize their style.

A great many **Rubiaceae** species are important commercially, *Coffea arabica*, alone, is sufficient to make the gold centers of the world aware of **Rubiaceae**, but there is quinine, ipecac, the red dye, madder, and a number of other dyes. From an ornamental standpoint we cherish **Rubiaceae** for gardenias, bluets, sweet woodruff, partridge berry, and a number of other less familiar ornamentals. For exhaustive lists of species see *The Royal Horticultural Society Dictionary of Gardening*, Bailey's *The Standard Cyclopedia or Gardening* as well as other encyclopedic horticultural works, Gray's *Manual of Botany*, and similar area taxonomic references. Among the genera more commonly encountered are:

Adina	*Crucianella*	*Nertera*
Asperula	*Galium*	*Oxyanthus*
Bouvardia	*Gardinia*	*Pentas*
Catesbaea	*Geophila*	*Phuopsis*
Cephalanthus	*Hoffmania*	*Pinckneya*
Cinchona	*Houstonia*	*Platycarpum*
Coffea	*Ixora*	*Rudgea*
Coprosma	*Mitchella*	*Serissa*

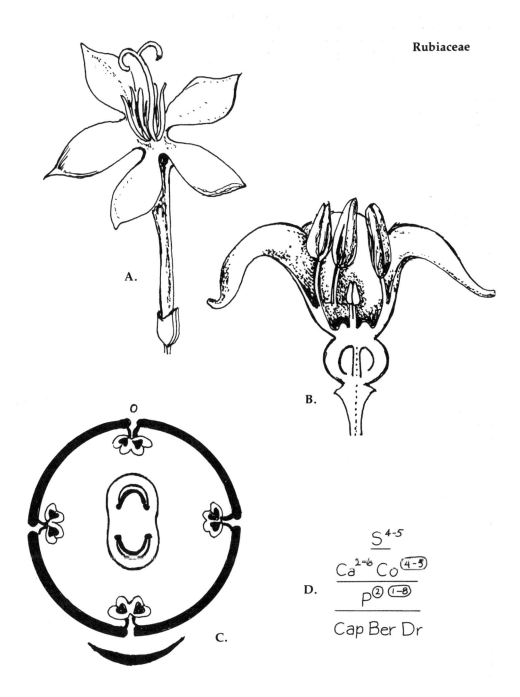

$$S^{4-5}$$
$$Ca^{2-6} Co^{\boxed{4-5}}$$
$$\overline{P^{\textcircled{2}} \boxed{1-8}}$$

D.

Cap Ber Dr

Madder Family

A. Sketch of a coffee, *Coffea*, flower, typical of madder-type flowers. **B.** Longitudinal section of a madder flower, *Rubia tinctorum*, clearly illustrating epipetaly (stamens inserted on petals) and hypogeny (inferior ovary = flower parts inserted *above* the ovary). **C.** Floral diagram for *Rubia*. **D.** Floral formula for the Family.

233

Rutaceae Rue Family

The 1,600 or more species of **Rutaceae** are grouped into about 150 genera, and are found in tropical, sub-tropical, and temperate regions, especially in Africa and Australia. Most are shrubs or trees, some are herbaceous. Leaves usually alternate, sometimes opposite, simple or variously cut or compound, usually with pellucid glands (visible as dots when leaves are held to the light) and abounding in a pungent or bitter-aromatic acrid volatile oil, stipulate or with no stipules, often evergreen. Flowers complete, rarely unisexual, usually actinomorphic (radially symmetrical) rarely zygomorphic, calyx of 5 or 4 sepals, free or somewhat connate, overlapping in bud; petals 5 or 4, free; stamens 10 or 8, rarely more, sometimes fewer, inserted at the base of the *gynophore*; pistils separate, 2 to 5, or a compound pistil of 2 to 5 carpels (carpels sometimes free below and united above), styles commonly united or cohering, ovary(s) superior, each cell with 1 to 5 ovules; the ovary is raised on a disc-like projection of the receptacle called the *gynophore*. Fruit a capsule opening by valves as *Ruta*, rue, or fleshy and indehiscent, as *Citrus*, orange, or separating into fruitlets, rarely winged, as *Ptelea*, hop tree.

The scented, gland-dotted leaves, the usually pentamerous (sometimes tetramerous or very rarely trimerous) flowers with stamens usually double the petal number, and with the pistil (of sometimes more or less separate carpels) inserted on the gynophore, give relatively easy field characteristics. Study flowers of rue, prickly-ash, and any citrus or hardy-orange to become familiar with structural variations within this family. In handling these you also will learn that aromatic does not necessarily mean pleasantly scented, as orange. Incidentally, some individuals develop severe dermatitis from the oils of some species in the family; *Dictamnus*, gas plant, is particularly infamous. But it is an interesting plant because on hot, absolutely airless summer evenings the volatile oil vapors collect in sufficient quantity about the plant that they can be ignited with quite an impressive flash.

Some cultivated and wild genera in the **Rutaceae** include:

Acmadenia	Choisya	Euchaetis	Poncirus
Acradenia	Chomelia	Evodia	Ptelea
Acronychia	Citropsis	Feronia	Ravenia
Adenandra	Citrus	Fortunella	Ruta
Aegle	Clausenia	Geijera	Severinia
Agathosma	Coleonema	Macrostylis	Skimmia
Almeidea	Correa	Medicosma	Spatelia
Atalantia	Crowea	Melicope	Spiranthera
Balsamocitrus	Cusparia	Murraya	Ticorea
Barosma	Dictamnus	Orixa	Toddalia
Boenninghausenia	Diosma	Peganum	Triphasia
Boronia	Diplolaena	Peltostigma	Wendlandia
Calodendron	Empleurum	Phebalium	Xanthoxylum
Casimiroa	Eriostemon	Philotheca	Zieria
Chloroxylon	Erythrochiton	Pilocarpus	

The economic uses of various **Rutaceae** products go back to the dawning of civilization. The diversity, fish poison to perfumery, is great!

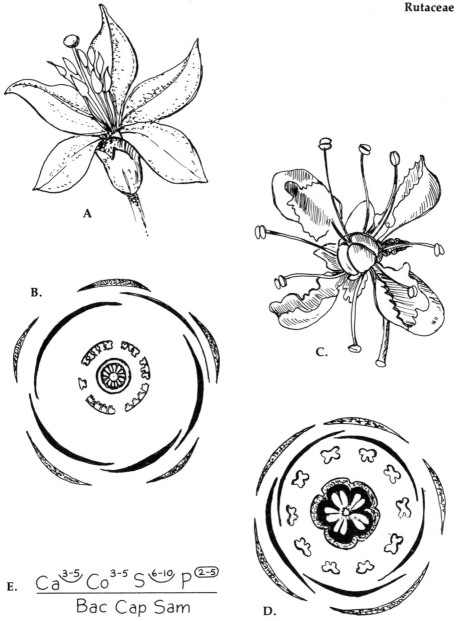

Rue (Citrus) Family

A. Flower of orange (*Citrus*). **B.** Floral diagram of *Citrus*. **C.** Flower of rue (*Ruta graveolens*). **D.** Floral diagram of *Ruta*. **E.** General floral formula for the Family.

Salicaceae Willow Family

The two genera of **Salicaceae** include at least 400 species, most of them willows. Some authorities add a third (Asiatic) genus, *Chosenia*. All are trees or shrubs, most occur in the North Temperate zone, reaching into the Arctic; generally deciduous, leaves alternate, simple, with stipules. Wood soft and light, bark with little colorless sap, bitter. Catkins with either staminate or pistillate flowers (amentiferous), with a single flower at each bract; flowers greatly reduced; perianth lacking or reduced to a small disc or to a few glandular scales; stamens 1 or usually 2, or rarely more, filaments slender, free or more or less united; ovary sessile or short stalked, 1-celled, with 2 to 4 parietal placentae, stigma 2 or 4-lobed; ovules several to many. Fruit a 1-celled capsule, 2 to 4-valved, seeds with much silky down.

Catkins of the willows (*Salix* spp.) are upright in most cases, those of the poplars and aspens (*Populus*) usually are pendulous. Field characteristics include the alternate, simple, deciduous leaves with petioles often glandular (and flattened in many species of *Populus*) and with either leaf-like and persistent stipules or scale-like and early-falling stipules. The bitter bark (at all seasons) is characteristic, as are the dioecious flowers in catkins, the glandular disc which supports stamens and pistils, and the "fly away" seeds with their silky "cotton".

The two genera of **Salicaceae** are *Populus* and *Salix*.

Many species of both genera are decorative; various species yield numerous medicinals, tannins, dyes, and charcoal of high quality.

Willow Family

A. Staminate catkin of willow, *Salix*. **B.** and **C.** Staminate flowers of two species of willow, showing great reduction. **D.** Pistillate catkin of willow. **E.** and **F.** Pistillate flowers of two species of willow, each reduced to a 2-carpellate compound pistil with subtending bract. **G.** Floral formula for the **Salicaceae.**

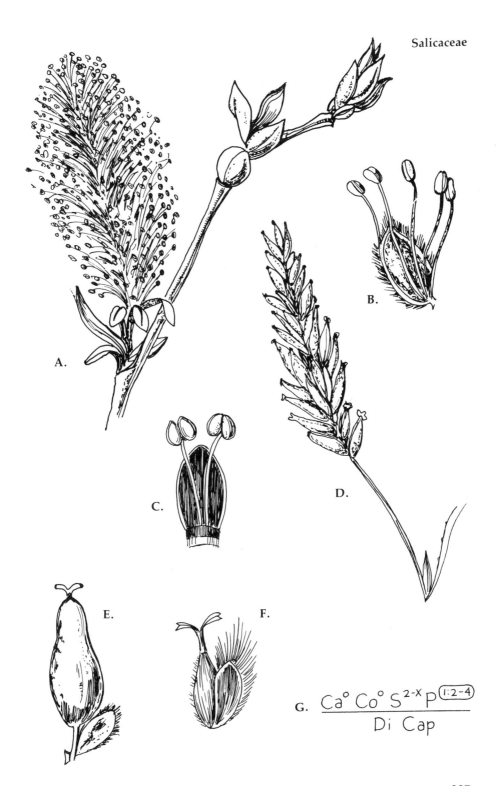

A.

B.

C.

D.

E.

F.

G. $\dfrac{Ca^{\circ}\ Co^{\circ}\ S^{2-X}\ P^{\boxed{1:2-4}}}{Di\ Cap}$

Sarraceniaceae Pitcher-plant Family

Seventeen species in the three genera make up this quite small family whose members show relationships to the **Droseraceae, Nepenthaceae, Papaveraceae,** and **Nymphaeaceae.** Plants occur usually in turfy or marshy bogs. They are herbaceous, with basal leaves highly specialized into elongated (or short) "pitchers" with tubular mouths and rounded lids. Flowers on naked scapes, rising above the foliage; perfect, regular, sepals 4 to 5, free, imbricated; petals 5, overlapping and deciduous (lacking in *Heliamphora*), hypogynous; stamens many but apparently neither spiral nor cyclic; ovary superior, 3, 5, rarely 6-celled; ovules many; a single style diverges into 1 to 5 stigmas. The fruit is a capsule.

The field characters are simple; look for pitcher-shaped leaves and for the clean scapes supporting rather flattened, brownish flowers that tend to face downward. You can't miss on this family.

Genera encountered in the wild or in cultivation include:

Darlingtonia (Extreme western U.S.)
Heliamphora (Guyana)
Sarracenia (Mississippi basin eastward to the Atlantic, U.S.)

The pitcher-plants are of no economic importance and as marshes and bogs are drained they become more scarce. Never purchase collected plants, but buy only plants you know have been propagated in cultivation. These are not easy for the inexperienced gardener.

238

$$\frac{Ca^{4\text{-}5}\ Co^5\ S^\infty\ P^{(3,5,6)}}{Cap}$$

Pitcher-plant Family

Field sketch of *Sarracenia*, illustrating characteristic tubular, hooded leaves.

239

Saxifragaceae Saxifrage Family

Mostly herbs, shrubs and trees of cool and cold climates, only a few members of **Saxifragaceae** grow in warmer portions of the world. The family includes some 650 to 1000 species distributed through 30 to 80 genera depending on the inclusion (as presented here) of Subfamilies **Grossularioideae** and **Hydranoideae**. Horticultural forms and artificial hybrids abound as many Saxifrages are highly sought after ornamentals. Many species are herbaceous or shrubby with alternate (sometimes opposite) leaves, sometimes more or less succulent, usually with no stipules. Flowers usually regular, perfect, mostly perigynous, sometimes hypogynous or epigynous; sepals 5 or 4, rarely more or less; petals usually inserted on the floral-cup, commonly as many as the sepals, rarely absent; stamens as many or twice as many as petals, inserted on the floral-cup, free; carpels commonly fewer than the sepals (the same number in *Penthorum*) free or more commonly partially united, 1 to 5, usually 2, often with the base embedded in the floral axis (floral-cup) or rarely definitely inferior. Styles as many as the carpels and usually free. Seeds numerous. Fruit usually is a capsule or berry. Often Saxifrages are tiny, alpine or subalpine plants suitable for the rock garden. The Latin name means "rock breaking".

Field identification of these usually depends on flower characteristics, though, by all means, look for the leaf arrangement, and often the lack of stipules will lead you to **Saxifragaceae** and away from **Rosaceae**, which is important! The rather limited number of stamens, carpels (simple pistils) fewer than sepals, and the usually perigynous arrangement of petals and stamens is characteristic. So is the 2-celled ovary where the pistil is compound, but this is by no means a fast-and-sure feature of the family. The withered floral parts often adhere to the developing fruit (as gooseberry) which is typical. In the latest literature the Subfamilies are given family status.

Genera of ornamental value or which may be encountered in the wild in the United States include:

Abrophyllum	*Deutzia*	*Philadelphus*
Anopterus	*Dichroa*	*Pileostegia*
Astilbe	*Escallonia*	*Platycrates*
Bauera	*Fendlera*	*Quintinia*
Bergenia	*Francoa*	*Ribes*
Boykinia	*Geissois*	*Rodgersia*
Brexia	*Heuchera*	*Saxifraga*
Calacluvia	× *Heuchereлa*	*Schizophragma*
Callicoma	*Hydrangea*	*Sullivantia*
Cardiandra	*Itea*	*Tanakea*
Carpenteria	*Jimesia*	*Tallima*
Cephalotus	*Kirengeshoma*	*Tiarella*
Chrysosplenium	*Lithophragma*	*Tolmiea*
Davidsonia	*Mitella*	*Valdivia*
Decumaria	*Parnassia*	
Deinanthe	*Penthorum*	

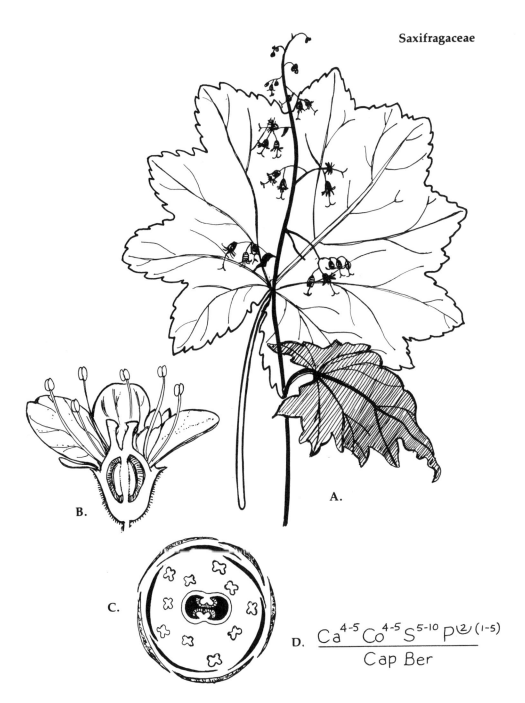

A. Field sketch of *Heuchera*, with palmately-lobed simple leaf and few-flowered cyme. **B.** Longitudinal section of *Saxafraga* flower. **C.** Floral diagram of *Saxifraga*. **D.** Floral formula for the Family.

$$\frac{Ca^{4-5} \, Co^{4-5} \, S^{5-10} \, P^{(2)\,(1-5)}}{Cap \; Ber}$$

Saxifrage Family

A. Field sketch of *Heuchera*, with palmately-lobed simple leaf and few-flowered cyme. **B.** Longitudinal section of *Saxafraga* flower. **C.** Floral diagram of *Saxifraga*. **D.** Floral formula for the Family.

Scrophulariaceae Snapdragon or Figwort Family

A few trees, some shrubs, and mostly herbs of **Scrophulariaceae** are grouped into about 3,000 species and more than 200 genera. Leaves in a few genera all are alternate, but in most at least the lowest leaves are opposite or whorled, and with no stipules. No species has truly regular flowers but some seem nearly so; flowers often in spikes, but never are truly terminal. Calyx synsepalous, mostly with 5 lobes or teeth, persistent, usually leaf-like; corolla usually zygomorphic, sympetalous, often two-lipped but sometimes nearly tubular or bell-shaped (campanulate); corolla lobes 5, rarely 4; the lips of the corolla are unequal, the upper one entire or 2-lobed, the lower lip often 3-lobed and spreading; stamens epipetalous and al-ternating with the lobes of the corolla, usually 2 pairs (didynamous), or 4 equal, or sometimes only 2 accompanied by a reduced sterile one; pistil superior, ovary usually 2-lobed, 2-celled, with single, often slender style and an entire or 2-lobed stigma; placentation is axial, and usually many ovules fill the cells of the ovary. Fruit is most commonly a capsule, or rarely an indehiscent berry. Many of these are bitter-narcotic plants.

Both the Figwort Family and the Mint Famiy have representatives with 2-lipped flowers which superficially are similar, but the Figworts all have a rather round, 2-celled usually many-seeded ovary, and the Mints have a deeply lobed 2-celled ovary which appears to be divided into 4 chambers, each with a single seed. Also, the 4 stamens, in 2 pairs, is characteristic of many Figworts (but in *Penstemon* only 2 stamens and a sterile one). The capsule, often opening by small pores, is another good field character for **Scrophulariaceae.**

Some genera in the Figwort Family are:

Adenosma	Craterostigma	Lindernia	Russelia
Alonsoa	Cymbalaria	Manulea	Schwalbea
Anarrhinum	Dermatobotrys	Maurandia	Scrophularia
Angelonia	Diascia	Mazus	Selago
Antirrhinum	Digitalis	Melampyrum	Seymeria
Aptosimum	Erinus	Micranthemum	Sibthorpia
Artanema	Euphrasia	Mimulus	Synthyris
Bacopa	Freylinia	Nemesia	Teedia
Bartsia	Gerardia	Odonites	Tetranema
Bowkeria	Gratiola	Oresitrophe	Torenia
Buchnera	Hebenstreitia	Orthocarpus	Uroskinnera
Calceolaria	Hemichaena	Ourisia	Verbascum
Campylanthus	Hemiphragma	Paulownia	Veronica
Castelleja	Isoplexis	Pedicularis	Veronicastrum
Celsia	Ixianthes	Penstemon	Walafrida
Chaenorrhinum	Jovellana	Phygelius	Wulfenia
Chaenostoma	Kixia	Picrorhiza	Zaluzianskya
Chelone	Lencocarpus	Rehmannia	
Collinsia	Leucophyllum	Rhinanthus	
Conobea	Linaria	Rhodochiton	

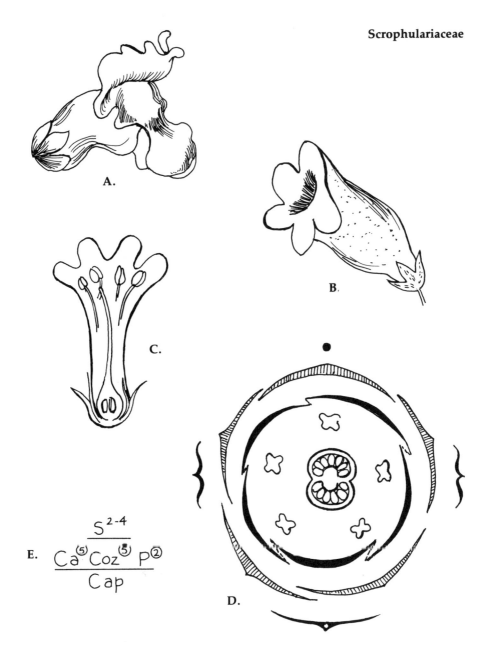

A.

B.

C.

E. $\dfrac{S^{2-4}}{Ca^{\textcircled{6}} Coz^{\textcircled{5}} P^{\textcircled{2}}}{Cap}$

D.

Snapdragon (Figwort) Family

A. Sketch of a snapdragon (*Antirrhinum majus*) flower showing the more or less regular calyx and the extremely irregular corolla. **B.** Sketch of a *Penstemon* flower. **C.** Longitudinal section of a *Phygelius* flower showing the two pairs (diadelphous) of stamens inserted on the tube of the corolla (epipetalous) and a typical "scroph" pistil, flask-shaped with a long, slender style. **D.** Floral diagram of mullein, *Verbascum*, atypical with its almost entirely free petals and with mostly 5 stamens, corolla only slightly irregular. **E.** Floral diagram for the Family.

Solanaceae Nightshade Family

About 85 genera, which contain more than 2,300 species, make up the Nightshade Family; these mostly are herbs, some erect or climbing shrubs; only a few are trees. Species are generally distributed through temperate and tropical regions with the greatest concentration in Central and S. America. Leaves mostly alternate (but upper sometimes paired) or occasionally whorled, simple or occasionally pinnately compound, entire, serrate, lobed, or dissected. Flowers axillary or cymose, often seemingly extra-axillary; complete, actinomorphic or rarely irregular; calyx synsepalous, 5 (rarely 4 to 7) -lobed or cleft or parted, persistent; corolla sympetalous 5-lobed, often rotate and showy, but in the family considerable variation occurs in form and structure, rarely more or less zygomorphic; stamens as many as the corolla lobes and alternating with them, 5 or 4 or 2+2 or 2 in zygomorphic flowers, epipetalous; superior compound pistil of 2 carpels (rarely 3−5 cells) closely united, 1 style and 1 stigma, with axial placentae with many ovules. Fruit a berry (as tomato) or a capsule (as flowering tobacco). Juice of these plants is colorless, foliage often is rank-smelling, foliage and fruits often are narcotic, often very poisonous.

The easiest field characteristic of this family is the folding of the corolla in the bud; quite often the joined petals are folded lengthwise, accordion-fashion (that is rim to insertion) below the ovary rather than being imbricate or otherwise; a plant with such buds and pentamerous flower parts (calyx, corolla, and stamens in 5's) and with the stamens epipetalous, and with a many-seeded, two-carpeled superior ovary with a single style and capitate or lobed stigma, is sure to be Solanaceous. Until you are fairly sure of genus and species do not taste the sap or any part because it may be toxic.

Among the numerous genera of **Solanaceae** commonly encountered in agriculture, horticulture, and in the wild, are:

Anthocercis	*Jaborosa*	*Retzia*
Atropa	*Juanulloa*	*Salpichroa*
Browallia	*Latua*	*Salpiglossis*
Brunfelsia	*Lycium*	*Saracha*
Capsicum	*Lycopersicon*	*Schizanthus*
Cestrum	*Mandragora*	*Schwenkia*
Datura	*Metternichia*	*Scopolia*
Duboisia	*Nicandra*	*Solandra*
Fabiana	*Nierembergia*	*Solanum*
Grabowskia	*Petunia*	*Streptosolen*
Hyoscyamus	*Physalis*	*Vestia*
Iochroma	*Physochlaina*	

Vegetables, as tomato, potato, eggplant, pepper, and less familiar sorts are members of this family; so are narcotic plants such as tobacco, belladonna, stramonium, mandragora, and many others; the poisonous species are legion. Fortunately, in this family many of the fine garden ornamentals are known by their generic names which have become the common names; Browallia, Datura, Petunia, Salpiglossis, and Schizanthus would be hard to recognize by any other epithet. Who can say that Latin is dead?

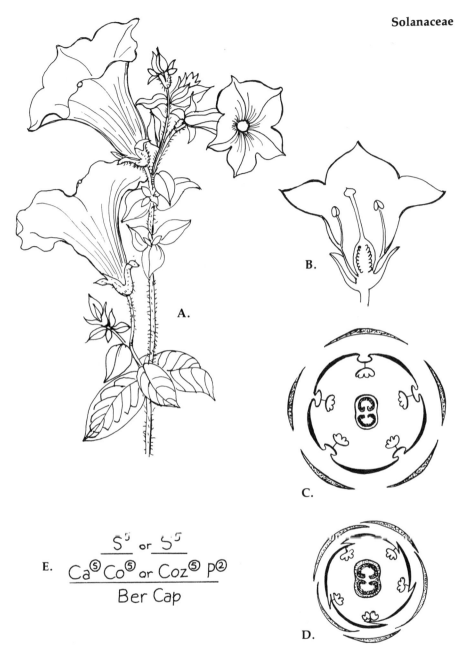

A.

B.

C.

$$\frac{S^5 \text{ or } S^5}{Ca^{\circledS} Co^{\circledS} \text{ or } Coz^{\circledS} P^{\circled2}}{Ber Cap}$$

E.

D.

Nightshade Family

A. Field sketch of *Petunia*. **B.** Longitudinal section of a petunia flower, stylized; note stamens inserted on the corolla alternating with the corolla lobes. **C.** and **D.** Two floral diagrams, potato, *Solanum tuberosum*, and ground-cherry, *Physalis alkekengi*. **E.** Floral formula, compounded, showing both a regular corolla with stamens inserted alternating with the lobes and the irregular corolla with epipetalous stamens.

Staphyleaceae Bladdernut Family

Sixty or more species in 5 genera, all trees and shrubs, make up this small family whose members are found in temperate N. America and Eurasia. Leaves mostly opposite, sometimes alternate; odd-pinnately compound, stipulate. Flowers perfect, regular, in panicles; calyx of 5 sepals separate or attached basally, imbricated; corolla of 5 petals, imbricated; stamens 5, free, alternating with the petals and inserted outside the large, central, cup-shaped disc; compound pistil of 3 carpels sometimes barely united in the axis (but sometimes fully united), long styles connate, sometimes separate; ovary superior, usually 3-celled, rarely 1-celled, a single or few ovules in each cell. Fruit a capsule, often deeply lobed, with leathery or fleshy walls, sometimes bladdery-inflated.

The compound, stipulate leaves, and the perfect, regular flowers with 5 sepals, 5 petals, 5 stamens, and a pistil of 3 mostly connate carpels which insert on a glandular disc serve to identify the family. These have much in common with the **Sapindaceae** in which family the genera now in **Staphyleaceae** were once included.

Commonly horticulturists encounter only the native N. American genus *Staphylea* but rarely in special collection are:

> *Euscaphis*
> *Staphylea*
> *Tapiscia*
> *Turpinia*

Styracaceae Storax Family

Twelve genera include about 175 species of trees and shrubs which are distributed from Brazil to Peru and Mexico, Virginia to Texas, Japan to Java, and 1 species, *Styrax officinalis* in the Mediterranean basin. These have watery sap and a stellate pubescence on young shoots and leaves. Leaves are alternate, simple, with short petioles, often evergreen, and exstipulate. Flowers solitary or in racemes or panicles, perfect, actinomorphic with some variation regarding the position of the ovary which often is superior but sometimes partially inferior with a floral-cup adnate at the base; calyx 4 or 5-lobed (rarely 4 to 8) or cleft, free or inserted on the shallow floral-cup; corolla 4 or 5-lobed (rarely 4 to 8), petals free or united at the base and hypogynous or inserted on the shallow floral-cup; stamens free or rarely somewhat united at the base, with long anthers, in a single series and as many as corolla lobes or 2 to 4-times as many, epipetalous (inserted on the corolla) or hypogynous; compound pistil of 3 to 5 carpels with a single style with 1 to 5 stigmas; ovary superior or often inferior with the base embedded in shallow floral-cup, 1-celled at the top and often 3 to 5-celled at the base with 1, rarely several, ovules in each cell. Fruit a drupe with fleshy or dry pericarp.

The floral characteristics of **Styracaceae** somewhat resemble **Ebenaceae**, but these have perfect flowers and the ovary is distinctive when multi-celled at the base and 1-celled at the top. The usually delicate-textured, white, mostly shallow bell-shaped flowers are characteristic.

Where hardy, many species of **Styracaceae** serve as fine ornamentals, including representatives of the following genera:

Halesia	*Pterostyrax*	*Sinojackia*
Pamphilia	*Rehderodendron*	

Aromatic resins (much used in churches as natural incense) are produced by some East Indies and Brazilian species of these; aside from that, they are best known as small ornamental trees with few insect or disease pests, but rather temperamental regarding environment.

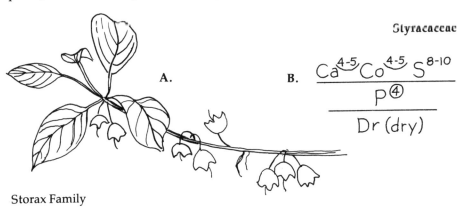

Styracaceae

$$\frac{Ca^{4\text{-}5} Co^{4\text{-}5} S^{8\text{-}10}}{P^{(4)}}$$

$$Dr \text{ (dry)}$$

Storax Family

A. Field sketch of the twig of snowdrop tree, *Halesia carolina*. **B.** Floral formula for the Family.

247

Tamaricaceae Tamarisk Family

This is a small family, 4 genera with about 125 species, all native to the arid areas of the Mediterranean basin and into central Asia; trees, shrubs, or rarely herbs, often with the general appearance of a heath due to the very small, sessile leaves. Leaves alternate, mostly needle-like or scale-like, sessile, exstipulate. Flowers small, actinomorphic, complete, numerous in spikes, or solitary; calyx of 4 to 6 separate (or barely united) sepals, persistent; corolla usually 5 (or 4 to 6) petals separate or barely connate at the base, imbricated, withering and drying persistent; stamens 4 to many, commonly equal to and alternate with the petals or double the number, rarely distinct, or mostly partially connate, filaments inserted on a more or less evident basal disc; compound pistil, styles 3 to 5, with small, lobed stigmas, or 1 with deeply 3 to 5-lobed stigma; ovary superior, 1-celled, with a few to several ovules. Fruit a capsule, usually with bearded seeds.

The ericoid appearance, withering-persistent petals, definite stamen number (relating to petals), and 1-celled ovary are distinctive field characteristics. Also the bearded seeds are typical. This family is included not so much for its horticultural importance as for the value it has in learning flower analysis techniques. Plants of *Tamarix* are relatively easy to find, and a careful study of the floral structure is most instructive.

Only three genera may be encountered: *Myricaria, Reaumaria,* and *Tamarix.* The latter is most common and is economically important within its natural range for tannin, resin, and oils.

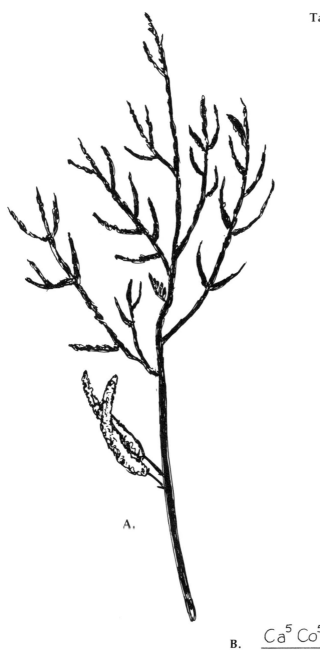

A.

B. $\dfrac{Ca^5\ Co^5\ S^5\ P^1}{Cap}$

Tamarisk Family

A. Field sketch of twig with scale-like leaves and almost catkin-like spike shaped racemes of tiny flowers. **B.** Floral formula.

Theaceae Tea (Camellia) Family

How good it would be to revert to the previous name for this family, **Ternstroemiaceae**, honoring Christopher Ternstroem, the noted Swedish naturalist of the early 18th Century. The 16 genera, about 200 species, which make up this family are tropical and sub-tropical trees and shrubs with alternate, simple, pinnately-veined, usually evergreen, exstipulate leaves. Axillary flowers usually solitary, or paired, mostly showy, actinomorphic, hypogynous, mostly complete, rarely staminate or pistillate; calyx of 5 (rarely 6 or 7) sepals, free or only slightly united (connate); corolla of 5 (rarely 4, 9, or many) petals, free or slightly united at the base; stamens usually numerous (rarely 5, 10, or 15), sometimes free, often united in small bundles, or sometimes united into a tube, and with filaments often united at the base with the petals; compound pistil with a single style or with styles as many as carpels; ovary superior, 2 to 10-celled, ovules 1 to many in each cell. Fruit a woody 3 to 5 (usually) locular capsule, seeds few, or drupaceous.

The simple, glossy, exstipulate, alternate, sometimes evergreen leaves are a good beginning field character. The showy flowers, with a 5-parted polysepalous, or barely synsepalous calyx, the 5-parted (or in horticulture, often many petaled), barely sympetalous corolla with attached clusters of stamens surrounding the commonly 3 to 5-celled superior pistil, give the final confirmation.

While only the species *Thea chinensis*, tea, is an important agricultural member of the family, several of the **Theaceae** genera include species of great ornamental value; among them are:

Camellia	*Gordonia*	*Ternstroemia*
Cleyera	*Hartia*	*Thea*
Eurya	*Schima*	*Tutcheria*
Franklinia	*Stewartia*	

As you become familiar with the structure of **Theaceae** flowers you will see similarities to those of **Hypericaceae** and **Guttiferae**, and also to those of *Actinidia* (**Dilleniaceae**) and *Stachyurus*, both of which once were included in this family. *Thea chinensis* is classified by some authors as *Camellia sinensis*, and some heretics transfer our beloved American *Franklinia alatamaha* to *Gordonia alatamaha*, and the British sometimes misspell the specific epithet "altamaha". Homeopaths will be interested to know that the bitter taste of tea is due to a glucoside, and its stimulating properties come from the alkaloid theine. Immature tea leaves are picked frequently; when quickly dried they make green tea; when piled to "sweat" and develop a uniform layer of mold, (a sort of controlled composting) then dried, they make the various kinds of black tea.

Tea Family

A. Budded and flowering branch of *Thea*. **B.** Flower of tea in longitudinal section. **C.** Floral diagram of *Thea*. **D.** Generalized floral formula for the Family.

251

Thymelaeaceae Mezereum Family

Annual herbs, shrubs, or trees with acrid, very tough and non-aromatic bark, in about 450 species grouped into 40 genera make up the **Thymelaeaceae**. Leaves are opposite, alternate, or scattered, simple, entire, and without stipules. Flowers usually in terminal spikes, panicles, or clusters, sometimes axillary; perfect or staminate or pistillate, actinomorphic; perianth of a single whorl, perigynous, usually with quite a long tube often with appendages in the throat, calyx lobes pronounced or not so, usually 4 or 5; stamens as many or usually twice as many as the perianth lobes and inserted on the throat of the tube; filaments usually short, in some stamens are included in the tube, in others exserted; pistil sessile or short-stalked, on hypogynous disc, 1 stye (short or exserted) or none with the single stigma sessile; ovary superior, usually 1-celled rarely 2, with a large, solitary ovule. Fruit a berry-like drupe, or a berry, or a nut, always indehiscent.

The best field characteristics include the single perianth elongated into a tube-shaped floral-cup, the epigynous stamens, the appendages in the tube, and the superior, 1-celled ovary with a single ovule. The careful study of flowers of two or three kinds of *Daphne* and the flower of the native American *Dirca* (leatherwood) easily establishes the characteristics of this family.

Among the genera of **Thymelaeaceae** encountered in cultivation or wild in the U.S. are:

Arthrosolen	*Lagetta*	*Stellera*
Dais	*Lasiosiphon*	*Struthiola*
Daphne	*Ovidia*	*Thymelaea*
Edgeworthia	*Passerina*	*Wikstroemia*
Gnidea	*Phaleria*	
Lachnaea	*Pimelea*	

Of these, most are of tropical or sub-tropical origin, but some are from the temperate regions of the world; a few have economic value, producing dyes, medicinals, or for fiber. The species of *Daphne* are first rate ornamentals but most are rather difficult, and the rice flower, *Pimelea*, is a good greenhouse or plant room subject.

Mezereum (Daphne) Family

Field sketch of *Daphne mezereum*, showing the lilac-like flowers of sepals (no corolla). Compare flowers of *Daphne* and of *Elaeagnus* to understand the differences and similarities between two related families.

253

Tiliaceae Linden Family

About 50 genera include the 450 species of herbaceous plants, shrubs, and trees which are widely distributed in the tropical and sub-tropical regions of the world, with few species extending the range into the North Temperate zone. Bark is fibrous, inner bark with mucilaginous properties; alternate leaves are mostly simple, entire, dentate, or lobed, often oblique at the base, and with stipules. Flowers actinomorphic (regular), hypogynous, usually perfect; calyx of 5, rarely 3 or 4, free or somewhat connate sepals which are deciduous; corolla of separate petals, as many as sepals; stamens 10 or more, hypogynous, filaments separate or barely connate at the base, or in fascicles of 5 to 10, often with staminoids, anthers 4-celled, opening by slits or pores; compound pistil with 1 style, stigma often lobed; ovary superior, 2 to 10-celled with 1 to several ovules in each cell. Fruit usually a capsule, or indehiscent and nut-like, or drupaceous.

The field characters for the single genus common in the North Temperate region, *Tilia*, are easy; the leaves are alternate, oblique at the base, simple, dentate. Flowers in a loose cyme, each hanging on an axillary peduncle which is united to a strap-shaped, membranous bract which is uniquely characteristic of the genus. To handily classify the tropical genera resort to floral characters, as defined above; in these, stamens commonly are in "tufts" and may be strongly reminiscent of the closely related **Malvaceae**, except for the incomplete fusion of stamen filaments and the deciduous sepals of **Tiliaceae**.

Among the genera of **Tiliaceae** encountered in gardens or conservatories are:

Antholoma	*Grewia*	*Muntingia*
Apeiba	*Heliocarpus*	*Sparmannia*
Entelia	*Honckenya*	*Tilia*
Glyphaea	*Luehea*	*Tricuspidaria*

For their mucilaginous qualities several species of **Tiliaceae** have been used for medicine; *Tilia* yields particularly fine lumber and primitive peoples have used its inner bark for cordage or cloth (hence the common name, basswood, for the bast fibers of the secondary phloem tissue). *Grewia* fruits are eaten in India. *Sparmannia*, *Entelea*, and *Luehea* are particularly ornamental in tropical gardens and warm conservatories, and *Tilia* gives northern gardens many species and hybrids, all splendid, ornamental shade trees.

B.

A.

C. $\dfrac{Ca^5\ C^{5-X}\ S^{\infty}\ P\ \widehat{(2\text{-}10)}}{Cap\ Bac}$

Linden Family

A. Field sketch of *Tilia* inflorescence with its leaf-like bract. **B.** Floral diagram.
C. Floral formula.

255

Ulmaceae Elm Family

About 200 species of trees, rarely shrubs, included in about 15 genera, which are found mostly in the temperate zones, rarely in the tropics, make up the Elm Family. Leaves mostly are deciduous (some evergreen species), alternate, pinnate-veined, usually oblique at the base, generally toothed, with stipules which fall early (fugaceous) leaving slight or distinct scars. Flowers small, regular, bisexual or unisexual, perianth of a single whorl (apetalous) of 4 to 5, rarely 3 to 8 sepals, sometimes slightly connate (fused) to form a campanulate (bell-shaped) calyx; stamens as many or rarely, twice as many, as perianth lobes, and *always erect in the bud*; pistil compound with 2 carpels, 2 styles; ovary superior, 1-celled, with a single ovule. Fruit a flat, more or less papery samara (as in elm), a drupe (as in hackberry), or a nut.

In the field look for woody plants with simple, usually toothed, pinnately veined, more or less ovate leaves, unequal at the bottom (oblique) with stipules which fall early, and alternately arranged. The sap should be clear, colorless, mostly neutral. This gets you clear of near relatives such as the Mulberry Family, and leaves you with look-alikes such as the lindens or some of the members of the rose family. Now proceed to flowers or to fruits. The tiny, reduced, flowers are easy once you have learned their make-up; study early spring specimens of various elms and hackberries. Also, the fruits are easy to recognize in several of the genera.

Among the **Ulmaceae** genera encountered in the wild or in cultivation are:

Aphananthe
Celtis
Hemiptelea
Planera
Pteroceltis
Ulmus
Zelkova

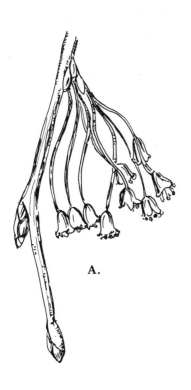

A.

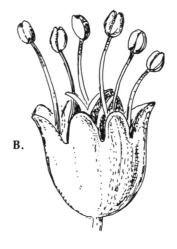

B.

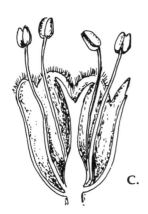

C.

D. $\dfrac{Ca^{4-8} \, Co^{\circ} \, S^{4-8} \, P^{(2)}}{Pg-Mo \; Sam \; Dr}$

Elm Family

A. Field sketch of American elm, *Ulmus americana*, twig with a cluster of flowers. **B.** A single flower, enlarged, showing the lobed calyx, extruded stamens, and two-lobed stigma. The corolla is lacking. **C.** A longitudinal section of an elm flower. **D.** Floral formula for the Family.

257

Umbelliferae Parsley Family

A vast family of more than 3,000 species in about 300 genera, these are in greatest concentration in the North Temperate zone but also occur sparingly throughout much of the rest of the world. They are mostly annual, biennial, or perennial herbs, some shrubs; plants usually have hollow internodes and usually the leaves are pinnately compound often recompounded until the foliage is plume-like; leaves alternate, rarely otherwise, petiole bases commonly sheath the nodes; exstipulate except for *Hydrocotyle* species. Minute or small flowers almost always are in umbels, rarely capitate, epigynous, regular (sometimes not so, see below), and perfect; sepals small and scale-like or mere teeth on the outer rim of an epigynous tube or disc, 5 or none, separate petals usually 5, on the rim of the epigynous disc, separate and often falling early; stamens 5, free, inserted on the inner rim of the disc and alternating with the petals; compound pistil of 2 carpels, with two styles often thickened at the base (the *stylopodium*); ovary inferior, 2-celled, with a single ovule in each cell. Fruit is a mericarp; this is an indehiscent, hard, woody, even bony, fruit firmly enclosed in the sheathing floral-cup, ridged and with oil-ducts between the ridges; these occur on the plant in pairs (to make up the schizocarp so important in classification of these plants), suspended from an extension of the floral axis (Y-shaped at the apex) called a *carpophore*. Because of the aromatic oil, fruits (indeed, the whole plant) usually is aromatic, as celery, parsley, myrrh, and others.

In the field the **Umbelliferae** can easily be identified as a family by small often white or yellow flowers in umbels, stems hollow between nodes, petiole bases sheathing the nodes, and with flowers or seeds as described above; often the scent is suggestive as is the divided foliage. Check out these points with a plant of wild carrot, *Daucus carota*, or garden parsley, *Petroselinum hortense*. Note that sometimes the outermost flowers of the umbel are larger, somewhat zygomorphic (irregularly shaped), and sterile. *Hydrocotyle* now is regarded as being in family **Hydrocotylaceae.**

Many members of **Umbelliferae** are of considerable importance in gardens and in agriculture; also, a considerable number of genera occur in the wild in the U.S.; among them are:

Aciphylla	*Conium*	*Meum*
Actinotus	*Coriandrum*	*Molospermum*
Aegopodium	*Crithmum*	*Myrrhis*
Ammi	*Daucus*	*Opopanax*
Angelica	*Didiscus*	*Osmorhiza*
Anthriscus	*Dorema*	*Petroselinum*
Apium	*Erigenia*	*Peucedanum*
Arracacia	*Eryngium*	*Pleurospermum*
Astrantia	*Ferula*	*Portenschlagia*
Athamanta	*Foeniculum*	*Seseli*
Azorella	*Hacquetia*	*Smyrnium*
Bupleurum	*Heracleum*	*Sium*
Chacrys	*Hydrocotyle*	*Thapsia*
Carum	*Laserpitium*	*Torilis*
Chaerophyllum	*Levisticum*	*Xanthosia*
Cicuta	*Malabaila*	*Zisia*

The economic value of various **Umbelliferae** is immense; several are important vegetables, others herbs of great merit. Several are extremely poisonous (including the hemlock, *Conium*, which put paid to Socrates), many others contain resins or gum-resins of considerable importance, including the foul-scented asafetida, used rarely nowadays in medicine, but still a favored *condiment* in Persia. Many members are fine garden ornamentals and some others are insidious pests.

Umbelliferae

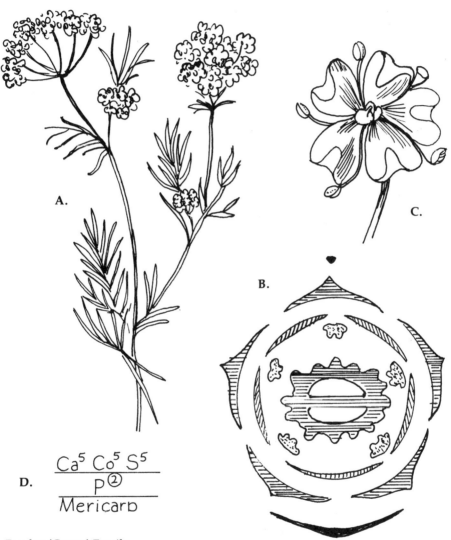

$$\frac{Ca^5\ Co^5\ S^5}{P\ ②}$$

Mericarp

D.

Parsley (Carrot) Family

A. Field sketch of chervil, *Anthriscus cerefolium*, showing the finely divided leaves and umbel inflorescence so typical of this family. **B.** A schematic interpretation of an Umbelliferous flower (no specific species). **C.** A single flower of caraway, *Carum carvi*. **D.** Generalized floral formula for the Family.

Urticaceae Nettle Family

A family of about 550 species distributed through approximately 45 genera of mostly tropical trees, shrubs, and herbaceous plants, the Nettle Family includes several notable ornamental plants as well as others with stinging hairs on the foliage and sometimes stems and other plant parts. The juice of the **Urticaceae** usually is watery, clear, and mostly the flowers are greenish, not at all showy. Those encountered in the North Temperate zone are mostly herbaceous. Leaves are simple, with stipules, usually with toothed margins. Leaves of ornamental sorts may be green or variously mottled maroon and silvery-green. Flowers, almost never perfect, those on individual plants either staminate *or* pistillate or plants monoecious (individual plants with both staminate and pistillate flowers), the very small, insignificant flowers borne in cymes (threadlike elongated clusters) in the axils of the leaves. The flowers of this family are greatly reduced; sepals represented by 2 to 5 lobes (usually 4 or 5); petals lacking; stamens as many as perianth lobes, filaments incurved in the bud but uncoiling suddenly when pollen ripens, anthers 2-celled; pistil with a simple stigma, reduced or no style; ovary simple with a single ovule. The fruit is a nutlet (achene) or a drupe.

Field characteristics include herbaceous character, opposite leaves glabrous or harshly hairy, with or without stinging hairs; stems often glassy or brittle, or sometimes tough and fibrous, sometimes (not always) square or ridged and sometimes with stinging hairs or harsh, non-stinging hairs. Leaves more or less elm-like. Flowers in string-like clusters (or "tufts") at the nodes. Flowers insignificant.

Some genera included in the Nettle Family are:

Boehmeria	*Laportea*	*Pourruma*
Debregeasia	*Myriocarpa*	*Urera*
Helxine	*Pellionia*	*Urtica*
*Humulus**	*Pilea*	

*The genus *Humulus* (hops) in American literature usually is *not* in the Nettle Family, but rather in the **Cannabinaceae**, Hemp Family. European authorities, however, often include it here.

A.

B.

C.

D. $$\frac{Ca^{4-5} Co^{0} S^{4-5} P^{1}}{Pf\ U\ Ach\ Dr}$$

Nettle Family

A. Field sketch of common nettle, *Urtica*. **B.** The greatly reduced male (staminate) flower of nettle. **C.** The female flower of nettle, also known as the pistillate flower. **D.** Floral formula for the Family.

Valerianaceae Valerian Family

Thirteen or more genera include the some 400 species of annual and perennial bland or often strongly scented herbs (plus a few S. American shrubs) which make up this family. Most of these are of temperate regions, especially in Europe and in S. America, but the genera *Valeriana* and *Valerianella* are well represented in the U.S. Leaves opposite, exstipulate, and often cauline, sometimes all basal. Stem leaves often pinnatifid or 1, 2, or 3 pinnatisect. Flowers small, usually in conspicuous cymose or capitate clusters, mostly white, pink, or red, perfect or unisexual, epigynous, zygomorphic (or actinomorphic); sepals minute, 1 to 3, tiny teeth, more commonly a ring at the rim of the epigynous disc, or developing as fruit develops to several plumose bristles (like a pappus); corolla sympetalous, tubular or funnelform, often irregular, 3 to usually 5-lobed or 3 to usually 5-cleft, sometimes saccate or spurred at the base; stamens 1 to 4, rarely 5, epipetalous but mostly fewer than the lobes of the corolla, mostly exserted; compound pistil usually of 3 closely united carpels with single slender style with 1 to 3 stigmas; ovary inferior, 1 to 3-celled, mostly with only a single locule with a fertile ovule and with 2 abortive or empty cells. Fruit an achene with adnate calyx (cypsela), sometimes crowned by a handsome radiate calyx, plumose or bristles or hooks.

In the field look for herbaceous plants with a sympetalous, epigynous corolla, stamens mostly fewer than the lobes of the corolla and epipetalous, and the distinctive 3-celled ovary with one fertile ovule in one of the cells which produces the typically one-seeded fruits. You will need a hand lens to make these distinctions.

Of the genera of **Valerianaceae** which may be encountered in gardens or in the wild in N. America, the following are commonest:

> *Fedia*
> *Kentranthus*
> *Nardostachys*
> *Patrina*
> *Valeriana*
> *Valerianella*

Valeriana officinalis contains a powerful nerve sedative with a peculiar odor, and spikenard, a very ancient drug and ointment, is obtained from the young shoots of *Nardostachys jatamansi*. Several species of *Valerianella* are known as "corn-salad" and used raw or as pot-herbs; some have escaped to become weedy in N. America. Two very beautiful species, *Valerianella ozarkana* and *V. bushii*, each originally with not more than five or six stands in S.W. Missouri and adjacent N.W. Arkansas are almost extirpated by the encroachments of civilization, with the last remaining stands completely imperiled by road right-of-ways. Unfortunately, neither is very amenable to culture out of its original habitat.

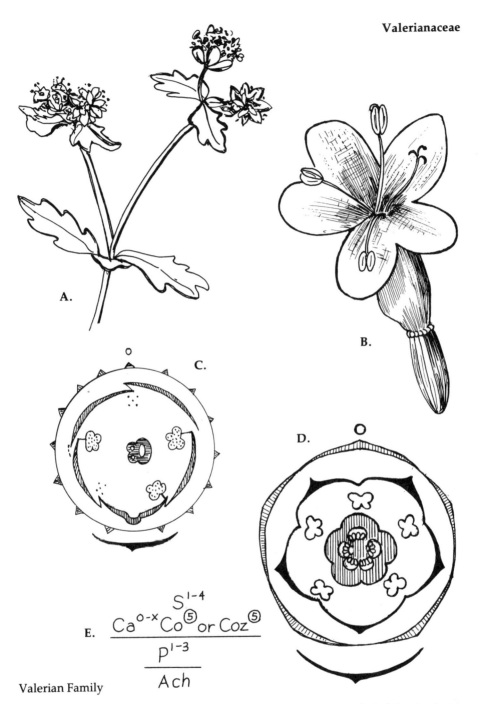

A. Field sketch of corn salad, *Valerianella olitoria*. B. Enlarged sketch of valerian flower showing slight asymmetry. C. Floral diagram showing zygomorphy in **Valerianaceae**. D. An actinomorphic (regular) diagram for the Family. E. Floral formula for the Family.

263

Verbenaceae Verbena Family

More than 3,000 species grouped into about 75 genera of annual or perennial herbs, shrubs, and trees make up this great family, the members of which are mostly concentrated in the temperate, sub-tropical and tropical regions of the southern hemisphere, but also with some species in the northern latitudes. The leaves are opposite or rarely whorled or very rarely alternate, simple or compound, often serrate and scurfy to the touch, and exstipulate. Flowers complete, in spikes, cymes, or panicles, usually rather small, and two-lipped or oblique, rarely regular, many brightly colored; calyx synsepalous, 5, rarely 4 to 8-toothed, sometimes lobes are uneven; corolla sympetalous, hypogynous, tubular with a rotate limb as *Lantana* or two-lipped as *Lippia*, (4 to) 5 lobed, with imbricate lobes; stamens mostly 4, didynamous (2 pairs of 2 separate stamens), or 2 with 2 or 3 staminoids, very rarely 5, epipetalous (inserted on the corolla tube) or very rarely hypogynous; compound pistil of 2, (rarely 4 or 5) closely united carpels, style clearly terminal (as distinguished from **Boraginaceae** or **Labiatae**) slender, with a small, often lobed or divided stigma; ovary superior, often entire with 2, 4 or 5 cells or 2 to 4-lobed and 2 to 5-celled with 2 ovules in each cell, or 5 to 10-celled by false partitions and cells with single ovules; fruit a drupe or berry, rarely a capsule.

This is a rather easy family to identify; the vegetative characteristics are suggestive; look for the often 4-angled stems, the opposite, usually scurfy-harsh leaves often simple and serrate, and in many cases a pungent (pleasant or not-so-pleasant) scent when leaves are bruised. The tubular corolla with lips or an oblique limb or 5 sympetalous petals, the didynamous stamens, *and especially, the more-or-less entire superior ovary with a single terminal style* brings you into the Order Tubiflorae and directly to **Verbenaceae.**

Most taxonomists recognize 3 or more sub-families in **Verbenaceae** and 1 or more of these is sometimes considered as a separate family.

Some of the more familiar genera in the **Verbenaceae** include:

Aloysia	*Clerodendrum* *	*Lippia*	*Spartothamnus*
Amasonia	*Cornutia*	*Monochilus*	*Stachytarpheta*
Baillonia	*Duranta*	*Oxera*	*Tectona*
Bouchea	*Faradaya*	*Petrea*	*Verbena*
Callicarpa	*Gmelina*	*Premna*	*Vitex*
Caryopteris	*Holmskioldia*	*Priva*	*sometimes
Citharexylum	*Lantana*	*Rhaphithamnus*	*Clerodendron*

Many of the more tender species of **Verbenaceae** have been used in medicine and our own *Verbena hastata* makes an acceptable bitters; *Aloysia triphylla* which was until recently *Lippia citriodora* is lemon-scented and the source of the essence "verbena". Other sorts have been used in food products and *Tectona grandis* is the source of teak wood. *Verbena officinalis* of Europe is a tonic but more noted for its uses in witchcraft; the lore of this goes back to the Romans and the Druids who used it in ritualistic ceremonies. We know the family best for its members which beautify our gardens, and many of us fail to take advantage of the wonderful blue flowers in late summer and early fall which the woody species and hybrids of *Caryopteris* and *Vitex* afford.

Vervain (Verbena) Family

Floral diagram of *Verbena officinalis*; the 5th stamen is indicated as aborted or missing.

Violaceae   Violet Family

More than 900 species of annual and perennial herbs, shrubs, and small trees, in 22 genera, comprise the **Violaceae.** These are distributed throughout the world except in the arctic regions; a few species are climbers. Leaves are usually alternate, simple (but sometimes deeply lobed or digitate-lobed), often serrate, and stipulate. Flowers commonly are axillary, often nodding; mostly zygomorphic, hypogynous, and commonly complete; calyx of 5 sepals, not petaloid, commonly separate or barely united, persistent; corolla of 5 petals, separate, the anterior petal usually spurred to form a nectary (rarely gibbous, e.g., swollen or bulging on one side); stamens 5, hypogynous or slightly perigynous, alternating with the petals, filaments short, anthers sometimes adnate or at least closely connivent over the pistil round the style, the filament frequently extending beyond the anther into a membranous wing; compound pistil of 3 carpels, the style often clavate (club-shaped), with a simple stigma turned to one side; ovary superior with a single cell, and with 3 parietal placentae with many ovules. Fruit a capsule with 3 valves. At least two genera, *Hybanthus* and *Viola*, include species which produce cleistogamous (hidden) flowers at the base in late summer; often these are underground, and are apetalous, more or less reduced to a large ovary with great quantities of seeds.

In the field the irregular flowers, the peculiar stamens (study flowers of several kinds of violets, violas, pansies, and if possible, the green-violet) with their crested, or joined, filaments, and the 1-celled, 3-placentae ovary, are characteristic. American kinds all are herbaceous.

Among the genera of **Violaceae** which may be encountered in cultivation or in the wild are:

Corynostylis	*Ionidium*	*Schweiggeria*
Hybanthus	*Melicytus*	*Rinorea*
Hymenanthera	*Noisettia*	*Viola*

The species of an earlier genus, *Alsodeia*, have been transferred to *Rinorea*. While in foreign countries a few species of this family have been used medicinally, most are considered as ornamentals, and the largest number of these is in the genus *Viola*; as the Violas hybridize readily in nature, distinguishing species sometimes is extremely difficult. In most cases, the American violets are with little or no odor, the European ones are sweetly scented.

D. $$\frac{Ca^5 \, Coz^{4+1} \, S^5 \, P^{\boxed{1-3}}}{Cap \; Ber}$$

Viola (Violet) Family

A. Field sketch of common violet. **B.** Longitudinal section of *Viola* flower. **C.** Floral diagram of *Viola*. **D.** Floral formula for **Violaceae**.

Vitaceae Grape Family

Mostly shrubs climbing with tendrils, or small trees, or fleshy, cactus-like, desert plants in about 700 species in 12 genera; these grow mostly in tropical and sub-tropical regions, but also extend into the temperate zones. Leaves large, simple and often deeply lobed, or compound, with stipules. Inflorescence usually a much branched cyme, borne (with tendrils) opposite a leaf, sometimes partially tendril-like. Flowers regular, perfect or monoecious, very small and greenish; calyx minute or truncated, with 4 or 5 (rarely 3 to 7) lobes; corolla of 4 to 5 (rarely 3 to 7) petals, separate *or united at the tip* and falling as a whole, *petals very deciduous;* stamens 4 or 5 (rarely 3 to 7), free, and opposite the petals, and inserted at the rim of the disc or in marginal lobes of the disc; pistil superior; ovary with 2 cells (rarely 3 to 6), with 2, rarely 1, ovule in each cell, style 1 or none, stigma capitate or discoid. Fruit a juicy berry usually with several rather small horny seeds.

The woody vines with cymes of small green flowers and tendrils opposite the leaves generally indicates this family. The details of flower structure confirm identification, especially the reduced calyx, the early-falling petals (novices sometimes find specimens with all petals fallen and mistakenly think them to be apetalous), and the small, free stamens opposite the petals. The 2-carpeled berry is distinctive, when present. Some of the desert species of *Cissus* are particularly confusing, with fleshy, cactus-like, angled, jointed, or terete stems; some have tubers or tuberous bases. With these, floral characteristics and fruit are very important for identification.

Among the genera commonly encountered in the **Vitaceae** are:

Ampelocissus	*Cissus*	*Rhoicissus*
Ampelopsis	*Leea*	*Tetrastigma*
Cayratia	*Parthenocissus*	*Vitis*
(sometimes listed as	*Pterisanthes*	
Columella)		

Vitis, the vine, or grape, is one of the most ancient plants come to live with man, supplying food, drink, and shade for his arbor when living became gracious; as the old German ballad has it, it wasn't drinking that brought about man's downfall, but eating! The woodbines and Boston-ivy adorn our houses and gardens, and the many beautiful tender forms of *Cissus* and species in related genera make superb house plants.

Grape (Vine) Family

A. Field sketch of *Vitis*, with leaf, tendrils, and inflorescence. **B.** Grape flower in longitudinal section. **C.** Flower without the floral envelopes (perianth). **D.** Floral diagram of *Vitis*. **E.** Floral formula for the **Vitaceae.**

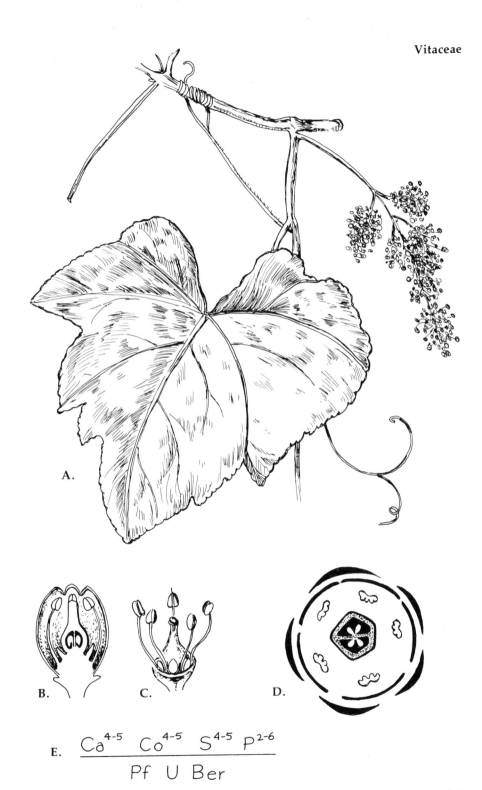

A.

B.

C.

D.

E. $\dfrac{Ca^{4\text{-}5}\ \ Co^{4\text{-}5}\ \ S^{4\text{-}5}\ P^{2\text{-}6}}{Pf\ \ U\ \ Ber}$